My Father's Final Journey

A Heart Surgeon's Memoir

David L. Galbut M.D.

Dedication

This book is dedicated to
my mother,
Bessie Galbut

My wife,
Gita

And my daughters,
Riki, Elle, Dani, Elana, Rachel and Nili

These three generations of women are simply the best and
have given me immeasurable love and inspiration.

Dedication 2

Acknowledgements 5

Foreword 7

Prologue: Under the Watchful Eye of the North Star 9

Chapter 1: The Warmth of My Father's Hand 22

Chapter 2: Falling in Love All over Again 31

Chapter 3: Limitless Promise and Impending Grief 46

Chapter 4: The Creative Force of Optimism 63

Chapter 5: Always the Captain 91

Chapter 6: Zayde and Bubby 110

Chapter 7: With Strength Will Come Peace 133

Chapter 8: Days to Remember 153

Chapter 9: Generation to Generation 181

Chapter 10: A Slow-Moving Cowboy 211

Chapter 11: Dinner on the Patio at Sunset 225

Chapter 12: A Downhill Spiral 254

Chapter 13: Cardiac Surgery and Kickboxing 275

Chapter 14: A Time to Act 301

Chapter 15: Sleeping Fast 319

Chapter 16: My Father's Final Journey 337

Epilogue: The Kaddish 358

A Personal Note 371

Acknowledgements

The year of writing this memoir has been a labor mostly of love which would not have happened without the assistance of several individuals. I have accomplished little in my life that is not in large part attributable to the encouragement and support of my wife, Gita. During doubtful moments, she was certain and when the hours of tedious work became days, she was patient. Thank you for believing in me and for being my soul-mate.

My mother, Bessie Galbut has continued to be the matriarch of our family, teaching the essence of courage and the art of giving. Although difficult and at times even painful, she shared her innermost feelings wanting this story to be told accurately.

My brothers Robert, Al B., and Russell have been and continue to be my best friends. The love and loyalty which we share is unique even among siblings. There is strength in unity and I was encouraged to be the author of perhaps our story.

Our daughters Riki, Elle, Dani, Elana, Rachel, and Nili are the center of Gita's and my universe .Not only have you become G-d fearing, kind and purpose driven adults, but you are my inspiration. Perhaps this memoir is mostly for you to remember,

I must express gratitude to Leonard Nash, a creative writing consultant, who became my tutor. During my year of writing, I learned from a master the art of showing and not telling a story. I am grateful to Mitch Kaplan of Books and Books of Miami for introducing us.

Finally, a special thanks to Garret Macrine, an author in his own right, who was instrumental in the publication of this second edition. I greatly appreciate your friendship and kindness.

Foreword

There was a dream that belonged to my father. In addition to raising six daughters with his wife and becoming a world renowned heart surgeon, he wanted to author a book. Perhaps chronicling his father's terminal illness and death was not exactly what he had in mind. Nevertheless, a masterpiece was born. Please don't be mistaken-this book is not only about death or loss. On the contrary, it celebrates the life of a family patriarch. It is a book of love that delves deeply into the emotions a person experiences in one of the most intense periods in the journey we call "life". This narrative is riddled with many of life's greatest lessons. It offers a glimpse into the mind and soul of an extraordinary person undergoing the heart wrenching experience of being present in a parent's final journey.

My grandfather or Zayde as we called him received his dismal prognosis, and I witnessed how my father struggled to strike a balance between his role as a loving son and as a medical advocate. I had seen my father react in circumstances of stress, high anxiety and even sadness. For the first time, he was in a state that words cannot describe. In what I consider an effort to cope and even survive the pain and uncertainty, my dad made consistent diary entries. These entries were delivered to me via email as they were written. During the first year after my Zayde's funeral, my dad revisited and rewrote these entries creating this memoir.

My father's willingness to share this vulnerable part of himself touched my heart. My sisters and I each share a unique bond with our dad-one in which he has made each of us feel like his favorite. This beautiful story made the connection even deeper.

As I read the written words of my father, I was enlightened. It became clear to me how my father was motivated by his dad. This book affords the opportunity to really comprehend how each of life's events from birth is a building block of the human soul and spirit. In the most humble way, Zayde played a pivotal role in constructing the man my father is today.

Similarly, my sisters and I were infused with an unconditional love growing up that only a parent can truly ever possess. A parent can only pray to be bidden farewell by children with the same amount of love, respect and adoration exhibited toward Zayde during his final moments.

Daniella Galbut Kuhl

Prologue: Under the Watchful Eye of the North Star

It's 1953, and I'm sitting on the porch overlooking the back yard of our thousand-square-foot government project home in Coral Gate, a Miami subdivision where I live with my parents, an elderly Romanian woman who helped care for me and my three brothers, and a malamute mix named Brandy. I'm four years old. The porch, more of a "stoop," really, is about three feet wide. I'm sitting on the second step. My brother Robert, a year older, sits on my right, and to my left on the lower step sits my two-year-old brother, Al D. Across our collective lap lays our youngest brother, Russell. His head lies cradled in Robert's arms, his torso and legs draped over me and beyond the porch.

Dad holds his Yashica camera and directs us to smile, our eyes squinting into the heat of the afternoon sun. The stage is set, with my father's four sons intertwined, dressed in dungarees and striped cotton shirts. My father snaps several shots and says, "This is a beautiful picture."

My father attends law school at the University of Miami during the day and works nights as a short-order cook at Al's, a 24-hour diner on Fifth and Washington in Miami Beach. My mother, who grew up in New Orleans, works days as a bookkeeper

*and salesgirl in Three Sisters, a moderately priced clothing store
on Miracle Mile in Coral Gables.*

This is the story of my father's final journey. In October
2005, much of our family celebrated the Jewish holiday of Sukkot
in Israel. My parents were married in 1946, and until April 2005,
they enjoyed the best of health, independence, and vitality. This
ended when my mother developed symptoms of chronic
obstructive pulmonary disease, or COPD, a respiratory illness that
left her breathless, inactive, and nutritionally spent. She received
outpatient treatment until her condition deteriorated further,
requiring hospitalization for severe shortness of breath.

After a two-week diagnostic and treatment regimen, my
mother was discharged, but her health deteriorated further. In the
following weeks, she convinced herself that her life was ending,
even though her doctors had detected no malignancy or infection.
My typically upbeat parents grew hopeless, and their despair
spread throughout our large family.

By mid-June, my mother was convinced that she was at
death's door. Having discussed her approaching death with my
father, my mother called me on Saturday June 18th, the Sabbath,
and advised me that her death was imminent, and could I please
come over and say goodbye.

I arrived at their house, just a few blocks away from my Miami Beach home. I entered their grand bedroom though its double doors. My father sat at his table, reading a copy of *Model Railroader Magazine* and glancing intermittently at my mother, who sat in a chair beside her bed. The tube from her portable oxygen tank was draped over her shoulder, looped over her ears, and connected to a pair of delicate nasal prongs.

In the large den beside the bedroom, my mother stored her extensive collection of success and self-improvement books spanning some fifty years. She read everyone from Norman Vincent Peale to Anthony Robbins to Dr. Phil. In the den, she managed everything manageable in their lives, from their social calendar to their daily household financial matters. It was also where my father, chairman of Hebrew Homes, a chain of nonprofit nursing homes, conducted his work. The original location on Collins Avenue is in the heart of what the world now calls South Beach.

Opposite the den near the bathroom stood the tables where my father pursued his hobbies of assembling model trains and building dollhouses and model sailboats. The well-lit room has always been a main gathering point when we visited my parents. Typically, the larger formal holiday dinners were held at my house, or my brothers' homes, but my Mom and Dad's house was typically our base for family meetings and one-on-one visits to discuss private family matters. All in all, this happy, bright room was the heart and soul of my parents' home, but that June afternoon, something was changing.

"David," my mother said, her weak, cracked voice muffled by the oxygen machine, "I'm going to die soon, and I don't want you or Robert signing my death certificate. I called you here because I want to say goodbye." My older brother Robert, a Miami Beach pulmonologist, had been my parents' physician for the past twenty-eight years.

"Mom, you're wrong. This isn't your time, but I'd like to readmit you to another hospital for a reevaluation."

Before the Sabbath ended, I drove my mother to South Miami Hospital, where I am Chief of Cardiac Surgery, and admitted her into Intensive Care. "The angel of death is not in this unit," I told my mother. "You're safe tonight." She didn't smile, and in fact, she didn't say anything.

For the next eight days, Mom received antibiotics, anti-inflammatory agents, and respiratory therapy. She couldn't eat for the first four or five days, but she gradually took solid food and she began speaking in full sentences, rather than in short, breathless phrases. She also regained the beautiful smile we hadn't seen for a month, but she remained weak, having lost about seventeen pounds, down from her lifelong plateau of 125.

Once the infection subsided and her pulmonary function improved, we transferred her to a rehab unit where she remained another two weeks, working vigorously, gaining weight, improving her strength, and rebuilding her muscle tone. Through occupational and physical therapy, my mother relearned how to use her hands and she began walking again.

***

When my brothers and I were growing up, Mom never permitted card playing in our house. She'd grown up in a home where gambling was forbidden, probably a consequence of an addicted gambler somewhere in our past. Even so, there she was in the rehab unit, sitting at a table with her vocational therapist, learning how to play gin rummy. It was as if she had been reborn, sitting at the table and interacting with someone who had been a complete stranger only days earlier, her mind and body engaged.

In the rehab, she also rode a stationary bicycle, lifted weights, and walked increasing distances in the gym. She also began an unorthodox treatment—what physicians often call an off-label indication—with methotrexate, a chemotherapeutic agent often used for severe arthritis or connective tissue inflammatory disease, for the purpose of blunting whatever asthmatic or inflammatory component remained in her system.

My mother's COPD involved an asthmatic component, all of which impaired her ability to clear secretions from her lungs, making her more susceptible to infection. That was my medical assessment, but as her son, I knew that Mom's recovery also had much to do with her belief in God, her readiness to accept her destiny, her love of family, and her determination.

As Mom completed her rehabilitation, my two younger brothers, Abraham, whom we call "Al B," and Russell prepared the house for her return by eliminating the rugs and wall coverings. Throughout the house, the housekeeper dusted the many shelves of old books, the artwork, and other surfaces likely to contain allergens. We had the floor of their master bedroom resurfaced with a pine laminate, we replaced the king-sized bed with twin adjustable beds, and we moved all remnants of my father's hobbies (which invariably collected dust and many of which contained varnishes and other chemicals) to their converted garage. For that section of the bedroom, my father purchased a round table with padded wheeled chairs that moved about easily on the new wooden floor. He also installed a small basketball backboard and hoop, the sort you might find in a first grade classroom, or a college dormitory, for the purpose of encouraging Mom's ongoing coordination therapy. The room also contained permanent and mobile oxygen delivery systems, a nebulizer for her various treatments, and a hospital-quality vibration vest designed to clear her lung secretions. My father and my nurse practitioner organized a computerized daily menu of no less than twenty medicines, including dosing information and delivery times. For my mother's return home, my father and my younger brothers had assembled a new environment, one that approximated the purpose of the rehab unit, including twenty-four hour care to ensure continuity and to allow my father to remain her husband rather than become her caretaker. Out of respect for my mother's need for peaceful sleep, my father, a wiz at multitasking, prepared a nearby bedroom to watch TV, build his model sailboats, and to read, all of which he pursued late into the night. This was the first time they would sleep in separate bedrooms.

Throughout my mother's illness, Dad remained supportive and committed to seeing his wife of fifty-nine years return to good health. At South Miami Hospital, he sat with her every day from morning to night. He shared his cafeteria meals with her, accompanied her to physical therapy, observed her progress, and while she rested, he slept in the chair beside her bed, and sometimes when she fell asleep in the chair, he napped in her hospital bed. His optimism was crucial to her recovery, but at times he was overbearing. His great love for my mother kept him from fully understanding the gravity of her illness. In fact, one consulting physician commented that my mother would be better off in a nursing home, away from my father's domineering spirit.

I confronted that physician in the corridor outside my mother's room. "I appreciate your concern, but let's consider the nature of my parents' relationship. They must be together whenever possible," I said. "It's what motivates my mother to fight through this day after day."

"Yes, but you're father is impossible."

"With all due respect, you don't understand my parents. I'm willing to defer on most medical matters, but my mother's after-hospital care is not up for discussion."

As a heart surgeon for twenty-five years, I've learned that doctors must be willing to understand the family dynamic and to observe the *whole person*. Sure, some patients benefit from being away from their families awhile, but my mother's life was defined by her mission of caring for my father, and vice versa. Separating them during her recovery would have destroyed my mother's essence and mission. Allowing that to happen would have been inconsistent with my responsibility of honoring my father and mother—and it would have conflicted with my responsibility as their medical advocate.

Mom returned home after the Fourth of July holiday and she continued to improve, aided by her determination and by Dad's commitment to her routine of nebulizer treatments, physical therapy, and medication. Besides her physicians at South Miami Hospital, Mom's care also included the attention of my older brother Robert, the pulmonologist, and my younger brothers, Al B and Russell, who managed the schedules of the around-the-clock aides. The routine imposed on my parent's lifestyle, but Mom needed help. As the summer rolled along, Mom's weight returned to normal and she continued her physical therapy. Most importantly, she had been blessed with a second chance to continue on as our family matriarch.

In September, we prepared to celebrate Rosh Hashanah, the Jewish New Year. During the preceding year, we had celebrated my daughter Elana's marriage to her husband. At this point, my eldest daughter Riki and her husband Miki had three children. My second daughter, Elle and her husband Jamie had two children with a third on the way. My third daughter, Dani and her husband Josh had one child and another due in April. My fifth daughter, Rachel, was about to become engaged to her high school sweetheart, Ethan, and my youngest daughter, Nili, who was fifteen, had just finished ninth grade.

I met my wife Gita during my graduate training at Columbia Presbyterian Medical Center in New York. Ever since, she has been my soul mate, sharing my dreams and adventures. During our three decades of marriage, we have raised six bright and beautiful daughters, and I credit Gita for most of our success as parents. As a heart surgeon, discipline and control is inherent in the training. When I was a younger man, Gita accommodated my desire to have a son, but today, I recognize my foolishness. For my fortieth birthday, Gita asked me what present I wanted for that momentous occasion.

"Another child to grow old with," I said.

"Only if you accept in advance that the child will be another girl."

"I accept," I said, assuring her that I would be genuinely happy no matter what. Our sixth daughter was born within a year and we named her Nili Matanah. In Hebrew, her second name means "gift." And that's exactly what she is.

As Rosh Hashanah approached, Gita and I planned to meet Russell and his family, who would be observing the actual holiday in Israel. My four married daughters would remain in America, but Rachel and Nili were coming with us. In early October, Gita and Nili flew to Israel with my father, who believed this would likely be his last chance to visit the Holy Land. Rachel, a rookie teacher in an early childhood program, flew with me several days later to meet Gita, Nili, my father, Russell, and his family.

As I observed the holiday in Miami with our other children and their families, I prepared for the New Year and prayed for my mother's recovery, prayers filled with repentance and earnest requests for God's grace. I also expressed great gratitude for the gifts our family had been granted in the prior year, most notably my mother's improving health. The coming months, however, would offer challenges we never anticipated.

Dad's insistence on taking this trip perplexed me. My parents' only separation had occurred during Dad's tours of active duty during his many years in the Naval Reserve. Even then, his Navy trips formed the basis for our family vacations. During these two-week trips, he spent a week in the classroom, and a week at sea aboard a battleship or aircraft carrier. Each year, we spent two weeks in officer's quarters at either Norfolk, Virginia; the Naval War College in Newport, Rhode Island; the Naval Station Mayport, near Jacksonville, Florida; or at the Pentagon. This was our routine from 1954 until 1962. For my brothers and me, these trips included carefree days of baseball, basketball, and swimming on the various naval bases. With movies at a nickel each, we spent many evenings in the company of Glenn Ford, Richard Eagan, Jane Mansfield, and John Wayne.

Always the navigator, our father wanted us to understand the relationship between lighthouses and the contours of the harbor, so we toured every base we visited by land and by sea. My father was a proud Naval officer, having reached the rank of lieutenant-commander by the time of these road trips, and ultimately captain by the time of his retirement in 1980.

He enjoyed shopping in the commissaries, where items were available at cost, for most of our clothing and school supplies for the coming year. But what I enjoyed most were the tours my father gave us aboard the U.S. Navy's greatest warships, many of which I had read about in school, including the S.S. Alabama, the S.S. Missouri, both of which had been commissioned during World War II. As a young boy, I was in awe of the mighty steel structures, representative of our great country, and I was proud of the respect my father received as a high-ranking officer.

We never flew on these trips, but rather we drove from Miami with our belongings tucked away in either a small trailer or a rooftop carrier. Dad always made sure we saw the scenic attractions along way. We often spent time in the Smokey Mountains and the Blue Ridge Mountains and in the Luray Caverns in Virginia. Along the way, we toured many historic cities and towns such as Savannah, Charleston, Williamsburg, and New Orleans—just to name a few—and we frequently visited the Smithsonian Institute and the many other Washington, D.C. landmarks. In those years, the Interstate highway system—largely the brainchild of President Eisenhower—was still evolving, so we relied primarily on slower, scenic routes such as US-1 along the east coast. We spent our days, and even some evenings, on the road, but most afternoons, as evening approached, my father would pull into a private motel along the highway. He insisted on places with a swimming pool because he knew we needed to exercise and play. We swam together in the late afternoon or early evening and then ate the dinner we'd brought along in our cooler, or we'd enjoy a meal of fish and vegetables in a local restaurant.

It's the summer of 1958. I'm nine years old and we're driving to Newport, Rhode Island in a Cadillac convertible my father borrowed from a private investigator who works for him. We're pulling a small U-Haul trailer with our luggage and other stuff that wouldn't fit into the trunk. Needing to make up time, Dad drives most of the night while my brothers and Mom sleep.

"How do you know where you're going?" I ask my father.

"By the stars," he says.

I look up at the endless stream of stars hovering above our open car. "But the stars seem everywhere," I say.

"There are many stars, but the North Star never changes position. Look, it is the brightest star. That's why the North Star functions as a point of stability and reference." My father tells me about his experiences as a navigator in World War II and how he was responsible for an entire ship, and how at night he relied on the stars for both light and direction. It all seems complicated, but I feel safe in the presence of my parents and my brothers in the confines of this huge big car speeding along the highway under the watchful eye of the North Star.

Chapter 1: The Warmth of My Father's Hand

My father wanted Mom to join us on the Israel trip. We all did, but despite her improved breathing, she couldn't fly, given her susceptibility to respiratory infection and the inevitable disruption of her respiratory therapy, which required several hours per day.

"Dad, are you sure about going to Israel now?" We were standing behind my car, alongside the two large suitcases Dad had just carried from the house.

"David, we both know this could be my last overseas trip. It's very important to me. Robert and Al B will look after Mom. She'll be fine."

At least Dad wouldn't be traveling alone. He would fly with Gita and Nili. At the time, I was unaware that Dad had asked Robert to determine the Hebrew names of a list of sixty loved ones for whom he wanted to pray for their health and happiness at the grave of the great rabbi, Baba Sali, 1890-1984 CE, who orchestrated his Moroccan community's immigration to Israel. My mother, of course, topped my father's prayer list.

Baba Sali's tomb is located in Netivot, some ten miles north of Gaza, an area governed by the Palestinian Authority. Of the many historic gravesites my parents had visited over the years, they had found the grave of the Baba Sali to be most enduring and spiritual.

My joy upon arriving in Israel was tempered by Gita's news that my father had fallen in the bathtub in Tiberius the weekend before and that since their arrival in Jerusalem, he had spent most of his time in the hotel room. When I arrived, Dad was sitting in an armchair reading the *Jerusalem Post*.

After we greeted each other with a hug and a kiss, and once we caught up on the past week, including my update on Mom's progress, I asked Dad if I could examine his back.

"It's nothing, David. I'm fine."

"I'm sure you are, but the thorax is my specialty. Let me take a look. No charge."

I pulled up Dad's shirt and examined the left side of his back and saw moderate bruising. I suspected that he had fractured several ribs, but I didn't believe he required emergency care. Treatment would involve rest and pain relievers. Even so, something just didn't add up. A few broken ribs didn't seem like enough to keep my father secluded in a hotel room. And sure enough, it wasn't.

The next morning, my father still planned to visit the Baba Sali's grave. He would travel there with his first cousin, Allen, ten years his junior. Allen, who had also come to Israel from Miami, had grown up in my father's home, where he was always treated like a brother and son. They had remained close, and I know Allen felt great love and loyalty for my dad. In fact, some twenty years ago, Allen's life changed forever as the result of a call he made to my father. After many years in Los Angeles, Allen had become discouraged by the monotony of his business endeavors and by his recent divorce. Sensing Allen's need for family and a new start, my father convinced him to come to Miami. Allen subsequently lived with my parents for a few years, during which time he met his current wife and began a new career. His loyalty to my father was without bounds, and so on that trip to Israel, Allen didn't hesitate when my father asked him to accompany him on his final journey to the grave of Baba Sali.

That morning, despite his discomfort, Dad seemed agile and energetic. At breakfast in the hotel restaurant, he ate heartily and was excited about starting his day. My mother had given Russell the responsibility of making sure my father ate sensibly, given his diabetes. Russell grudgingly accepted the task, but Dad wasn't in the mood to hear about his dietary restrictions from Russell, who gave up trying after my father's first and last outburst on the matter over a big plate of pancakes and strawberries.

Upon their return about three o'clock that afternoon, Allen told me about their journey. At the Baba Sali's gravesite, my father had prayed, and undoubtedly he recalled the twenty or so visits he had taken to Israel with my mother and all the time they'd spent touring the holy sites. At the chapel alongside the gravesite, he encountered the attending rabbi and gave him his list of sixty names, along with a cash donation, after which he and Allen and their driver returned to the hotel.

"Your father was terribly uncomfortable, the whole two-and-half-hour drive, but he was determined," Allen said. This was the afternoon before the beginning of Sukkot, the holiday in which traditional Jews eat and study in a temporary hut that commemorates the forty years the Jewish nation traveled in the desert prior to entering the land of Israel. The holiday symbolizes man's dependence on God and the transience of his existence.

Back in 1982, my adventurous parents spent six months on sabbatical, so to speak, living in Jerusalem on the same block as Prime Minister Menachem Begin on Brenner Street. Although they didn't meet him, each Saturday evening, from their balcony, they could see the Prime Minister and his family celebrate the completion of the Sabbath on their own balcony in a festival of song.

That year, each of my father's four sons and their families spent three weeks in Israel, living with my parents in their three-bedroom rented apartment, where I believe Gita and I conceived our fifth daughter Rachel. During that trip, I witnessed the tremendous enthusiasm my parents had for sharing their excitement for Israel with their children and grandchildren.

My parents attended an immersion or "Ulpan" Hebrew language course for immigrants, and they took multilingual bus tours reserved for new immigrants. They intended to return to Miami, but they wanted to approximate the feeling of *living*, rather than *traveling*, in Israel. My mother, who speaks Spanish and Hebrew fluently, understood the tour guides much better than my father could, but his intuition and book learning helped him appreciate the history and culture, and in short order, he memorized the geography of the country. As a young navigator in the Pacific Theater in World War II, aboard a small destroyer, my father utilized his knowledge of astronomy and navigation, and his unfailing memory, to guide his ship through the vast, treacherous enemy seas.

During their six months in Israel, my parents attended Shabbat services at the Western Wall, and my father joined a Sephardic minyan (a group of ten or more men who pray together). My father, New York born of Russian descent, had little prior exposure to the Sephardic community, but he found this particular minyan unexpectedly welcoming. This minyan was situated near the dividing curtains between the men's and women's section of the Western Wall, which permitted my parents to see each other during the prayer service and to pray together. The genuine warmth exhibited by the Sephardic congregants gave my parents the sense of belonging they had been seeking.

The only evening meal my father shared with us during the holiday was in the sukkah in the grand veranda of the David Citadel Hotel, overlooking the old city of Jerusalem. My father sat at the head of the table, his eyes closed. His heart was with us, but his mind was elsewhere. The night was balmy and cool, the food was extraordinary, and yet my father ate very little, which I took to be a reflection of his loneliness.

"This is a beautiful sukkah," I said, recalling the beautiful, grand sukkah he'd engineered at Beth Israel Synagogue back in Miami Beach, and the smaller—but not small—suikkahs he'd built for each of our homes as recently as a year before.

"I'm tired," my father said. He got up to leave the table, and I held his hand and accompanied him to his room.

In 1958, I'm nine years old. We recently moved from our little house in Coral Gate to a much bigger house on Royal Palm Avenue in Miami Beach, where we joined a new synagogue. My

Dad says most of the people there are German and Hungarian. After services, we come home and enjoy the Sabbath together. Then my friends come over in the afternoon and we play softball in the side street or in our large backyard, or we play basketball at Polo Park.

During Shabbat services, my mother sits in a separate section with the other women, and my father sits with me and my brothers, two of us on either side. Dad usually holds our hands or puts his arm around us, touching our backs.

One Sabbath morning—I'm sitting on my father's left and Robert is on his right. When my father takes my hand, I have this sudden feeling of embarrassment. I'm almost ten years old, not far from being a teenager.

"Dad," I said, "you know I love holding your hand, but sometimes we don't have to, like when my friends are around or if girls are nearby."

"David, I hear you, but it's mostly in your mind. When I touch you, I am conveying my love, but I understand."

***

For the next several months, I regretted saying that to my father, because nothing comforted me more than sitting beside him as he held my hand or touched my shoulder in the synagogue. In our family, "Stay in Touch," suggested a true human connection, and not just a popular slogan of the long distance phone industry.

And for the rest of my life, I will always feel the warmth of my father's hand.

The next several days, my father enjoyed only one meal a day, usually breakfast, downstairs in the hotel sukkah. He spent most of his remaining time in Israel in his room, resting and passing time with his family. I assumed that his bruised ribs had affected his mobility. Either way, without my mother he probably had little interest in sightseeing.

The TV was always on, and the door to the balcony overlooking the courtyard, swimming pool, and sukkah was always open. Each day, my father spent time reading the *Jerusalem Post* and adventure novels. His grandchildren would visit at different times, bringing along takeout lunches and dinners, most of which Dad didn't eat.

Meantime, Gita and I focused on Nili and Rachel, making sure that we all remembered to enjoy our visit, away from our daily responsibilities back home. One afternoon, we attended a groundbreaking dedication of Nof Zion, a private residential community with a panoramic view of the old city of Jerusalem, which Gita represents in America. For Dad, this proved to be a difficult outing, one that he completed out of respect for Gita and her professional endeavors.

My father's one evening event during the trip was the premier for a movie entitled *Ever Again*, a film narrated by Kevin Costner and produced by the Simon Wiesenthal Center. Russell and his wife Ronalee were major sponsors of the film. Many dignitaries from Israel and visiting friends attended the premiere. The subject of the film is the re-emergence of anti-Semitism in Europe. Despite the international slogan of "Never Again," regarding the Holocaust, this 2005 film illustrates that the threat to Jewish survival remains.

Although Dad was proud of his children's accomplishments, he chose to sit near the exit, rather than in the central row reserved for dignitaries and major donors. After the movie, he kissed Russell and Ronalee and insisted that he needed to skip the cocktail reception and retire to his room.

On October 25th I returned to Miami on Air Canada, along with Gita, Nili, Rachel, and my father. Throughout the flight, Dad didn't sleep much and ate little. He watched the movies for several hours, but he seemed to be thinking of other times and other places.

Chapter 2: Falling in Love All over Again

On Tuesday, we were back in Miami, preparing for the closing of Sukkot. Mom had stayed at Al B's home during our trip, and since Dad hadn't assembled the sukkah, they had stayed with my brother for the duration of the holiday.

"I'm not feeling well," my father said on the phone. "I have sharp abdominal pain when I move."

Within minutes, Robert and I each arrived at Al B's house to examine Dad.

"It could be diverticulitis," I said, referring to an inflammatory condition of the large intestine.

"Dad, you should be hospitalized," Robert said, "for a workup and so you can receive intravenous fluids and possibly antibiotics."

"Dad, would you like to be admitted to South Miami?" I asked, knowing Dad had been impressed with Mom's care.

"That's fine. I'm ready to go, David," my father said.

I drove him to the ER, where I ordered tests and contacted consulting physicians. The CAT scan of Dad's chest and abdomen documented the presence of four fractured ribs on his left side, a hematoma in the spleen—or possibly in the tail of the pancreas—and multiple defects in the liver, which appeared cystic and not solid. The ultrasound of the abdomen also documented that the blood flow to my father's spleen was compromised. The fall in Tiberias explained Dad's left rib fractures, but I couldn't accept the defects in Dad's liver, pancreas, and spleen as being the consequence of serious trauma. Three days later, however, his abdominal pain disappeared and we discharged him from the hospital.

Driving my father home, I received a call from the radiologist, who was unaware that I was driving my father back to Miami Beach. The radiologist explained that further analysis of the abnormalities in Dad's liver revealed a solid density suggesting the presence of a tumor. As I listened to the doctor's grave diagnosis, I looked intermittently between the traffic ahead of me and at my father, sitting beside me, enjoying a Beatles compilation as we cruised along US-1.

"Let's schedule a further evaluation, percutaneously," I said.

My father must have heard my grim orders, but he seemed blissfully unaware that I was speaking about him.

The first few days of November, I denied what appeared to be my father's death sentence, but the compelling factual information on the CAT scan haunted me. I wanted a few days to discuss these findings with Robert, Al B, and Russell, and I wanted to schedule the liver biopsy for the following week, but Russell hadn't yet returned from Israel.

At the Synagogue on Saturday morning, I discussed my clinical concerns with Robert and Al B.

"I can't believe it," Robert said. "I want to see the films and review them with the radiologists at Mt. Sinai."

"Let's gather all the information," Al B said, also reluctant to consider the harsh reality that the biopsy would inevitably reveal. "I'm confident that with God's help, it will be OK."

After the Sabbath, I called Russell in Israel and gave him the news I had shared with Al B and Robert. His silence during that phone call convinced me that he understood the gravity of Dad's future. "Russell?"

"I'll return immediately, and I'll support your recommendations."

On Tuesday, Robert accepted the grave prognosis after consulting with a radiologist at Mt. Sinai. He and I agreed to share the medical responsibility.

On Friday, November 4th, Dad returned to South Miami for a liver biopsy, and on Saturday I studied the slides with the pathologist. There was no doubt as to the diagnosis: the pathology was consistent with an adenocarcinoma, probably originating in the pancreas, which explained the mass, about the size of a plum, abutting the spleen.

I shared this information with Robert and Al B in the synagogue at the conclusion of the Shabbat prayers, and I met with Russell that evening in our parents' home. But first I sat with my mother in her room and explained that Dad apparently had a tumor involving the pancreas that had spread to the liver.

"Can it be removed?" my mother asked.

"We'll explore the possibility of chemotherapy and radiation therapy this week as there is no surgical option," I said. I hugged and kissed my mother. "We still have the opportunity for some quality days."

My mother, with enormous faith, and with unfailing love for my father, said, "It will be OK . . . let's get him home . . . we must do whatever we can."

That evening, I thought about irony and how life is so unpredictable, especially the times that have the most significance. How ironic for my mother to have been so sick, believing that the angel of death was in her room, and that her moment was approaching.

In the preceding six months, my father had accepted that he would likely outlive my mother, and even now, despite his diagnosis, he appeared stronger than she, vigorous and vital for a man in his eighty-fifth year. My responsibility for conveying his death sentence the following day agonized me. Over the past twenty years, I have performed successful heart bypass and valve replacement surgeries on seven uncles, aunts, and cousins. The question has always been whether surgeons should operate on family members, but it's not unethical when the surgeon's statistics support the decision, and so long as ego is left at the door. If the statistical outcomes suggest that I have the best results over time for a given procedure, then the only question is whether I can remain objective during a procedure. This has been facilitated by the stability of my team and the sincerity of my effort. Although no operation could save my father, I would not relinquish my role as his medical advocate.

I thought about how our lives would change, and I prayed that God would give me the strength to provide the honor and kind attendance my father deserved in the months ahead. He was Mom's soul mate, and as a father, he always showed unconditional love and support. He demanded integrity and loyalty and precision, but he understood his children and accepted their abilities and limitations. Dad believed in education, and he learned from life's lessons. He taught us by demonstration and action. He loved us equally, but he conveyed a special interest and bond with each son, making each of us feel like his favorite. Our responsibility to perform proactively and reactively would be challenged in the months ahead. The time had come for my brothers and me to realize our finest hour.

The responsibility of each child to his father's final journey is equal, but the actual performance may vary based on one's abilities and resources. Robert and I would oversee our father's medical care. Supervision of our parents' home care would belong to Al B and Russell. Creating a lasting testament to our father's contributions to Miami Beach and his love for the community would fall to the four of us in our daily work, while Russell prepared to accept the leading role in the enduring philanthropic memorials to our father.

Late Sunday afternoon, my brothers and I met in Dad's hospital room to discuss his diagnosis and possible treatment options. Dad was watching a Miami Dolphins game. My brothers were sitting beside Dad. I sat on his bed and held his hand. On Saturday, we had agreed that I'd be the spokesman for the four of us. Robert had reviewed the entire hospital record and he and I discussed the findings with Al B and Russell.

Waiting for the right moment to begin the conversation about my father's cancer, I remembered the winter of my ninth grade year, when I was fourteen years old.

The Optimist International Football League in Flamingo Park in Miami Beach is underway and I'm the second-string quarterback. My father attends all the games, and today I can see he's upset because I'm not starting. I can tell he's planning to discuss this with my coach. I walk over to him and say, "Dad, I'm not the starting quarterback, but it's OK."

"You deserve to play at least as much as that other boy."

"Dad you know that most games he gets a nosebleed and goes to the hospital. You'll see. I'll play most of the game." And just as I predict, the coach sends me in to replace our starting quarterback in the second quarter. My strength as a quarterback isn't my size. I'm tall and thin, and my arm's only average, but my throws are accurate and I have a knack for calling the right plays. In the fourth quarter, with our team behind 10-7, and knowing my father's was on the sidelines, I call a quarterback sneak, which gets us eight yards. The next play is a fake handoff to my halfback to the right of the center. I roll to the left and pass thirty yards to my receiver near the left, bringing us within twenty yards of the goal. On the third play, I fake a handoff to my right halfback, fake another handoff to my left halfback, and then I hand off to my wide receiver who crosses from right to left, and now he's free and clear for a touchdown.

After the game, Dad and I stop at the 7-Eleven on Alton Road and buy Coca-Cola Slurpees.

"You were terrific today," Dad says.

"Thanks, but I got lucky."

Driving home, my father goes, "I'm proud of how you played today, but I'm happy that you are well-rounded and that you have many interests besides sports."

We both knew football was not my future, which was just as well, as my high school didn't have a football team, although we did have a basketball team that competed against other private schools with similar enrollment. I played forward, and my skills were above average. Although I didn't play college basketball, I continued playing competitively in pickup games until recent years, when I took to coaching my daughters, four of whom starred on their own high school basketball teams.

"Dad," I said, during a commercial break in the Dolphins game, "you know how much we love you, and we realize how much you love us. Our lives wouldn't be what they are today without you."

"Yes, I know, David."

I moved closer to him, careful not to block his view of my brothers. "Dad, your fall in Israel resulted in some fractured ribs, but the investigation has revealed abnormalities in your liver. These areas were biopsied two days ago, and the results are consistent with a tumor. The origin of this tumor is probably the pancreas."

"Is this what Miriam had?" he said, referring his younger sister who had passed away two years before.

"Aunt Miriam's tumor was of an endocrine cell line. Yours is of the cell line that produces enzymes for digestion."

"We'll fight it," Dad said. "I'll have surgery. Just tell me what to do."

"Because it's in the liver, surgery is not an option. Chemotherapy is the best choice, and we'll explore whether radiation therapy might help."

Russell had tears in his eyes, Robert maintained a painful silence, and Al B, always the optimist, sat up straight, nodded his head, hanging on to some hope.

"Dad," I said, "other than this, you are healthy. Your body is strong, your mind is perfect, and we have time. You have five great-grandchildren on the way, Thanksgiving is coming up, and Hanukkah too. Your birthday is two months away, and this year I'd like to celebrate your birthday and mine together, and Rachel's wedding is set for the spring."

"I believe in miracles," Dad said. "When do we start the treatments?"

"We'll have a consultation tomorrow, and after that, we'll implant a port," which I explained is a self-sealing device implanted under the collarbone for the delivery of chemotherapy into the subclavian vein." Robert and I would research the best treatment and facility options. "Dad, is there anything that you feel you have not done, something you've missed?"

"My cup runneth over," Dad said. "My life is fulfilled."

Just then, the dietary aide arrived with a tray containing a tuna sandwich, a small salad, and a cup of apple juice. "It looks delicious," he said. "Thank you so much."

Each of us offered to spend the night, but my father insisted that he needed his rest and that he'd be fine alone. "It's late," he said. "You should all go now. You look tired."

We each kissed him, hugged him, and expressed our love, our voices mustering enthusiasm from pained spirits. Instead of driving straight home, I met my brothers at Al B's house. On the way, I thought about my need to consult with oncologists at the University of Miami Sylvester Cancer Institute. I would also send the digital imaging and clinical record to a gastroenterological oncologist at Sloan Kettering in New York for a second opinion.

In Al B's formal dining room, where our family traditionally celebrates the first night of Rosh Hashanah, we discussed three subjects. The first was The Land of the Living, a cemetery on the outskirts of Jerusalem. Our family section includes approximately 80 graves that Russell had acquired. We discussed the positioning of our parents, of ourselves, of our children, and the possibility of other gravesites being added. Our parents, ourselves, and our spouses were committed to being buried in this setting, and we wanted to offer the option to our children.

I knew I needed to participate in the cost, commensurate with the size of my family, taking into account my six children, their spouses, and potentially their children. This could easily be up to forty percent of the graves. "I'll contribute forty percent of the cost," I said, recognizing my fair share of this responsibility.

"Whatever you want, David," Russell said, "but I'm happy to do this."

"The cost should be evenly distributed," Al B said. "I feel like a parent to my nieces and nephews, so some of my allotted graves can also be saved for them."

In 1946, soon after the end of World War II, my parents married in my mother's hometown of New Orleans, where my father had once been a pre-med student at Tulane University. In 1939, at Rosh Hashanah services at Anshei Sfard, one of the oldest synagogues in New Orleans, he had met my future grandfather, who invited my father home for a holiday meal. He met my mother upon entering the house, and at first glance, he fell in love. He was nineteen and she was sixteen, already a high school graduate and working as a bookkeeper and credit manager at

Rubenstein Brothers, a fine men's clothing store on Canal Street. They had dated for about a year and half when America entered the war. Expecting to be drafted, my father enlisted in Naval officer's training school, a six-month program at Fort Schuyler in New Jersey. He graduated as an ensign, and was assigned to the Pacific Theater. During the war, his billet was that of a navigator aboard a destroyer.

My parents married in my mother's aunt's home, before fifty relatives and friends. They honeymooned in Havana, and began their new life in South Florida, where my father began working for his brother and father at their hardware store at Fifth and Washington in Miami Beach. He stocked shelves and performed various custodial tasks, but the business went bankrupt in 1950. Robert was two years old at the time and I was about six months. My grandfather passed away later that year, after which, my father, a beneficiary of the GI Bill, enrolled at the University of Miami Law School. By the time he graduated three years later, Al B and Russell had also been born.

The way I understand it, my father had been his mother's favorite and his brother had been their father's favorite. My father grew up immersed in sibling rivalry. Furthermore, I believe it was my father's need to bring closure to his unresolved relationship with my grandfather, who died suddenly in 1950 that prompted his leadership role in the development of Mount Sinai Memorial Park in Opa Locka, where my grandfather had been buried. Two years later, my father became the cemetery's president and helped establish the not-for-profit foundation to ensure the economic stability and strength of the facility for future generations. This effort coincided with the early years of his struggling legal practice and his commitment at home as a husband and father.

In the mid-1950s, we spent our Sunday mornings at the largely vacant cemetery. My mother looked after my younger brothers while my father handled the business affairs of the cemetery with the full-time secretary, Mrs. Albaum. He also worked on the geometry of the twenty-five-acre property, naming the roads and sections, and he handled the collections and the distribution of income to the six not-for-profit synagogues that shared in the ownership of the cemetery, which was then less than twenty percent occupied. Robert and I found the vacant acreage, which is now the site of thousands of graves, to be an excellent baseball practice field. We practiced throwing, catching, pitching, and hitting. We were one and a half years apart and grew up best friends.

That night at Al B's house, we discussed the need for estate planning, to ensure a legacy for our parents' descendants. To be safe, Al B and Russell, both attorneys themselves, agreed to seek outside counsel. Lastly, we discussed the issue of how we would coordinate the treatment plan and how we would respond to the options we would soon receive from Sylvester and Sloan Kettering. It was important that none of us regret doing too much, or that we might regret not trying some cutting edge, experimental therapy. The marker for our efforts would be prolonging the quality of our father's life and following his wishes.

The next day, I met with Dr. Citron, a senior oncologist at South Miami. "Although he's older, he's still vigorous," the doctor said. "I would give him the chemotherapy. He wants to fight this."

The evening before the procedure to implant Dad's port, I went into his hospital room. I needed to hear it from him one more time that he was comfortable with the treatment plan. "Are you sure you're ready to proceed with chemotherapy?"

"I'm willing to fight," my father said, "but either way, my life has been fulfilled. My greatest accomplishment is my family, and every moment I have is a bonus."

The next morning, my father received his port. When I visited him that night, Russell and Al B had just gone home. Dad was sitting in his bedside chair, eating a tuna sandwich. I was exhausted from the day, having performed a coronary artery bypass at South Miami, a lung resection at Aventura Hospital, and having seen at least thirty-five patients in my North Dade office.

"Dad, are you having any pain below your left collarbone?" I asked, referring to the site of his port.

"It feels fine," he said, "but I'm tired and I'd like to go home first thing tomorrow."

Entering my father's room, I'd noticed that someone had written "Beloved of God" on his dry-erase board.

"Why is this here?" I asked my father.

"I asked my nurse if she knew you, and she said yes, and so I asked her if she knew what your name means, and her response was no, so I informed her that David means *beloved of God*."

I kissed his forehead. "Dad, I love you," I said. "Gita will pick you up at about nine. I turned away and left his room, not letting him see my tears.

I visited Mom on the way home. "Dad's coming home tomorrow. He's in great spirits," I said, "and full of surprises. With God's help, the chemotherapy may be beneficial."

"I'm falling in love with him all over again," my mother said. "It's like I'm sixteen and it's the first time I met him. He was so handsome in his Navy uniform. I want him back home with me."

"It's going to be great having him home," I said.

Chapter 3: Limitless Promise and Impending Grief

In the morning, Gita helped my father check out of the hospital. "He's so weak, David," she said on the phone.

I regretted not being there, but that day I'd performed an abdominal aortic aneurysm resection in a morbidly obese patient. Despite my great difficulty in obtaining the exposure of the aorta in this 400-pound man, I remained focused and persistent and completed the procedure. Later in the day I met with the Director of Public Health from the Cayman Islands, who wanted to strategize about South Miami Hospital becoming a destination to Caymanian patients. Throughout my career, I have been active in the marketing of my practice, rather than relying exclusively on referrals from cardiologists.

I then prepped a patient from the Bahamas, scheduled for open-heart surgery in the morning, and I spent another ninety minutes in rush hour traffic, driving up to Broward County for Nili's first basketball game against the David Posnak Hebrew Day School at the Posnak JCC. I missed all but the last five minutes, but I noted Nili's happiness upon spotting me in the bleachers. On the ride home, Nili was upset because an excellent younger player who had outscored her that evening and had gained their coach's confidence as the team leader.

"Nobody believes in me," she said.

"You have to believe in yourself," I said, "and I believe in you. That should be enough."

"But you don't understand. I hate school and I have no friends."

"Sweetheart, despite my best efforts, I was never perceived as an exceptional student in school and I had few friends in my class, but I had so much love from my parents. When I was growing up, my father always expressed a profound interest in everything I did, and thanks to him, I learned to believe in myself."

"But you and Mommy don't always believe in me. Sometimes your belief depends on what I do."

"That's not true, Nili. My love is unconditional. You're beautiful, bright, and you're a great athlete. You don't appreciate it now, but I promise you will in the future. Perhaps I've forgotten how difficult it is growing up."

As Nili stared out the window as we drove, I shared my memory of competing in sports. "In one-on-one competitive sports like tennis, when the game could be lost on a faulty serve or a simple forehand shot, I'd say to myself, 'I'm Hymie Galbut's son.'

On occasion, I've even used this rallying for heightened concentration in my work when things don't go as planned."

"Really?"

"Your mother and I love you no matter what," I said. "Let that be *your* rallying call. To us you are the greatest."

Driving south along I-95 back toward Miami Beach, the soft music blended with the rush of the air conditioning and the sound of the road. I sensed Nili's stress diminishing, as if escaping through the open sunroof.

"Zayde will get better, right, with chemo or radiation?"

"We're beginning chemotherapy, but it's not that simple."

"Can't you just scoop out the tumor?"

"Sometimes that's all it takes, but not all cancers can be resolved surgically," I said, "particularly when the tumor is not localized. Zayde's cancer has spread to his liver, and his age is also a negative factor."

"If this cancer is the same as Aunt Miriam's," Nili said, crying in the seat beside me, "then, Daddy, you could also get cancer. I don't want that ever to happen to you."

Her tears touched my heart, and I began to cry also. And then I explained that when a person reaches old age, the angel of death often comes in the form of a cancer, a stroke, or a heart attack.

"Let's visit Zayde tonight," she said.

At my parents' house, Louisiana was massaging my father's feet. Dad always loved having his feet massaged, which was generally a chore accomplished by my mother, and occasionally by his sons when we were much, much younger. Louisiana, who had cared for Dad's sister a year earlier, was now a fixture at my parents' house. She admired my parents, who'd visited my aunt daily during her final six months. Louisiana, a pretty thirtyish Haitian woman was studying to become a licensed practical nurse at Miami Dade College. Mom appreciated Louisiana's professionalism and warm companionship. On any given day, they might discuss Louisiana's nursing courses, household budgetary matters, the stock market, and just about anything else.

Nili held my father's hand, smiled, and told him about the basketball season ahead. I thought how similar she is to Gita, so strong-willed and independent, probably the reason they sometimes struggle to get along.

Russell was there too, and we spoke to my mother in her study. "Mom," Russell, said, the estate planning is going beautifully. Al B is a great lawyer, and we'll complete the paperwork in the next few weeks."

"I want to preserve my independence and my ability to continue giving my money away." Mom was referring to the hundreds of financial gifts she distributes to members of our family annually. Her tone conveyed the authority she'd earned as the financial manager in her marriage and as a bookkeeper in her youth.

"You'll never have to worry about that," Russell said.

As Mom walked back to her chair, Dad struggled to stand up, and I helped him into the bathroom. I left the door open, so I could keep an eye on him just in case.

With tears in her eyes now, Nili asked my father if he needed anything.

"I'm OK," he said.

While Dad was in the bathroom, Mom completed her final nebulizer treatment for the evening, inhaling deeply from the mouthpiece connected to a medicated cylinder. Upon exhaling, she sometimes coughed uncontrollably.

Working the twelve-hour night shift, Louisiana had become an outstanding companion for my mother. She had also grown to love my father, having met him when he still had his full vigor, and now she was confronting his deterioration. I touched her shoulder. "You're one terrific person. Our family can't thank you enough for your kindness."

"Thank you, Dr. David," she said as my father emerged from the bathroom.

"Everybody, go home," my father announced, sitting down in his chair beside my mother. He picked up his remote control and searched through the channels. "It's late. I love you. I'll see you in the morning."

As we left the house, I put my arm around Nili and said to Russell, "We'll need a male aide for him within the week."

"I'll take care of it," Russell said.

Back home, I saw Riki who'd driven down from Hollywood; Elle and her husband Jaime, who'd returned from a New York vacation a day early; Dani and Josh and their daughter Yvonne, who'd flown down from Toronto. After a quick bite, Gita told me that Ethan was proposing to our fourth daughter Rachel. The romantic plan, unraveling as we spoke, involved a boat ride to Prime Grill, on the Intracoastal Waterway in Aventura, a visit to their new apartment on Meridian Avenue—adorned in flowers and candles—followed by Ethan's proposal. Rachel accepted, and the two of them went to my parents' home to share the news even before Gita and I received a phone call.

As Rachel described it, my father held her hand with a great smile, although his eyes remained closed as he sloped over in his recliner. Living for these moments, my mother gave Ethan and Rachel their first gift, a generous check to help them get started in their life together.

At the home of Ethan's parents, Debbie and Marty Wasserman, the rest of our family welcomed Rachel and Ethan as they arrived in their white limousine. The evening was filled with champagne toasts to the love of the childhood sweethearts, and to their bright, exciting future. But through it all, I caught myself wondering, "How can a moment contain both limitless promise and such pending grief?" In a transcendent moment, I hugged my three pregnant daughters, poised to raise their families together; and I observed Rachel's beauty, so much like her mother, but at the same time, I could not erase the finality of my father's illness.

My parents spent much of the next day together. In the morning, Ronalee took my mother to South Miami Hospital's respiratory therapy outpatient department to begin a twice-weekly exercise regimen. My mother also visited Dr. Rodney Benjamin, her pulmonologist, to discuss her medications. And once again, I met with Dr. Citron, who maintained that we initiate the chemotherapy. After a telephone interview with a specialist at Sloan Kettering, we elected to consult the expert in pancreatic cancer at the University of Miami Sylvester Cancer Institute.

At my parents' house, I found my father resting on his bed in the spot that for so many years had been my mother's, further from the bathroom. He rested comfortably, nearly asleep, as the hour approached 8:30 p.m. "How was your day?" I asked him.

"Riki and Elle were here with the kids. They played with the trains, and they ate potato chips, but I'm tired now," he added. "I could use a good night's sleep."

I examined him. He was not breathless, but his skin felt warm. I took his temperature and confirmed a low-grade fever. He denied any abdominal pain and his soft abdomen confirmed this. However, his legs were swollen more than ever, probably a consequence of fluid retention and reduced protein production, typical of a body in the process of breaking down. I kissed him on the forehead, wished him a good night, and spoke to my mother about her visit with Dr. Benjamin at the front door.

"He says I should exercise three times a week to continue improving and to build my reserve."

"That's how you'll help protect yourself from infection," I said.

Back home, Nili said her team had lost 40-36 to a team in Boca Raton. She'd scored 18 points. "Where were you?" Nili said. "I kept looking for you from the court."

"I'm so sorry," I said. "You know you *are* my priority." I admire doing more and saying less, but my actions have not always been true to my beliefs. At times I've accepted this incongruity because of the demands of my work, but in reality it's a rationalization.

"Nili, I've often told you that I believe in no excuses. One should do what he says. I'm sorry I let you down."

"It's OK," Nili said, but I knew it wasn't.

"You were the team's high scorer," I said. "The need to demonstrate excellence is a daily challenge, but your belief in your abilities must remain constant, regardless of the ups and downs."

"You mean *confidence*?"

"Exactly," I said.

At about 9 p.m., I got a call back from the gastrointestinal oncologist at Sylvester who'd been highly recommended by Sloan Kettering.

"The best regimen is Gemzar and Tarceva. The former is given intravenously on a weekly basis and the latter orally on a daily basis."

"What can we expect this to do for him?"

"If he responds, he'll have reduced symptoms of pain and a prolongation of life…perhaps a few months."

"What percentage of patients respond?"

"Maybe one-third," he said.

On Shabbat we had a full house, with the exception of Riki and her children. Enjoying the Friday night family dinner with our children and grandchildren was as good as it gets. Our large dining room accommodates about thirty people. Gita, Elle, Dani, and Elana had lit the Sabbath candles. The table was beautifully set with our best china and silver.

Lifting my favorite Kiddush cup, a gift from Gita, to sanctify the Sabbath with the blessing over the wine, I felt the Sabbath's ability to protect us from the daily stresses, and how it reminds us to reconnect with our families. These spectacular meals are among Gita's most radiant moments. We typically begin with gefilte fish or stuffed cabbage or Moroccan stuffed pike, followed by chicken soup replete with carrots, onions, parsley, and potatoes. We then enjoy coleslaw and a garden salad including artichokes, hearts of palm, and when it's in season, fresh avocado. Entrees typically include stuffed shoulder of veal, honey-baked chicken, and roasted beef ribs. After the wine and throughout the meal, we enjoy Rachel's specialty, fresh-baked challah. Dessert includes apple pie, chocolate cake, or a strawberry shortcake and a selection of seasonal fruits such as grapes, strawberries, blueberries, watermelon, and papaya.

At these feasts, Gita and I sit at opposite ends of our large table, overlooking Biscayne Bay reflecting the city lights, and we are like bookends, with our children and grandchildren seated between us. The children share what they are studying in school or we might discuss the week's Torah portion.

That night, I decided that for the duration of my father's illness, I would visit them every Friday night at the conclusion of our Shabbat meal.

After Shabbat dinner, Rachel and I arrived at my parents' house at about 10 p.m. Mom was playing Rummikub with Louisiana, while Dad slept in the second bedroom with the TV on. For twenty minutes, I watched him breathe. He didn't appear to be in any agony or pain, although his respiratory rate was rapid, and I sensed that his interest in life was waning. Here was a man who had always been in control, and in his youth was the strongest man I'd ever known. Could he endure what lay ahead and how would I fulfill my role as both a son and a physician?

I kissed my mother good night and walked home with Rachel, who discussed her sisters, her friends, and her upcoming wedding. Given Rachel's enormous understanding, I knew she was ready to deal with the challenges of marriage.

On Saturday, I attended early synagogue services, made rounds, and had Shabbat lunch at home. I visited Dad after the afternoon prayer and found him angry and agitated. He hadn't slept well the night before but had slept during the day and was relatively disgusted.

"Why wasn't my blood sugar corrected?" Up to this point, his type II diabetes had been controlled with oral agents and diet, but with the advent of his pancreatic cancer, the production of insulin continued to diminish and his frequent blood sugar checks revealed inadequate control.

"Dad, you've reached the point of needing insulin. This will control your blood sugar."

"What's the real cause of my problem?"

With love and tenderness, I reminded him that the tumor in his pancreas had spread to his liver and was therefore inoperable.

"Why am I always cold? Your mother keeps the thermostat too low."

"I believe the tumor may be responsible for a low-grade temperature, which is contributing to your feeling uncomfortable. I'm certain Mommy will adjust the thermostat for you."

I waited a few moments, conveying a willingness to answer any questions, but none came. "We're initiating chemotherapy tomorrow, and I promise that you'll have adequate medication to help you sleep and to keep you relaxed. The chemotherapy will help contain the tumor and hopefully minimize the symptoms. Proper nutrition will also be important, along with a positive attitude, which has always been your trademark."

As I left, I realized that the classic four levels of confrontation of terminal illness—denial, anger, acceptance, and resolution—can vary in sequence and intensity. Dad's *acceptance*, which he had demonstrated through comments of fulfillment with his family and the duration of his life, were now juxtaposed with his demonstration of anger.

On Saturday evening we attended a surprise birthday party at Aventura Lakes Country Club for Miki, my oldest son-in-law, who had just turned thirty-four. We enjoyed a Chinese dinner, disco dancing, and a chocolate birthday cake and fruit salad. At the function, my wife looked like she could have been Riki's sister. Elle, Elana, and Dani, my three expecting daughters, danced together in pregnant silhouettes, along with their sisters Riki, Rachel, and Nili.

My sons-in-law tended bar, perhaps oversampling the various spirits.

"Who's the designated driver?" I said.

Each one pointed to another and said, "He is."

Pointing to the dance floor, I said, "Aren't they beautiful? You guys are among the luckiest men in the world."

None of them argued with me for a second, and each assured me that their wives would be driving them home.

Early the next morning, Mom called and said my father had awakened angry and agitated. "I gave him his Xanax, but he hardly slept. Now he's saying it's time to die."

I arrived fifteen minutes later with a visiting nurse, who was coming to the house twice daily to check Dad's blood sugar, which was 300 today, and to administer his insulin.

By now my father seemed calm as he sat in his recliner beside my mother's chair in their bedroom.

"The chemotherapy has a great chance of giving you more quality time," I said. "You have six great-grandchildren on the way, plus Rachel's wedding. You have a shot, Dad, because you're strong." I heard my encouragement, filled with half-truths, but in the end, I hoped it would all be worth it.

"OK, David, but how can I sleep better?"

"We'll find the right medicine," I assured him.

At ten o'clock, we had the birthday party for my two grandchildren, Yve and Eme, born a week apart two years before.

"He's my life, David," she said, "and I know I must stay strong so I can be here for him."

My mother is a righteous woman with the highest level of mental strength and conviction in God's benevolence. "You'll be strong," I said, "and your kindness will help minimize his suffering, and we'll pray for a miracle with the chemotherapy."

Later that Sunday morning, at 10:15, Al B brought my parents to our house for the last party my father would attend in our home, on a day in which musical "Happy Birthday" balloons containing motion-activated sensors, ricocheted off the walls and ceilings.

My parents sat to my left, in their established place, at our dining room table. I paid particular attention to my father, almost quantifying his caloric intake. His plate contained pickled herring in white sauce, part of a vegetable omelet and half of a toasted, scooped-out bagel. He drank orange juice and coffee, and after the meal, Yve and Eme sat on their great-grandfather's lap before their Carvel "Princess" cake adorned with pink candles.

After the girls received their gifts, my father decided to lie down. I helped him over to the black couch in our large family room overlooking the bay. He reclined and fell asleep, as he had done hundreds of times before during the twenty years we've been in our home.

My mother pulled me aside. "Dr. Benjamin insists that I don't go to the chemotherapy unit with your father."

"He's right, Mom. You have to save your strength and minimize your exposure to bad germs."

"I'm living on borrowed time," she said, referring to how she had expected to encounter the angel of death the previous June. "When one's spouse leaves, the second one is not far behind."

"That's often true, but I believe God has given you improved health for a reason. You still have a mission. Your family needs you, Mom."

"It's all in God's hands, but yes, I want to carry on your father's work."

I'm five years old and it's around 9 a.m. on a Saturday. My mother is dressed in colorful summer cotton. My father is dressed in a suit and holding my mother's hand. I hold my father's other hand as we march the five blocks from our home to Temple Zamora.

Along the way, we pass the front yard of a house where the grass is different. It's greener and thicker than the surrounding lawns. The grass is being attended to by an elderly man who I can see takes great pride in his gardening.

"Lazy man's grass, right?" my father says.

"Botanists call it centipede grass," the homeowner says. "Everybody else around here has St. Augustine, which is fine, but I wanted something a little different."

"You have a beautiful lawn," my father says.

As we continue toward the synagogue, I say, "I can't walk anymore. I'm tired." I know that if I complain enough, Dad will lift me onto his shoulders. As we continue walking, I complain to my father, "My feet hurt."

"Walking is the easiest thing in the world," Dad says. "Just take one step after another, and before you know it, you'll arrive at your destination."

After the birthday party, I gathered in our kitchen with Ronalee, Gita, and with the three girls carrying new life—Dani,

Elle, and Elana—along with Rachel, to complete the cleanup. We discussed my father's upcoming days. I explained what was in store for him, including the possible benefits of the chemotherapy, and how we must look at each day as a gift with specific goals. Later that month we would celebrate Thanksgiving at Russell and Ronalee's house. Beyond that, our goals for my father included welcoming six more great-grandchildren (my three new grandchildren, Robert's two, and Al B's one.) I looked forward to seeing Dad hold these babies as they arrived over the next six months—with at least two coming in December.

That evening, about 6 p.m., I visited my parents. Rachel had already been with them much of the afternoon. Dad sat in his recliner beside Mom's chair, watching the second half of a football game. Gita had brought a container of vanilla Häagen-Dazs, and she sat with my father for about fifteen minutes, feeding him spoonfuls of ice cream.

"Thank you," he said, "that was delicious. And thank you for the wonderful day. The function was great. I love being with the kids."

Chapter 4: The Creative Force of Optimism

Most Sunday mornings, Gita and I take a long walk together. In recent weeks, we had taken to parking somewhere on Alton Road north of Lincoln Road, and walking south along West Avenue from 20th Street and discussing the upcoming weeks. I was preparing to attend the American Heart Association convention in Dallas. I had spent a year setting up the Florida marketing for AngioNew, a New York company developing a machine that delivers a noninvasive treatment option for angina. In Dallas I would visit the AngioNew booth and discuss the marketing strategy with the owners. Pending the response of the specialist at Sylvester, my father was scheduled to begin chemotherapy in my absence.

"Perhaps you should cancel the trip," Gita said.

"It's the largest annual meeting for cardiologists in the world. In any event, it's just a day trip, and I'll keep my phone on," I said, comforted by the fact that Gita would be with my father throughout the day.

"OK," Gita said. "I was planning to be with him during his chemotherapy treatments anyway."

"Thank you," I said. I kissed her cheek and placed my arm around her waist.

On our walk that Sunday, Gita reminisced about her own father, who had succumbed to esophageal cancer fifteen years earlier. He had been treated with a surgical resection, and once the cancer returned, he received chemotherapy. Gita never missed his treatments, which he tolerated well. The last months, he too experienced great love from his family, and I believe he found peace in his heart. I functioned as a son-in-law who became a son. I also remained his physician throughout his battle and I attended to him in his final days, hours, and minutes.

I flew to Dallas Monday morning. AngioNew had set up a booth where they demonstrated the product to cardiologists and other health care providers from across the country and around the world. The purpose of my trip was to study the competition and to present my marketing plan for the state of Florida. Although my body was in Dallas, my mind was back at Sylvester. Every hour, I called Gita, who was waiting with my father and Russell for the first consult with the specialist. That day, my father's physical exam revealed a temperature of 101, which raised the clinical question of cause, which was either an infection, or perhaps it was indicative of tissue breakdown from the tumor. Until this was clarified, the chemotherapy could not begin.

"David," Gita said on the phone, "He's devastated."

"What do you mean?"

"Actually, Russell just came back into the room … here," she said, "I'll let you talk to the doctor yourself. She handed the doctor her cellphone. "Tell my husband what you just told us."

Without a perfunctory greeting, the doctor said to me, "Based on the two CT scans, your father's tumor is galloping from the end of October into the first week of November. There's little chance of the chemotherapy being effective."

"What? Is my father there?"

"Yes, and your brother is here too."

"What else did you tell him?"

"I explained that the side effects could include nausea, diarrhea, weakness, and shortness of breath. I question whether chemotherapy is advised. In my estimation, he has less than a month to live and he should consider this in making his decision."

"How's my father taking this?"

"He told me to give it to him straight."

"I'll return this evening," I said. "The family is committed to chemotherapy, and to resolve the cause of the fever, I want him admitted for evaluation and blood work." Further, I suggested that if the blood cultures had no growth, that we should accept the cause as being tissue breakdown from the tumor and begin the chemotherapy at once.

When a patient says, "Give it to me straight," that doesn't give the doctor carte blanche to shoot the patient in the head, particularly when the patient has some semblance of well-being. Besides, how can a doctor foretell that a patient has one month or three months? Statistics and averages don't always fit an individual patient. The importance of a sense of mission and hope, along with family support, dramatically influence an outcome. With my patients, I emphasize statistical expectations, but I always add the importance of three factors: the patient's commitment to recovery; my ability to achieve peak performance from myself and my team; and last but perhaps most important, God or destiny. Any heart surgeon who thinks he controls the world cannot be a top performer.

After my last meeting, I took a cab to the airport in the late afternoon for my return flight to Miami. The specialist had reluctantly agreed to follow my wishes regarding my father's admission for tests, and Gita informed me that Dad was shaken but that he insisted upon his belief in miracles and that he wanted to proceed with the chemotherapy.

"Gita, let me speak with Russell," I said.

"Of course," Gita said, handing my brother her phone.

"We need to determine the cause of his fever," I told Russell, "but we've got the wrong oncologist."

"The guy's a son of a bitch without heart," Russell said.

"I don't believe his conclusions," I said. "I'll speak to the Chief of Service when I get back. Give Daddy encouragement and tell him I'll see him later tonight. I'll come straight from the airport."

On the flight from Dallas, I remembered the summer I sold mangos with an older boy in Coral Gate. We used the red wagon my parents had given me for my fifth birthday to carry the mangos we collected from nearby homes. Upon arriving home several hours later that Saturday afternoon, I walked into the house, announcing that I'd earned fourteen cents. My mother, infuriated by my entrepreneurship on the Sabbath, took off her shoe and struck my backside with her heel. "We don't work on the Sabbath!"

This reminded me of the unity of my parents. Although my father's background was more secular, he participated with my mother in her desire to raise their family in an environment consistent with Orthodox Judaism. In return, my mother accepted Dad's commitment to the Navy and to community service.

I also thought about how Robert had won the American Heart Association Summer Scholarship, and how during that year,

Dad had chaired the fundraising campaign. And I thought of Al B and his early stuttering. Our father admitted that he too had stuttered, but overcame his impediment by forcing himself to remain silent until he had determined exactly what his words would be. Despite a year of speech therapy, it was Dad's mentoring that helped Al B become a clear thinker and an excellent speaker who later became a Navy lieutenant in the Jag Division.

And I thought of the weekly photos Dad had taken of Russell and his childhood friend Ruben, who'd lived in our house for about a year, and how they progressed from being overweight to becoming fit and trim. Over the course of four months, my father kept them on calorie-restricted diets and encouraged them to take long walks and to perform basic exercises. One summer, Russell, who was about nine at the time, accompanied Dad for his two weeks of active duty in the Navy Reserve while the rest of us remained in Miami. Being the youngest is often difficult, but the time they spent alone together helped Russell appreciate Dad's love for all his children. And the regimented environment of the base in Norfolk, Virginia gave my youngest brother a sense of discipline that he's never lost.

Flying back from Dallas, I also pondered the early years with my father and how he treated Mom like a queen, always demonstrating that the best action a father can do for a child is to love his mother. Even so, to outsiders he often appeared autocratic and controlling. His upbringing had been dysfunctional, with a father and mother who played favorites with their children, and he hadn't gotten along with his older brother, but he always loved his younger sister Miriam. I also pondered my father's great love for his children, his commitment to never show favoritism, and his efforts to ensure our safety and success.

When Russell's was in high school, Dad went to war with the Hebrew Academy principal who had accused my brother of plagiarism. Russell, who was not always appreciated for his unique approach to school, had been no stranger to the principal's office. On this occasion, Dad insisted that Russell rewrite his paper in the principal's office, with the chairman of the English Department and my father present. The resulting document was consistent with Russell's initial submission. Embarrassed, it's safe to say that the principal continued his ongoing grudge against my youngest brother. Realizing the principal's negative opinion of Russell, my father asked the school's founding rabbi to write Russell's recommendation letter to Cornell University's School of Hotel Management, where he earned his bachelor's degree before later becoming a C.P.A. and later, an attorney.

For whatever reason, on that nonstop from Dallas I also recalled how Dad encouraged my growth as a public speaker. In seventh grade, I volunteered for the school's annual oratorical contest. I chose a monologue of jokes for my three-minute presentation. The contest was attended by the entire junior high student body. The first four contestants wore suits, white shirts, and ties. They were well-prepared and spoke beautifully. When I was called upon, I walked to the podium, dressed casually in khaki pants and a short-sleeve blue shirt. Peering into the audience, I realized that I was not ready to participate. I began crying and sat down.

Afterward, one of the judges approached me. "You have two days to prepare yourself better."

That evening, during dinner, I told my parents about the day's debacle.

"You will become a great speaker," my father said.

After two nights of writing and rewriting my new presentation, and hours of rehearsal before the hallway mirror, I presented with greater confidence and was properly dressed, but I still had much to learn about public speaking.

Several months later, my father entered me into the Optimist International Oratorical Contest. The National Optimist Organization earmarks boys between the ages of twelve and fifteen, and organizes national football, basketball, and oratorical contests in order to develop character, performance skills, and leadership. The contest was held by the ten individual Optimist clubs in Dade County. The winner from each club then competed on a regional level. Beyond that, an elite few progressed to the state and national level. The subject of the five-minute oratorical speech was, of course, a derivative of optimism. The topics my three years included "Optimism, Ingredient for Leadership," "The Creative Force of Optimism," and "Optimism, Basis for Freedom."

In preparation, I spent long hours writing speeches, and to rehearse, I walked around the neighborhood, speaking out loud. Or I would stand before a mirror, going over it repeatedly until I was satisfied. Although a participant was only supposed to compete in one Optimist Club contest, my father enrolled me in as many club contests as were required for me to ultimately win. One year, this included three different clubs in different parts of Dade County. With his encouragement, I scrapped my notes and memorized my speeches. I committed to becoming a great speaker, and I knew that the best speakers didn't rely upon notes but rather spoke to the audience with sincerity. One evening during my second year of participation, in a fancy Coral Gables restaurant, the audio system was too magnified for the participants. As I spoke, I came closer to the microphone, ignoring the ricochet of sound within the small room, which must have irritated the audience. Afterward, my father took me to Dairy Queen, where we each got a vanilla cone. "Tonight, David, you spoke great, but you were deceived by the microphone, which was like a snake."

"I don't understand."

"The key, David, is to be in touch with your surroundings and not be influenced by disruptive forces."

That was the most important ice cream cone I've ever had.

The summer after tenth grade, when I was fifteen, Dad sent me to Ohio State University, in Columbus, for the Summer Center for Communicative Arts. Ohio State boasts an enrollment of about fifty thousand students, about ten thousand of whom are on campus during the summer. I was there to study debate in a program designed for high school debate and theater students. The National Forensic League chooses a topic for the year. I will never forget the 1963 topic: "Should nuclear weapons be banned from proliferation?"

Back home in the confines of Miami Beach, I attended a private Jewish school, and there I was in Ohio, thrust into the heart of Billy Graham Country, where the popular evangelist preached in a month-long crusade at a football stadium about an hour away.

There were maybe five Jews among the eighty-something participants in the debate program. Early on, I felt lonely and displaced, but within a week, I became quite popular among the other kids. For the six weeks of the intensive program, we lived in college dormitories. The summer program was divided into two three-week sessions, each culminating with a formal tournament. The other students all belonged to their high school debate teams, but at the Hebrew Academy we had more of a non-competitive public speaking club.

Two days before the tournament, my father called. "I'll see you tomorrow," he said.

My father and I spent the day and evening together. We walked throughout the campus and he told me how proud he was of my efforts and accomplishments, and he expressed his belief that I was a great speaker and that life is wonderful if one takes advantage of opportunity.

"Have you ever doubted me?" I asked my father.

"You're my son, and no matter how you perform in the tournament, it won't matter because the act of being here and competing is simply enough."

Over dinner in a campus cafeteria, I said, "Dad, really, why did you come?"

"I had business in Ohio," he said.

"What kind of business?"

"Important business," he said.

And with that, I understood.

***

Upon arriving home from Dallas, I drove to Sylvester, where Dad had been admitted for the fever. Since the morning flight, I couldn't shake the guilt of leaving town on the morning of my father's first visit with his oncologist. He always put his children first—he flew to Ohio to see me participate in a lousy debate—but rather than attend to him during his chemotherapy, I flew to Texas for a doctor's convention.

A beautiful smile lit his face, and I could see again that I was still the little child he'd always loved unconditionally.

"It's not your time," I said. "Your mind and body are strong, but I believe the fever is contributing to your exhaustion."

"That oncologist is a putz," Dad said.

My father's second floor room overlooked a large oak tree and a manicured garden. One could assess the strength of the wind by the dance of the leaves.

"Dad, the two X-rays are apples and oranges. One came from a newer generation machine, producing greater definition. It makes a precise comparison impossible."

My father's eyes locked on me, searching for any sign of hope.

"We believe in miracles," I said, and I reminded him of the story of his beloved sister, Miriam, and how the chief of oncology at Mount Sinai had given Miriam less than a week to live. After I adjusted her narcotic medication, she lived another seven months.

"Dad, what do you feel about your life? Is there anything that you wish to do at this time?"

"My cup runneth over. I have accomplished everything that I need to accomplish."

"Is there anything special you want from your sons?"

"You have already given me the greatest joy," he said. "Please, David, go home and rest."

"I'm hungry, Dad. Let's eat together first."

I ate a sandwich Al B had picked up.

"I want to get home and be with Mom," he said. "She's unhappy being there alone."

As I kissed my father good night, I thought, here lies the most powerful, knowledgeable, perceptive man I've ever known, and tonight is no different. I touched his forehead, and his temperature seemed normal. "Tomorrow will be a better day," I said.

In the morning I called Mom during my drive to South Miami Hospital to perform coronary bypass surgery on a professor of neuro-ophthalmology from the University of Miami.

"I thank God for my beautiful life with your father," my mother said.

That day, Russell and Al B spent several hours with my Mom and Dad at Sylvester, along with an attorney handling their estate planning.

I called Dad after my morning operation. "How are you feeling?"

"Great," he said. "Your brothers are here, with counsel, working on the estate. Gita brought a great lunch for everyone from Tasty Delight."

That afternoon his blood and urine cultures came back negative, prompting the infectious disease consultant to discontinue all antibiotics. There was no longer any reason for my father to be hospitalized, as the tests had been concluded and his IV had been disconnected. Nevertheless, the oncologist was still reluctant to accept the cause of the fever being tissue destruction from the tumor, and so he refused to initiate chemotherapy.

Within the previous year, I had first met Dr. Joseph Rosenblatt, Director of Hematology/Oncology at Sylvester, at a charity dinner for Chai Lifeline, an organization that supports families of children with cancer. At different times, we had each been honored for our service to cancer patients. I decided to pull rank and solicit Dr. Rosenblatt to become my father's oncologist. I couldn't allow any physician treating my father to demonstrate such heartlessness as what he heard the day I was in Dallas. With such thoughts in his mind, my father would spend his remaining days living like a dead man.

"Now that bacterial infection has been ruled out, it's probable that the fever is the consequence of the tumor burden," I maintained. "And if this so, then chemotherapy may be of benefit."

"Let's discharge your father tonight," Dr. Rosenblatt said. "We'll do a chest X-ray in the morning, and if that's negative, we'll begin chemotherapy."

With Dr. Rosenblatt's order, my father's nurse sent him home with me and Rachel at 10:30 that evening. In my parents' driveway, I admired my father's strength as he approached the house, marching up the steps of his home with his walker. Mom waited for him on the top step, where she gave him a big kiss on the lips. "It is so wonderful to have you home, Hymie. I love you."

"It's wonderful to see you too, Miss America."

Dad sat in his electric recliner, designed to offer massage and to raise him to a standing position. He dozed off with a smile, surrounded by Mom, Gita, Al B, and four of his grandchildren, Brian, Erica, Kimberly, and Rachel.

Leaving the house that night, I pondered the actions of the man everyone outside the family knew simply as "Captain Galbut."

That night, Mom called at 3:50 a.m. At that hour, no call is good.

"Your father fell in the bathroom."

"I'll be right there," I said. Then I called Russell, woke up my son-in-law Jamie, and we went to the house. The lights were on and the televisions were blasting in both bedrooms. We found my father resting on the bathroom floor with a blanket over him.

"Did you feel faint?" I asked.

"I just lost my balance. I turned around and fell, and now I can't get up."

Jamie and I, along with Al B and Russell, who arrived a few minutes after we did, lifted Dad from the floor and helped him to the bed. I sensed from the power in his grip as he held onto us that he still had good strength in his upper extremities. Once he was in the bed, we cleaned him up, got him into fresh pajamas, and gave him a new pillow. He had a fever of 102, so I gave him a dose of Tylenol.

"Dad, does anything hurt you?"

"Go home, everybody," he said. "I'm fine now."

"Tomorrow we have a big day…three hours from now. Hopefully we'll begin the chemotherapy. Are you are up for it?"

"I'll see you bright and early," Dad said.

In the morning, we arrived at Sylvester to find a sea of people waiting for tests, diagnoses, consultations, and chemotherapy. I wondered how many were getting treatments in vain, how many would recover, and how many would appear to recover, only to be disappointed a few months or many years down the road? But perhaps the act itself permits some reaction to the illness and some semblance of personal contribution to healing.

Dr. Rosenblatt confirmed my hope that here was a doctor with knowledge and a heart. "Your father looks strong," he said, "and not too impaired from the ravages of his disease at this time. And we can't overlook the care and support from your mother and everyone else."

"Absolutely," I said.

"And I know your wife is quite involved too."

"She's amazing," I said. "She loves him very much. We all do."

Dr. Rosenblatt invited me into his office to review the laboratory data. The blood and urine cultures were negative, and with the radiologist, we reviewed Dad's morning chest film, which showed no evidence of obvious infection or pneumonia. We also reviewed Dad's CT scan.

"There is a large amount of disease in the liver," Dr. Rosenblatt said. "I don't treat many GI tumors," he added as we walked toward the chemotherapy treatment unit. "I specialize in lymphomas, but one of my greatest successes involved a patient with an inoperable liver cancer?"

"What type?"

"A cholangiocarcinoma, which I treated with a complex regimen including aggressive chemotherapy and high-intensity radiation. Ultimately, a liver resection was performed in France. Given the circumstances, no surgeon in America would accept the liability."

"As an American surgeon, I can certainly empathize. The tort system is out of control."

"She's still alive, five years later."

"That's quite an accomplishment," I said, knowing that my father was not a candidate for surgery. "By the way, I believe my daughter Nili is a classmate with your son Joshua at the Hebrew Academy."

"Yes, I met her in Hollywood, where we live. She's very beautiful. I'm sure you understand Hebrew," he said.

I nodded.

"Regarding your father, Dr. Rosenblatt said, *Hashem Yazor*," which I knew meant, "God should help."

Dr. Rosenblatt picked up a phone at the nurse's station and dictated his consult, including orders for a full treatment of Gemzar. He then reviewed his orders with the head oncology nurse.

As my father was wheeled from the waiting room into the treatment bay, I overheard the nurses at the desk expressing curiosity as to who Hymie Galbut was, and what was the basis for the special attention from the chief of service. I thanked the head nurse and said, "I've only heard great things about your unit, and we're glad to be here."

In the treatment area, we spotted, Billy Sotchkin, an old family friend who, for over a decade, had been receiving chemotherapy for multiple myeloma, a form of blood cancer. "I'm sorry to see you here, Hymie."

I was saddened by their ensuing dialogue, and tears filled my eyes. Billy saw this and put his arm around me. I felt better, and then my father, with a knowing smile, held Billy's hand in a handshake, massaging the dorsum—the back of his hand—expressing great affection, and in doing so, I was reminded of how my father was the master of keeping in touch and of delivering the right touch.

For several minutes, Billy reminisced with us about how he came to Miami from Cuba in the late 1950s, and how his father had run a sundries shop within Al's Corner, which my grandfather had founded. This was a wandering complex of businesses located on the southeast corner of Fifth and Washington. Al's Corner, or "Al's" as we always called it, included a drugstore featuring candy displays; playing cards and poker chips; cigarettes, cigars, and pipe tobaccos; an auto tag agency; a postal annex; a pinball arcade; and a twenty-four-hour diner. Completing the corner to the south was a walk-up pizzeria and bakery, and to the east, there was a barber shop and hardware store. The outdoor newsstand, beneath an aluminum overhang, sold hundreds of the latest newspapers, comic books, baseball cards, and magazines of all sorts, including a section off limits to kids, which isn't to say my brothers and friends and I didn't flip through those items sometimes.

"I've always loved the Galbuts," Billy said, recalling how Russell, as a young child, sat on his lap and learned how to count change. "Your brother Russell was always fascinated by the mechanical cash register and by the trick of taking dollars and returning nickels. That was your brother's first lesson in business."

"You're a true inspiration and a wonderful friend," I said.

Refusing, to leave my father's side, Gita asked Maria, Dad's nurse, how much longer it would be until the treatment began.

"We're at the mercy of the pharmacy," Maria said.

Russell and I went downstairs to the cafeteria for some sandwiches and drinks. We returned maybe twenty minutes later.

"The sitcoms here are terrible," my father said.

"We'll get him an iPod," Russell said.

Gita adjusted Dad's blanket and reclined his chair.

Maria, our chemotherapy nurse, prepared the skin overlying his port with a Betadine swab, and she placed the needle into the port that would deliver his anti-nausea agents prior to administration of his Gemzar.

Before the treatment began, I raced down to South Miami Hospital to implant a defibrillator, after which, I saw about twenty-five patients in my office. Gita later informed me that about halfway through, the port failed, and the flow of the chemotherapy ceased. Concerned about completing the chemotherapy dose and unable to clear the port successfully, Maria had elected to give the remaining Gemzar through a peripheral IV. I was comforted by Gita's familiarity with the process, as she had accompanied her own father during his illness, and I was grateful for the calming influence she brought to my father's first treatment.

During this time, Robert was in Israel, visiting his newlywed daughter and son-in-law. While there, he visited the Baba Sali's nephew, Rabbi David Abuhatzera, who resides in Nahariya in northern Israel. Less than a year later, in the summer of 2006, the area was heavily bombed by the Hezbollah from Lebanon. During the meeting, Robert and Rabbi Abuhatzera discussed our father's health. Robert has since described their discussion to me in great detail.

"My father has a pancreatic cancer that has spread to the liver. I know the outcome is dismal. Are there any prayers or recommendations?" Robert asked.

"You must have faith," the rabbi said, "and you must be devout in the performance of good deeds and learning, and then your father will live."

Upon Robert's return, I saw him at our parents' house. I'd gone there with Rachel, as had become our custom after our Sabbath meal at home. Robert was distraught over how much Dad had deteriorated in the past week.

"What else did you and the rabbi discuss?"

"Knowing my specialty, he had a lot of questions for me about lung disease. All in all, he has an astute understanding of medicine."

"Did you come out of the meeting believing that Dad will survive?"

"I felt better. I know that the legacy of his life will live on, and I believe that's what Rabbi Abuhatzera meant."

During our visit, Dad was alert and sitting beside Mom in their room, enjoying the company of his family. Robert, his daughter Erica, her husband Ari, along with Rachel and myself, sat with my parents on chairs and on the edge of the bed. Dad reported that he'd enjoyed a hearty Shabbat meal.

"How was your chemotherapy, Zayde?" Erica asked.

"Piece of cake," he said. "And every day I'm feeling better."

Robert and I observed new swelling in Dad's left arm, probably from the chemotherapy, which after thirty minutes had created discomfort at the site and was subsequently discontinued, with the other half of the dosage being delivered through a peripheral IV. This puzzled me, as the port had functioned properly for the administration of antibiotics during his hospitalization. My guess was that the length of the needle had been inadequate and that some of the chemotherapy had entered the subcutaneous tissue, which would have explained his discomfort. Dad was also complaining of weakness in his arm as a consequence of its increased weight.

"Dad, I believe the subclavian vein under the collarbone is thrombosed or has a clot. This is the large vein which drains your arm." I understood, of course, that people with malignancy are highly coagulable, but I didn't emphasize that point. I then instructed Dad and his aide on the importance of elevating the arm and need for gentle massage of the hand and forearm.

"Dad, you might require a blood thinner," Robert added. "Let's observe this finding over the next twenty-four hours to determine whether we need an ultrasound for diagnosis and subsequent treatment."

As I studied my father's swollen left hand, I thought about his skill as an artisan and his left-handedness. As a youngster, he'd told me about his desire to become a surgeon, and how World War II had interrupted that dream.

As a toddler, my earliest memory involves a train set on the oak floor of our living room. In the years that followed, Dad spent countless hours building things, including models of airplanes, ships commemorating the World War II Navy fleet, and in later years, once he had granddaughters, he created highly individualized dollhouses, paying keen attention to detail, down to the miniaturized family photographs hanging on the walls. As a further expression of his fascination with the sea, Dad built dozens of wooden sailboats that he shared with family members and special acquaintances. One day he left a particularly beautiful sailboat at my office, with a gold plaque at the bottom: "With Much appreciation from a grateful patient," and it was signed "Tom Peterson." That was my dad's pseudonym, which he sometimes used in the course of business or when doing investigations for his clients. My office is decorated with many awards and plaques, but that sailboat is my most meaningful memento.

Despite Dad's love of boats and the sea, model trains were his favorite passion. Dad's thousands of model trains included entire lines, from the Baltimore and Ohio; the Florida East Coast; the Continental, Union Pacific, and even some railroads of his own design including The Galbut System, which he created in 1983, the year I joined Dr. Thomas Gentsch, a senior heart surgeon and a founder of the Miami Heart Institute.

During my early practice at Miami Heart, I participated in the treatment of twenty women who had previously undergone saphenous varicose vein stripping for cosmetic reasons. These women now required bypass surgery, and the routine approach of using the leg veins for the graft was not possible. Dr. Gentsch had developed a procedure in which the cephalic vein from the forearm was enhanced in size and thickness by being connected to the radial artery two to three weeks prior to surgery. In addition, these patients had the two internal mammary arteries from under the sternum used as conduits. We studied these twenty patients and noted excellent results following their surgery. I decided to review the data and prepare a written presentation, believing that the success was a consequence of using the enhanced arm vein.

As a medical student at the University of Pennsylvania, as an intern at Harvard University, and during my surgical residency at Columbia Presbyterian, I had published several academic articles, including one involving insulinoma, a cancer of the pancreas in which excessive insulin is produced, and another on transplantation of the pancreatic cells responsible for producing insulin. So in 1983, when the Florida Medical Association held its annual meeting at the Diplomat Hotel in Hollywood, Florida, I appreciated the opportunity to present our findings on the use of the cephalic vein in female bypass patients, which I thought would help me achieve some recognition for myself as a young attending at Miami Heart Institute.

Upon reading the brochure and the application materials, my father noted the section for artistic presentations. In those years, as part of its effort to encourage physicians to be well-rounded, the American Medical Association and its state organizations encouraged physicians to pursue interests outside of medicine to compensate for their exceptional job stress.

"I'll apply for us to make a presentation in the artistic section," my father said.

"What would we create?" I said. "We're not painters. We don't draw."

"But we are creative," he said.

The Miami Beach Railroad Dad designed included a model HO locomotive, two boxcars, and a caboose mounted on tracks affixed to a slab of polished mahogany. The boxcars appeared ready to carry building materials, symbolizing Miami's 1980s growth boom. The blue and white trains representing the city colors of Miami Beach included a decal my father designed, ordered, and applied to the trains. The round emblem featured "Miami Beach Railroad," and "The Galbut System." We presented the trains within an enclosed case, accompanied by an engraved plaque which read, "David L. Galbut, M.D., a cardiac surgeon in Miami, has been a long time hobbyist with a particular love of railroads. A native of Miami Beach, he has a great appreciation for this city."

There was much discussion of our scientific findings during the convention, but within six months, I realized that our high success rate with this patient group was not the result of our use of the cephalic veins, but rather, the two internal mammary or chest wall arterial grafts, versus the customary practice of using thigh and leg superficial veins. I concluded that the arterial conduits, verses venous conduits, were the preferred grafts in coronary bypass surgery. Over the next seven to eight years, and statistics involving some 2,500 patients, our group pioneered the use of two mammary (or chest wall) arterial grafts. On average, these patients lived to a normal life expectancy, using US Census Bureau information. There was no significant increased risk in using the two arterial grafts compared to the leg superficial vein, which had been the standard method since the 1970s. Furthermore, we could perform this procedure in higher risk patient populations, such as the elderly, diabetics, and women (who tend to have smaller arteries, which are technically more difficult to manage), without an increased rate of complications.

Recognizing the superior results of this conduit, we helped establish the use of bilateral internal mammary artery grafts as the ideal operation in coronary bypass surgery. I have had the privilege of presenting this information at several national meetings of cardiac surgeons, and today, surgeons worldwide agree that the internal mammary artery graft confers patient longevity and contributes to lasting clinical improvement. In 2004, when President Clinton had quadruple bypass surgery, three of his grafts were accomplished using the internal mammary artery conduits.

As much as I enjoyed being a scientific presenter at the 1983 meeting of the Florida Medical Association, I also appreciated the recognition I received for winning first prize in the artistic competition.

"You outdid yourself," I told Dad after the convention as I handed him my blue ribbon. "They gave me the award, but you're the true recipient."

"I've shared my love of trains with you, but you haven't had the time to pursue it. Let's just say we're both winners."

As Rachel and I left my parents house in the aftermath of Dad's first chemotherapy treatment, my daughter shared her excitement over her upcoming wedding, scheduled for May 28th at the Doral Country Club, home to the famous PGA tournament, but I couldn't stop thinking about my father's swollen left hand.

Chapter 5: Always the Captain

Growing up, I envisioned becoming an attorney, just like my dad, but during my senior year of high school, he confessed that he loved the law but had grown disenchanted with the practice of law, which probably explains his dedication to community service. And then, during the summer between my freshman and sophomore year of college, I came down with infectious mononucleosis and was hospitalized for a few days with jaundice. I was intrigued by the medical environment, especially the physicians and nurses in white garb dedicated to the noble service of healing. By this time, Robert was into his pre-med studies and his enthusiasm inspired me. Thus far, I'd been planning to major in political science in preparation for law school, but during my sophomore year I turned my focus toward pre-med.

In later years, my father reminded me of his early dream of becoming a surgeon. The winds of battle had interrupted his college education, and the aftermath of war set him on a new path. But as Dad's law career progressed, he became jaded by the two intrinsic fallacies of the American judicial system. For one, he learned that the objectivity and integrity of a judge is not guaranteed. Secondly, he realized that juries are not always comprised of a defendant's peers. Nowadays, people of lesser education and lower economic capability serve on juries to a disproportionate degree. To a large extent, those of higher socioeconomic and educational status use their professional responsibilities as a basis for dismissal from jury service.

In the last decade of my father's career, he specialized in probate and estate law. He was a favorite assignee of many judges for pro bono cases. Despite his growing dissatisfaction with practicing law, especially toward the end of his career, he was grateful for how his legal career had provided for our family. As an attorney he counseled thousands of clients, many of whom I've met through the years as patients or in social gatherings, and the majority have recounted a matter my father handled for them. Without exception, they have recalled how my father had eased the pain of a divorce or probate case, or how he'd seen them through complicated life events from home purchases to overseas adoptions.

My father never suggested that I not become an attorney, but I could tell that he had ultimately grown bored with the practice of law. Fearing boredom myself, and needing to face even greater challenges, I chose not just medicine, but surgery, a field in which errors bring the gravest of consequences. Furthermore, cardiac surgery is a field in which the premiere practitioners don't reach their prime until their 50's. To achieve this goal, constant learning and refinement of practice is necessary. Although I've sometimes been frustrated with the practice of medicine, I've never been bored.

I am now twenty-seven years old, completing my second year of surgical training at Columbia Presbyterian, and I'm discouraged. I've completed medical school at Penn and my internship at Harvard. I know I'm a talented physician, but I'm not meeting my expectations in the operating room. Surgery is both an art and a science. The art is taught by mentors and attending surgeons in much the fashion of an apprenticeship. The resident stands across the operating table from his professor or surgical attending. The resident's right hand coordinates with the attending's right hand and the left coordinates with the attending's left. The vast majority of surgical residents are right-handed. In fact, right-handedness was once a mandatory dictum for surgical residents. Within the past ten years or so, some left-handed surgeons have progressed through surgical training programs, but not too many. My attendings expect the dominant player to be my right hand, but it's my left hand. My surgical teachers frequently don't understand the awkwardness of my movements because they often forget that I'm left-handed.

I'm in Miami in November 1976, celebrating Thanksgiving with my family.

"Tell me about your progress," my father says.

"I'm probably better off trying emergency medicine."
I explained the difficulty of learning the art of surgery because of my left-handedness.

"David, you're approaching this all wrong. You being left-handed can be an advantage. Most right-handed people see the world according to their perspective. Telephones, scissors, can openers, stick shift cars... you name it. The world is designed for right-handed people."

"How is this supposed to help me?" I say.

"A left-handed person can see things differently. And not only that, but you can become ambidextrous. A left-handed person can learn to use his right hand with equal proficiency."

"How can you be so sure?"

"I've seen people who lost their right hand learn to write with their left. And I know people who've had strokes learn to compensate with their opposite side."

"But surgery is a lot more precise than writing."

"Sure, most surgeons are right-handed, but they're limited to where they can stand alongside a patient, but a surgeon who becomes ambidextrous can deal with surgical problems

independent of position and can truly become technically
outstanding."

Upon returning to Columbia after Thanksgiving, and during the ensuing years, I forced myself to use my right hand, which allowed me to approach the surgical field from any position. This solution ultimately helped me become a good technical cardiac surgeon. You see, cardiac surgery requires being on the patient's right, but the field is limited by the anesthesiologist, who stands at the head of the table, and by the heart-lung machine, which is often to the right of the patient, near the operating surgeon. In addition, the anatomy of the heart necessitates the surgeon to approach it from the right side. In my practice, I open the chest with a knife in my right hand, and open the arteries from the back of the heart with my right hand. In complex cases, I can use either hand to excise valves. Although I predominantly sew parts of the heart with my left hand, I can perform acceptably with my right hand as well.

As surgeons, our craft involves great hand-eye coordination, with a keen understanding of mathematical planes and the intersection of points for dissection and reconstruction. To supplement my general surgical training at Columbia Presbyterian, and to enhance my ambidexterity, I often operated in the dog laboratory. To supplement my cardiac training at the University of

Miami, I spent many nights in the Medical Examiner's lab consulting on gunshot victims. This was in the early 1980s, a particularly violent period in Miami's history. During my year as Chief Resident, working twenty-five days a month, including fifteen nights, I treated the majority of patients presenting with gunshot or stab wounds to the chest. The Chief Medical Examiner sought my opinion in complex cases involving multiple bullets. Studying the deceased person's organs *in vivo*, or "as they are in life," helped me perfect my understanding of human anatomy. And toward the end of the year, I spent many hours at night in the autopsy lab dissecting and reconstructing hearts and lungs within the chest cavity, often focusing on improving my right-hand agility. Upon completing my cardio-thoracic residency, I was confident that I had achieved a superb level of surgical training, for which I felt partially indebted to my father, a left-handed artisan himself.

My father wasn't a surgeon, but he never steered me wrong. His lesson was simple: "Don't blame others...just solve the problem." It was a lesson he frequently taught us through example...

I'm nine years old, and it's a Sunday morning in September. We're driving to the Mount Sinai Jewish Cemetery for a day of public remembrance. It's customary before the high holidays for Jews to visit the graves of the departed. My father has scheduled a communal gathering in the cemetery with many rabbis available to say prayers for individual departed loved ones, and there's a large tent that will house three hundred people for a communal prayer. Robert and I are looking forward to manning the Coke fountain, which provides a mixture of seltzer and Coca-Cola syrup. Seeing as how we've arrived two hours early, my father moves through the cemetery with the gardeners as he inspects the grounds to be certain that all the grass is cut, the trees are properly pruned, and that there's no debris. When he finds a footstone that's off-center, Dad bends down to pick up this footstone, and I see how powerful he is, six feet tall and two hundred pounds of muscle. As he places the footstone into its proper position, he splits his pants right through the seat. Robert and I giggle at this, but Dad isn't laughing. Controlling my laughter now, I wonder, if Dad will blame the gardeners or the attendants.

Instead he says to us, "Tell your mother I'll be back in thirty minutes as I run home to change. It's a beautiful day, and we'll have great success this afternoon."

As I watch him race to the car, I realize that the unexpected will always occur, but one's response must be controlled and individual responsibility accepted.

On Saturday mornings, I go to the synagogue and then race over to the hospital for rounds, but today I decided to visit my father first thing in the morning. At the house, I found Dad sitting on his chair with his eyes half closed. His swollen arm was partially improved, but he was in a state of mild confusion, probably the consequence of a 3 a.m. Restoril. He had eaten very little in the past day.

"Are you hungry, Hymie?" my mother said. "What would you like for breakfast?"

"The moon diet," he said.

I was convinced that he was hallucinating. And as we spoke awhile longer, with my father wavering between partial slumber and wakefulness, he referred to what astronauts eat, which includes a high-caloric, low-volume diet. I believe in my father's mind, a lower volume diet was more tolerable as he experienced early satiety, which meant the first few bites of whatever he ate made him feel full.

I sat with my mother at her dining room table, where she admitted that she acknowledged that these were my father's last days. "It breaks my heart," she said.

Until now, that dining room had rarely been the site of such serious conversation. Mostly it had been a place for dining and joyous song.

"Mom, do you believe in the world to come and in the fact that we will all be together?"

"It doesn't ease the pain of seeing the man I love suffer," she said.

I reached for a cashew nut from a crystal bowl left over from the night before. "Dad denies pain. Sure, he complains of being less mobile, and his arm is swollen, but I think he's comfortable."

"I wish I could care for him myself," Mom said. She had recently begun a week of Tobramycin inhalation treatment, which we hoped would decrease her coughing and level of secretions, but she ran an increased risk of developing a resistant strain of bacteria.

"That's not your mission," I said. "Just continue being his loving wife. The aides know how important he is to you and all of us, and from what I've seen, he commands a relationship of respect with them. That's why they call him the Captain."

"He'll always be the Captain," Mom affirmed.

After morning prayers at the synagogue, I went to the hospital for rounds, spent the afternoon at home, and that evening, I returned to my parents' house with Gita, and Elana, who was now nine months pregnant. Again I found Dad sitting in his chair and quite drowsy. He asked to stand up in order to urinate. Louisiana held him on the left and I held him on the right as we lifted him into position so he could try urinating into a bowl. I asked Gita to turn the water on, after which, he was successful. Then he returned to his chair and closed his eyes. He insisted that he still wasn't hungry, but Gita brought him a dish of vanilla bean ice cream.

"Delicious," he said, after Gita had fed him a few spoonfuls.

Determined to bring him a little pleasure, so I began a Hebrew songfest, including the 23rd Psalm: "Though I walk through the valley of the shadow of death…" and songs of jubilation, including "Jerusalem, City of Gold," "Israel, a Living Nation," and his favorite, *"Kol Haolam,"* the English version of which includes, "The world is a narrow bridge, and the essence is not to be afraid."

I held his hand, and he moved his head back and forth, nodding in harmony with the music. I looked at my mother, sitting attentively and smiling, and at Gita and Elana, seated on the bed. There were three pictures on the wall. In the middle one, Dad is in his early 40s, wearing his white-dress Navy uniform. To the left was a picture of my mother and father at a recent dinner celebrating their 54th anniversary, the two of them are dressed in suits, facing each other, holding hands, and smiling. In the picture on the right side, my father is completing the final letters of a Sefer

Torah, in honor of their 50th anniversary. At that party, he and my mother had dedicated a Torah scroll to the community. Upon the completion of a new Torah scroll, which takes many months by a gifted and pious scribe, the last letters are traditionally filled by male members of the community under the scribe's tutelage.

Robert had returned home and we recited the Havdallah prayer, which separates the Sabbath, when the stars come out, from the rest of the week. The beautiful prayer, which my parents loved, is conducted in the glow of the light from a braided candle, along with a silver cup of wine and a container of aromatic herbs. Fire is a pure element, and looking at one's hands in that light, he is reminded to make certain that his hands are clean and that they be used for noble purposes. The aromatic spices savored in those waning moments recall the sweetness of the Sabbath day.

The Havdallah prayer was one of the few Hebrew prayers my father enjoyed chanting, and in his later years, his doing so each Saturday night became a great source of joy for my mother and for all of us. Having grown up poor, Dad didn't have the opportunity to learn Hebrew, so it was truly a foreign language to him. With the blossoming of the Artscroll phenomenon—an extensive collection of Hebrew works with linear translations into English—my father became knowledgeable about Judaism and felt more comfortable learning Hebrew, with Mom's encouragement.

That night, my father told Rachel that his prognosis was dismal. "The putz tells me that I'm not doing well," Dad said, referring to the specialist who'd been so cruel in his assessment. With his eyes partly closed, my father added, "But I'll fight this."

After rounds on the Sunday before Thanksgiving, I visited Dad around noon. He was watching an NFL pre-game show on CBS. The Dolphins were scheduled to play the Cleveland Browns that afternoon. Dad said he'd slept well, having taken a Restoril around 9:30 the night before. For his throat inflammation, or pharyngitis, a consequence of the chemotherapy, Robert had prescribed an antifungal oral suspension. His breathing was mildly labored and he was using supplemental oxygen.

"Dad, do you often think about your parents and other ancestors?"

"They were great people," he said, "educators, poets, scholars—just great people."

My grandfather could read the newspaper seven languages: Portuguese, Yiddish, Russian, Lithuanian, German, English, and Hebrew. Mom said my grandfather weighed 148 pounds "soaking wet," and that he often wore a white coat with maroon pants. "He looked like Bogart, with strong arms, and he always made people laugh."

I also know that my grandfather enjoyed watching boxing at the Fifth Street Gym, where Muhammad Ali later trained. In time, my grandfather earned the title "Honorary Mayor of South Beach" for his many philanthropic acts, including helping poor people make funeral arrangements, and feeding the prisoners at the old Miami Beach jail, adjacent to the old Miami Beach Police station, an area familiar to anyone who has ever enjoyed stone crabs at Joe's.

The love of my father's early life was my grandmother, Bessie, daughter of Rebecca Reisen, and sister to Abraham and Zalman Reisen. They grew up in Belarus, and were prominent in the history of twentieth century Yiddish culture. Zalman, a famous etymologist, remained in Vilna, Lithuania and became the author of the first lexicon of the Yiddish language. He died in the early 1930s, at the hands of the Russians. Prior to this, Abraham and Rebecca had immigrated to America in 1915. Abraham Reisen, a prolific Yiddish poet and writer, became an editor of *The Jewish Daily Forward*, which began as a socialist paper and which still exists today. Rebecca raised Bessie to be the ultimate family matriarch. Bessie's father was Morris Sklar, of Russian ancestry.

I didn't ask about my father's brother, knowing that they hadn't been close, but I did ask about Aunt Miriam.

"Another time, David," he said, and from the crack in his voice, I regretted asking the question.

To change the subject, I said, "Dad, you think the Dolphins have a chance against the Browns." On the TV, former Miami quarterback, Hall of Famer Dan Marino and his pre-game colleagues were breaking down the ins and outs of the day's games.

"Depends how bad they want it," he said. "Either way, they're not going to the Super Bowl."

In 1972, the year the Dolphins had their perfect 17-0 season, my father attended many of the games. I was a medical student at Penn, but I remember speaking with him on the phone about the excitement back in Miami. He told me about Coach Don Shula, and how he was such an inspirational leader and how he'd become an instant hero in South Florida. During a visit home, Dad and I attended a Sunday afternoon game at the Orange Bowl.

"Dad," I said, sitting there in comfortable December sun, a folded program in my lap. "You think a perfect season is possible?"

"I don't know, David, but if it does happen, it will be a blessing and a curse."

"Why?" I said, looking at my father, his eyes shaded by the brim of his Dolphins cap.

"Sure, it would be a source of pride for the team and the community, but it's a curse too because it will never happen again. Their hunger to succeed will never be the same."

At this point, I was about a year into medical school, and was bound for surgical training. Success in a surgeon's career involves a somewhat predictable sequence that cannot be altered. Four years of medical school, a one-year internship, four years of residency, two to three years of specialty fellowship, after which one typically joins a practice, where one usually receives further mentoring from a senior physician and attempts to learn from his mistakes, which in the case of a heart surgeon, inevitably involves death.

"Do you think physicians can have a perfect season?"

"We don't know when success will come in the course of any journey," my father said. "What we do know is that you must ride the current, maximize its thrust, and as you enter the future, every day must count if you are to be successful."

"But life's not like that," I said. "It's not a crescendo of success after success."

"Of course not. Life is a continuum, but we can't choose when success comes. Some people enjoy their greatest success in their twenties, others in their sixties or seventies, and some are never blessed with success. But the challenge after a success is to keep going."

In later years I have remembered that conversation with my father in the stands of the Orange Bowl, during what would, in fact, become the first perfect season in NFL history, a record that has so far endured. Of course my father was right. Although the Dolphins won their second straight Super Bowl in 1973, they endured several losses that season. More importantly, I've realized that order in life can never be determined, but the players must participate one hundred percent at all times. In my career as a heart surgeon, I've been involved in probably five thousand open-heart procedures, and I've had three runs in which I've had a hundred consecutive cases without a death. Each time, I've enjoyed a great sense of having accomplished the extraordinary, but the next hundred cases inevitably involve mortality as a counterbalance. The challenge after an exceptional run is to continue doing the best for my patients and not be distracted from the pursuit of excellence when a bad result occurs.

In his pre-game comments, Dan Marino compared his high-achieving teams of the mid-1980s to the current Dolphins squad, and I could tell he was happy to be dressed in a suit.

"I've had enough David," my father said, snapping me out of my football daydream. "Will you use a gun or pills?"

"Neither," I said. "It would create a tarnished image in the eyes of your grandchildren. Furthermore, we're not at that stage. There's still hope."

"What if you're wrong?"

"Dad, I promise that I'll be there with you, but your time hasn't come. This destructive thinking is premature. You've denied having any pain."

"OK," he said, noticing that the game had begun.

"Let's watch the Dolphins and see what they do today," I said, reaching for his hand.

During halftime, I left the house to run an errand with Gita, all the while thinking how something had changed. Perhaps he'd seen the Angel of Death and now realized his fate.

At 4:30, Robert called. "Daddy wants to talk to you," my brother said. "He feels like it's not worth it, says he wants to give up."

When I arrived moments later with Rachel, Robert said, "He looks at you as a decider."

"We all are," I said, but I knew what he meant, and perhaps I had expedited his chemotherapy, and maybe that's why he wanted to discuss the decision-making role with me." In the room, Dad sat, asked to stand, returned to his chair, and asked to stand again. His mouth was sore and his swallowing was difficult. His level of anguish and disgust had visibly increased in just those couple of hours.

"David, let's finish up," Dad said to me. "There is no point in any of this. I want a service at Riverside, and then I'll be taken to Israel. The most important thing is to console your mother."

"Dad, we must try another round of chemotherapy, which is coming in two days, and Thanksgiving is around the corner. You can do it, and I believe you'll even have the privilege of seeing some newborn great-grandchildren in December." Rachel massaged my back, and I felt tears in my eyes.

"Your mother and I love all four of you, and we're ecstatic to have shared so much in your lives."

"Dad, you've influenced all of the important decisions in my life." Now the tears streamed from my eyes.

"You don't have to say anything David. I know."

After my afternoon rounds and a quick dinner with Gita and Rachel at a restaurant on West Avenue, I returned to my parents' house with Rachel, Elana, and Nili. *Desperate Housewives* was on the TV. Everyone, including Radcliff, Dad's new primary home health care aide, watched the show with him.

It was Russell who'd hired Radcliff, a Haitian man of about forty. He came to us with fine references. He was professional in his appearance, arrived to work in a spotless white uniform, and with an unobtrusive manner, he cared for Dad, and in effect, the rest of us, with a soft touch.

I sat in the dining room and read the Book of Psalms, written by King David. I read the section for Monday, and thought of the consolation, which for centuries has been experienced by the desperate of so many different religions. Mom sat down and told me how Robert had been committing an enormous amount of time caring for my father since his return from Israel. "He says Dad's sugar is well-controlled with the insulin."

"I know, Mom. Robert's a great physician."

"Al B was here several times today. He keeps asking to take Dad for a ride to check on the Hebrew Homes and that new office building he's buying on Biscayne Boulevard."

"What's Daddy's response been?"

"He's thinking about it. He says he'll go when he has more energy."

That day, Russell had brought a cassette player for Mom to listen to the positive thinking tapes she had collected over the years. We listened to one tape and I saw the strength in Mom's eyes, even in the face of this situation. "The days are full and furiously paced," I said.

"We'll make the most of each one," she said, "however many we have."

Chapter 6: Zayde and Bubby

I awoke Monday morning at 6:00. I was tired and I'd lost a few pounds, but I was looking forward to Thanksgiving. I planned an early visit with my father, followed by a coronary bypass procedure at South Miami. I entered my marble shower, which I've done just about every morning for the past fifteen years since we remodeled the house, and stepped into a puddle of shampoo residue. My foot slipped from under me and I crashed to the floor. I landed on my left arm, jamming my two middle fingers against the marble bench, and bruising my left backside. Fortunately my head had only minimal contact with the marble. My first thought: what had I broken? My mind flashed back to my father, lying in a similar prone position, on his back in his own bathroom just a few days earlier. I stood up, steadied myself against the stone wall, and saw—and felt—that the nail on my middle toe was essentially sheared off. My left hand tingled and a black and blue subungual hematoma appeared on my left ring finger. My elbow was sore, but everything moved properly.

Like most surgeons, one of my greatest fears has been a physical injury that could impair my ability to perform. As I began my shower, the bleeding in my toe stopped. My elbow and backside were tender, but I could stand up straight. As for my hand, I believed I could function, given that my thumb and index finger were spared, but the incident got me thinking about my father. Did he begin each day, flat on his back, thinking, "Why can't I get up? What is happening to me? Why is my left arm so heavy? Why is my body disappointing me?" Wrapped in a towel, I shaved, and then I got dressed and began the race of my day.

At my parents' house, I helped Dad from his bedroom to the bathroom. Whereas I was prepared for a long day at the hospital, he faced a day of sitting in his chair. Despite a low-grade fever, undoubtedly from the tumor, he appeared invigorated.

"Radcliff is a very good driver," Dad said. "We saw all the sights that I've loved through the years. Plus there's lots of great parking spaces at that hour."

"The Captain slept poorly last night, but at 5:00 a.m., he said he wanted to take a drive. He said, "'Wake up, Bessie, we're going to South Beach.'"

"I wish I could have joined you," I said, thinking about my fall in the shower and how fortunate I was that my injury hadn't been worse. "Tomorrow is a big day with your 7 a.m.

chemotherapy. Take your Restoril at 9 p.m. so that you'll awaken refreshed at 5:30."

Mom walked me to the front door, she appeared extremely happy. "Your father amazed me with his enthusiasm for our early morning adventure, and I loved it."

Despite the pain in my left fingers, I got through the day's surgeries, rounds, and my office appointments. I forgot about my bruised backside until the long ride back to Miami Beach late that evening, which reminded me to start checking my shower floor for soap and shampoo each morning.

I visited Dad at 10:15 p.m. Elana was playing Rummikub with Mom and Louisiana. My niece Erica, sat with my father, holding his left hand, and I held his right. The Green Bay Packers and the Minnesota Vikings were involved in a close battle on Monday Night Football. Keeping a close eye on the game, my father also engaged in conversation with the women, talking about one of their favorite topics: shopping.

"They call the day after Thanksgiving 'Black Friday,'" Dad told Erica, referring to the official beginning of the Christmas shopping season. "Look at all these ads," he said, reaching for the stack of newspapers beside his chair.

"Is there one for Bloomingdale's?" said my father's 23-year-old granddaughter, reaching for the ads.

"The stores open at 6 a.m. with an abundance of merchandise at cut-rate prices for the day in order to gauge what the shoppers want for the season. If there's even a 2%-3% reduction in sales, it could impact the overall economy. With all the hurricanes we've had this year, we need a strong Christmas season."

"Zayde, are you saying I should buy things to bolster the economy and be a good American?"

"Sure, have a good time, but don't try to save the country all by yourself."

"I'll be at the Aventura mall at 5:30 a.m.," said Erica, who's a smart shopper, just like my own daughters.

"Here, Hymie," Mom said, handing Dad his Restoril. He swallowed the pill, but rather than prepare for bed, he wanted to remain in his chair awhile. "Go home, David," he said. "You've had a long day…you've had a lot of long days lately. I love you, and I'll see you in the morning."

"Six a.m. sharp," I said.

At the round table beside the basketball hoop in the bedroom, Mom and Elana and Louisiana continued their game of Rummikub.

"Louisiana knows how to play, and Elana is a master player," Mom said, but I could see she wasn't giving up. With two cubes remaining, she was committed to fighting to the very end.

Rummikub involves numbered tiles in a combination of colors and sequence, and the object is to have none left at the end. Along with her bookkeeping, Rummikub kept Mom's mind sharp. It also provided her the fantasy of logic and order and strategy amid the unpredictability of real life.

***

Gita and I arrived at my parents' house at 6:20 a.m. As would become our custom, my brothers and I helped Dad into one of our cars and caravanned to Sylvester, driving away from the sunrise across the Julia Tuttle Causeway toward Miami. At Sylvester, we spent the first forty minutes in the outpatient chemotherapy waiting room.

"The trains must be taken care of," Dad said.

"I know," I said.

"I was thinking we could hire a professional model railroad builder to complete the layout in the garage," Russell said.

My father nodded, but I sensed disappointment. That should have been *his* job.

"Dad," I said, "much of it will be a treasured heirloom for your grandchildren and great-grandchildren." Despite the beauty of the extensive collection, I doubted how well his passion might be conveyed to generations who hadn't personally studied model-making with The Captain. An accumulation of model trains can be inherited, but how does one bequeath passion?

The secretary sent us to a laboratory down the hall for the hematocrit and platelet test. Fifteen minute later, while I stood at the reception desk in my scrubs and white coat, I said, "If it would help move things along, I could draw the blood myself."

"That won't be necessary. We'll be with your father right away."

I wasn't sure if she thought I was a shoe salesman wearing a stolen physician's coat, but within minutes, the technician drew Dad's blood, after which we learned that his levels were favorable—no significant decrease as a consequence of the first chemotherapy five days before. One hurdle down. Even so, Dr. Rosenblatt decided that the second chemotherapy treatment should not be given for at least seven days following the initial treatment with Gemzar. Thanksgiving, which was two days away, precluded the opportunity for chemotherapy in the outpatient unit, so Dr. Rosenblatt arranged for a Friday appointment in the inpatient unit.

"We discussed the left upper extremity edema and clinical evidence of phlebitis. Dr. Rosenblatt ordered an ultrasound. We brought Dad down to the Vascular Laboratory, where the ultrasound confirmed a thrombosis of the axillary, subclavian, and left internal jugular veins involving the upper arm and lower third of the neck. The basilic and cephalic veins were free of any clots.

Dr. Rosenblatt said, "Let's increase the Lovenox to 120mg a day."

I agreed, hoping that this standard treatment would improve the swelling in Dad's left arm. In the hall between the lobby and the vascular lab on the first floor, I spent some time with Dr. Joseph Rosenblatt. "I grew up in Israel," he said. "My parents were of modest means compared with my children, who are growing up in luxury."

"I'm from Miami," I said. "My parents were poor early on, but my father began making a good living when I was ten or eleven. How'd you get interested in oncology?" I said.

"My mother was sick with breast cancer when I was growing up," he said.

"You must have really loved her," I said.

He nodded but didn't elaborate.

"I really appreciate your getting involved," I said. "We're intense, but I promise we'll also be calm, respectful, and disciplined in our communications with you. It's just that when it comes to my father's care, I'm hoping I can expect nothing less than my own personal standard, which includes being available 24x7 for my patients and their families."

"I'm learning about your family, and I realize that if you weren't so intense, you wouldn't be so successful."

At this stage in my life, praise is not essential nor necessary, but Dr. Rosenblatt's words assured me that he appreciated that he was treating an extraordinary man facing the greatest trial of his life.

Gita, Robert, and I helped Dad into Robert's car for the drive home. The rest of my hectic day included a carotid endarterectomy, rounds, and office visits. Then I drove to Kendall for Nili's basketball game, a loss to one of the top teams in the division.

I visited Dad at 9:20 p.m. As I opened the door and entered the house, I heard the melody of my son-in-law singing psalms. He was sitting beside Elana, who was now thirty-six weeks pregnant. The recent ultrasound suggested the baby weighed 6-1/2 pounds. Side by side in their bedroom chairs, my parents napped. They were at peace, hopefully having the most pleasant of dreams.

Radcliff and I helped Dad to his feet and guided him toward his room. On his mattress, he lay curled in a semi-fetal position. We placed the oxygen tubes into his nostrils and tucked his blanket around him. I lay beside him for a minute, placed my hand on his back, and told him how much I loved him.

I'm eight years old in the summer of 1957. We've just returned from our summer Navy vacation to the Pentagon. I spend much of my time at a day camp at Polo Park in central Miami Beach, but some days I pass the time in my father's office, reading comic books, saying hello to clients, and going with my father at least once a day, but sometimes twice, to the Dade County courthouse on Flagler Street. It's a beautiful building that reminds me of the some of the architecture we've seen in other big cities. I can tell that the law is important, as my dad has to climb about forty steps just to enter the first floor of the courthouse, the tallest building in town. In fact, it's the same forty steps no matter what direction we approach the building from. I wonder if it's because the law is supposed to be balanced for everyone, no matter where they're coming from.

I chase my father up the steps, racing to keep up as he takes two to three steps at a stride. My father is greeted by just about everyone, from the shoeshine boys to the sundries attendant selling cigars and candy, to the court assistants, clerks, stenographers, fellow counselors, and judges. "Hi, Mr. Galbut," "Good morning, Hymie, how are you? .... Hymie, it's great to see you."

"Dad," I say in the elevator, "it's like you know everyone here."

"Greet everyone with a smile, David," he says. "It costs nothing, and besides, a great principle in life is that little people become big people." We exit the elevator on the fifth floor and enter a courtroom. I wonder if my father is referring to my being a child who will grow up someday.

Through the years, I've reflected on that lesson. When I returned to Miami to practice heart surgery, many of those "little" people my father had greeted with affection had since become leaders in our community. A typical conversation with many a patient would be, "Are you related to Hyman Galbut?"

"He's my father," I would say proudly.

"He did me a service. He's a wonderful man. Is he still alive?"

"Yes, he is," I would say. "He's still in Miami Beach and doing well."

"Please give him my regards. He wouldn't remember me, but I'll never forget him."

By now, Dad had fallen asleep. I whispered, "Have a restful night." I stood up and watched him lying there, so vulnerable, so far from the lofty courthouse steps.

At the front door, Mom said, "What has the oncologist been saying?"

"He believes the situation is poor, with a formidable quantity of cancer in his liver to overcome, but he's committed to following Daddy's lead in going forward with the chemotherapy."

"Is it helping?" she said, eager for the slightest sign of hope.

"Over the past five days, his temperature and chills have improved," I said, realizing the gravity of description. "But I think the chemotherapy will help more in the weeks ahead.

The day before Thanksgiving, Gita and I walked to my parent's house and found Dad watching TV. Earlier he'd taken a few short walks around the house with Radcliff. Mom was busy at her desk, organizing envelopes, letters, and checks. A bookkeeper in one capacity or another since her first job at fifteen, Mom had been fulfilling this role for the past sixty-eight years. She was exemplary in her attention to detail and organization, certainly a solid foundation for her newfound passion for Rummikub.

The next day, I arrived at Mom and Dad's house at 2:45 to bring Dad to Russell and Ronalee's penthouse apartment for our Thanksgiving feast. My mother was dressed in a finely tailored navy blue skirt and formal white blouse with a large belt, emphasizing her slim, unchanging waistline.

Dad appeared comfortable and alert, but he wasn't dressed. "I'm not going," he said.

"Everyone's expecting you."

"I don't want the kids seeing me like this, looking like death warmed over." He was sitting in his recliner, watching a football game.

I sat beside him and held his swollen left hand. "Dad, you don't look that bad. Furthermore, to your family, you'll always be the leader." I felt it was important for him to attend, as this would undoubtedly be his last Thanksgiving.

"David, my mind is made up. Mom will read a letter which conveys my thoughts."

I am seven years old and I'm with Robert who is eight. It's Wednesday night, which for us represents active duty for my father at the Navy Base in Miami, located on the Miami River, opposite the Merrill Stevens yacht building company, near the bridge on Northwest 12th Avenue. The Navy Base is a two-story building with classrooms, a recreational area with a ping-pong table, a barber shop, a medical clinic, and a small auditorium. Outside is an area for marching and a flagpole, and there's a dock with a small, stationary boat, used for training purposes. Every Wednesday night, my father does his active duty here. He has just become a lieutenant commander and his first job, or "billet" as he calls it, is to command a reserve surface division. He is responsible for recruiting and training high school students. These are typically unsuccessful students, many of them dropouts, given a chance to join the Naval Reserve and then be mainstreamed into the active U.S. Navy.

It is 8 p.m. The training started at 6 p.m. and continues until 9 p.m. In our usual fashion, Robert and I get haircuts for 10 cents. In the past, I've asked Dad why we need haircuts every two weeks, as I'd rather hide my large ears with longer hair.

"I cannot have the barber doing nothing, so your hair must be cut. The barber needs to do something in order to feel productive."

While I'm playing ping-pong with Robert, which we always do here, a bell sounds, directing the recruits from the different classrooms to meet in the large common area. Approximately fifty young reservists pass by us. Robert and I stop playing ping-pong and watch them. Standing at the front of the room, my father introduces himself as Lieutenant Commander Galbut. He describes the history of the Surface Division, which these new recruits are joining. This Miami Surface Division is part of the Southeastern United States, in which there are thirty-two units. My father reviews last year's history, in which this unit ranked 31st from the top, or 2nd from the bottom.

"I wasn't here then, but as I understand it, many factors contributed to our unit's failure." Then he says, "As your new commander, I will not tolerate failure. I demand success. We will all demand success, and before I complete my billet, this Miami Surface Division will be second to none. When you are at the bottom, you have only one direction in which to go."

Afterward, Dad, still dressed in his formal whites, takes Robert and me to Valenti's, located on the Miami River. We come here most weeks after the Navy training for pizza and salad. In the entrance, there's an oil portrait of Mr. Valenti's late father, who founded the restaurant. Dad always enjoys seeing that picture.

"Commander," Mr. Valenti says. "We're honored to have you and your sons in our restaurant."

Of course my father turned that division around, and within a year, they achieved the number one ranking in the southeast. Through the years, I've been awed at how determined a person my father was, not just in his role as my dad but in his professional and military life. And even in his illness, he was no less determined to maintain his authority. As much as it saddened me to know that he would miss our last Thanksgiving together, I realized that there was no way I was going to get him off that chair and over to Russell's.

By the time everyone arrived, there must have been forty-five relatives and guests in Russell and Ronalee's home, a two-story penthouse, with views of the Intracoastal Waterway and the Atlantic Ocean. We sat around the magnificent Thanksgiving table in the living room, complete with menus and table cards, noting our assigned seats. Hand-drawn cutouts of pilgrims, turkeys, and corncobs adorned the table.

During appetizers, which included a mixed salad with chopped walnuts, my mother stood at the head of the table and addressed all of us. "Thanksgiving is a time for families to be together and to share love," Mom began. Your father, your Zayde, has decided to give each of you a letter to always remember, along with a special gift. He wants us to be happy, as this is a beautiful holiday of Thanksgiving. All of us have so much to be thankful for." She spoke these words with enthusiasm and without tears. "Such special gifts should be shared during life." Then she called upon Robert to present the letters.

But before he presented the envelopes, he welcomed Uncle Label, my mother's brother, a rabbi and retired professor. Uncle Label offered us a Jewish perspective on Thanksgiving, noting that this holiday had been established by Abraham Lincoln in 1863. He added that the concept of "thanksgiving" is accounted for in our daily prayers, but on this special day, American Jews should give special thanks to God, celebrating their good fortune.

Beginning with the youngest members of our family, one by one Robert called each of us to come forward and receive our letters. Everyone, including the seven infants, were accounted for, and Robert offered something specific about each person as he handed out the envelopes. Each great-grandchild and grandchild, along with my brothers, myself, and our wives came up and received an envelope and a kiss from Mom.

After everyone had received their envelope, Robert read Mom and Dad's letter, which they had dictated to Russell, and which Russell had written on a sheet of notebook paper:

Bubby and I are giving you this check as a special gift this year for Chanukah. As you know, we have recently been battling sickness and old age. We want this Chanukah to be special for all of us. We do not desire, nor will we accept, any sorrowfulness for us. We have lived wonderful lives in which you have played a special part.

We love each member of our family in our own special way, and we want you to always remember your heritage. We have always provided you with love and understanding. We ask that you remember our closeness through the years and we desire that this family remain so long after we are gone. Passover and other holiday events should always be spent together when possible.

We are the happiest, proudest parents, grandparents, and great- grandparents who ever lived. While all living creatures must pass on, not

all have ever truly lived. However, we have lived,
and will live forever, through you and your children
and your children's children. This is in no way a
sad reality but a beautiful one.

You are a shining example of what family is
all about. Be a beacon to your children, and light
their paths throughout their lives. Remember that
life is to be lived fully, doing the things that God
wants you to do and being all that you can be.

Love,

Zayde and Bubby

Upon receiving his envelope, Russell, through his tears, managed to say, "Our lives have been wonderful. Among our greatest gifts have been our parents."

When our turn came, Gita and I received our envelope and kissed my mother, and I knew she was waiting for my remarks. "What is the most universal sentence in Judaism?" I said, employing the Socratic method, as I am prone to do on such occasions. There was silence, but I sensed their interest. "It is the last sentence that should be contemplated prior to death," I offered as a clue. "It is the last sentence said by the twelve sons of the patriarch Jacob at the moment of his death."

Rachel responded, "*Shema Yisrael* ... Hear O Israel, the Lord our God, the Lord is One."

"Exactly," I said, and then I added, "I've often wondered if there are special moments in the daily prayer when requests and entreaties are best received by God. One of the moments is after saying *Shema Yisrael*." I continued with a more recent historical perspective. "Many young children and infants whose parents were lost in the Holocaust were raised in Catholic orphanages across Europe. The Jewish Agency, a Zionist organization charged with finding these children, sent investigators to these orphanages and had the children assembled. It was unproductive to ask these children about their parents, as they had been indoctrinated by the orphanages, and many were infants when they had been separated from their parents. The investigators would shout, 'Hear O' Israel, the Lord our God, the Lord is One.' Any child who closed his eyes and/or mouthed the words or responded in some observable way, would be identified as a Jew." I continued, "This sentence represents a Jew's commitment to the faith of his father, and it is this commitment that ensures the continuity of the Jewish people."

I concluded my remarks with a few words about my father. "Just recently I asked my father—your Zayde—whether there was anything he had not yet done, and do you know how he responded? It was a beautiful answer. He said to me that he has done it all. He has no regrets. He has had a great life, and he is most proud of all of us, his family."

As I looked around the table, I saw tears in the eyes of many of the children. The youngest were silent, not fully comprehending my sadness. Gita signaled that it was time for me to conclude. "In the weeks ahead, as we demonstrate our love for our father—our Zayde—let us all remember that what is most important to him is for us to preserve the unity of our family. What we have in common is far greater than our differences," I concluded. "Let's all make a pledge as we share this magnificent meal to keep our family strong, just as our father—our Zayde—has taught us."

After our extraordinary Thanksgiving buffet, Al B spoke about the importance of having someone at the helm. "Without a leader," Al B said, "the Diablo or Satan or the Devil can enter and take the role and wreak havoc."

Perhaps Al B's presentation was a little graphic, but his design was a strong endorsement for family unity, and it came at a time when we most needed to hear it.

After the meal, Mom left early to be with my father. At Ronalee's insistence, Gita and I returned home with leftover turkey, squash, salad, and pumpkin pie, enough to last us a couple of days. Fact is, we rarely bring home leftovers. When I was child, we often had reheated leftovers at home, which I don't recall fondly, but we couldn't afford to waste anything. As an adult, I've enjoyed the luxury of freshly prepared food at every meal.

Then I went to visit Dad. He was sitting in a different position in the bedroom, closer to the raised office area. The Denver Broncos and Dallas Cowboys game had gone into overtime. Dad wanted a sleeping pill, as he was scheduled for chemotherapy in the morning.

"I would start with an Ambien," I said. "And if you wake up before 2:00, take another." Then I added, "Dad, you look wonderful tonight." He was sitting with Elana on his left. Mom was moving about, attending to business in the office. I sat on his right, while Rachel massaged his feet.

"You could be a great masseuse," he told Rachel. When Eric, Al B's eldest son arrived, he lay on the bed and asked for the TV remote control. We watched the conclusion of the football game together, which ended a few minutes into overtime on a Broncos field goal.

"I've learned to love football because of your father," Mom volunteered. Actually she had attended quite a few games with my dad at the Orange Bowl and in later years, at Joe Robbie Stadium, which is now called Dolphin Stadium. But mostly she enjoyed watching the games with him on TV.

In a quiet moment, I said to my father, "Dad, you made it through Thanksgiving. Next you'll see the birth of two more great-grandchildren in December. Beyond that, let's look forward to your birthday in January, and then more great-grandchildren will be born in February, March, and April."

"I have no future," my father said. He didn't mention any pain, but said he had become uncomfortable sitting in his chair."

"Your future is now…we need you, Dad. Let's be positive for tomorrow's chemotherapy. Let's see what it does for us."

"I love you," he said. "Go home and be with your family."

As I walked out of his room, I said, "Happy Thanksgiving, Dad. I love you, and I'll be with you tomorrow." I said the words enthusiastically, but my heart ached.

Not yet ready to leave the house, I gravitated toward the wall of ten fabulous wedding photographs, one for each of my parents married grandchildren. These 18" x 24" photographs, each ensconced in a museum-quality frame, on the curvilinear wall in the dining room, The Galbut Gallery, if you will, which also features an amazing photographic collage of hundreds of family photographs within one 36" by 36" lacquered frame.

This being Thanksgiving, I was drawn to the image of my eldest daughter Riki's wedding which took place here in Miami Beach on Thanksgiving Day in 1997. Four nights before the wedding, my father conducted a rehearsal for the sole purpose of composing the wedding picture at Temple Emanuel, on Washington Avenue across from the Jackie Gleason Theatre of the

Performing Arts. When my father was a Miami Beach commissioner in the early 1960s, he had been instrumental in bringing Jackie Gleason and his weekly TV program, featuring the June Taylor Dancers, to Miami Beach.

Facing the raised bema of the grand synagogue, where the family wedding photograph would be taken, my dad revised his diagram, noting where each and every family member would pose, with the bride and groom featured in the center of the front row. I understood his disappointment from two prior weddings, when the family picture became a lengthy fiasco in which some family members were inadvertently excluded, and in which the bride and bridegroom were relegated to the back row or were otherwise not the focal point of their own wedding picture.

During the rehearsal, I said, "Dad, most wedding rehearsals are done with the rabbi in order to organize the procession, the music, and the actual wedding ceremony."

"David, the procession will go on, and for a few moments, we'll all share in Riki's joy, but the family picture will last forever. It must be staged to perfection. Besides, you know better than anyone that you must *plan your work* so that when the time comes, you can *work your plan*. The picture must be staged and accomplished to perfection."

Upon viewing that beautiful picture featuring my parents and the newlyweds in the center, flanked by Gita and me on each side, along with brothers and wives, nieces and nephews, and the little children up front, I realized that the photograph represented a pinnacle moment for my father. The large framed print represents the best of what he had accomplished. As the photographer flashed the pictures, Dad was not satisfied until everyone was silent, focused, and peering toward the camera with a great smile. Afterward, Dad told the photographer that he expected proofs of these pictures within a week. And right on schedule, the proofs arrived, the perfect image was chosen, and my father ordered many copies. And that will forever be my image of my happiest Thanksgiving.

Chapter 7: With Strength Will Come Peace

The next morning, my father and I met Russell at Sylvester Cancer Institute. Dad had slept well, with some assistance from his Ambien and Xanax. The outpatient chemotherapeutic unit was closed due to the holiday, so Dad received VIP attention from the charge nurse of the Inpatient Unit. In addition to orchestrating the chemotherapy, the charge nurse used Activase, a powerful clot buster, to clear Dad's port so it could be used for today's treatment. At Dr. Rosenblatt's insistence, Dad received Zofran and Gemzar in an inpatient room.

That morning I made several observations. To everyone, Dad said "Thank you," and he greeted everyone with his warm and beautiful smile. And after the treatment, Dad told the charge nurse, "I feel better." Who says that after chemotherapy? But sure enough, Dad rose from the bed with enthusiasm, ready to go home.

In the car, we played an Israeli CD that included the song "Hazak Shalom," which means "With strength will come peace." Strength must be mustered from all sources, including the support of loved ones, but perhaps the greatest source comes from within—strength only God can provide.

At the house, Gita gave Dad a plate of vanilla ice cream atop a Belgian waffle, and then he rested in his chair in the bedroom. Gita and I returned home for Shabbat. As she prepared for the festive meal, I showered and dressed for the synagogue. Knotting my tie, I considered how in a lifetime, the sad moments should be fewer than the happy times, and to help make this so, we must make every day count and cherish every moment. In Dad's view, today was a good day. He enjoyed time with family, listened to beautiful music, we had lunch together, and he had a little chemotherapy mixed in for good measure.

After services, Gita, Nili, Rachel, and I enjoyed Shabbat dinner at my parents' house. Mom sat in her usual seat at the head. Dad's seat beside her remained empty, as he rested in the bedroom. Robert was with us, but his wife Rita was visiting their grandchildren in Chicago. We were also joined by my cousin Joanie, and by Eileen Chaiffetz—a longtime family friend and legal associate of Al B's. Rachel, Nili, Gita, and I were also there. We enjoyed a delicious meal, which included a magnificent roast from Gita's kitchen, along with some Thanksgiving leftovers, which I must say were delicious as well. Even though Dad was in the other room watching TV, Mom seemed happy just having him home.

Saturday evening, Gita and I returned to my parents' house, along with Elle's husband Jamie. Robert, Al B, Eileen, and Elana also arrived. To conclude Shabbat, we said Havdallah in my parent's room. My parents sat in their usual chairs, where Dad watched the end of a University of Miami vs. University of Virginia football game, the outcome of which would determine whether Miami received a Bowl bid. He turned away from the game to participate in the Havdallah prayer, which we all recited before him in the bedroom. When the spices were passed to him he said, "These are fresh, I know, because I put the cloves in the spice box myself a few weeks ago."

"Yes Hymie," Mom said, "that's your job and don't you forget it."

Walking home that night, Gita asked me, "Are you feeling sad or depressed?"

"No," I said, "it's been an exhilarating Shabbat. Seeing Dad's tranquility yesterday, how he came home relatively unscathed from his chemotherapy, gives me a sense of satisfaction. The future is harsh, I recognize that, but there is sweetness in these days."

"Kind of like the sweetness of the spice box," Gita said.

I returned to Mom and Dad's house late Sunday afternoon, just in time to help Radcliff bring Dad back into the house after their drive to visit Al B in the new office building he'd acquired on Biscayne Boulevard. In the dining room, Mom told me how Al B had given the largest corner office to his son Eric. For my dad to see Al B perform this generous act was an acknowledgment that the lessons he'd taught would live on.

After Dad used the bathroom, he settled into his chair to catch the second half of the late NFL game. Mom told me that in the morning she'd walked around the block with Louisiana, and that in the afternoon, she'd spent time with Rachel, who'd been studying for the art history course she was taking at Florida International University.

At 6:30, Dad said he'd like to eat at the table. Elana had brought us dinner from Shemtov, a kosher pizza restaurant on Arthur Godfrey Road. My father stood with some assistance, but pushed off from the chair mostly on his own and used his walker as he stepped toward the dining room and took his seat, which he hadn't occupied in over a month. He was flanked on his left by my mother. Radcliff sat to his right. I sat with Gita near Elana and Rachel. Robert, his daughter Erica, and her husband Ari sat across from us.

At first my father seemed comfortable, but he ate little, didn't say much, and soon he wanted to return to his chair in the bedroom. Pending acceptable laboratory results, his next chemotherapy session would be Friday morning.

That evening, for the first time, I sat with my mother and Louisiana in an attempt to learn Rummikub, but so much was going through my mind, including issues regarding my practice, that that I couldn't focus on the game. "Mom, I promise that I'll learn someday, and we'll enjoy playing together."

"It's important to laugh in life," Mom admonished me. "And you should know that Elana and Rachel are both excellent players."

I stepped into the bedroom to check on Dad.

"A lot of weirdos," he said.

"What's that, Dad?"

"This show, *Desperate Housewives*. It's very popular."

"What's it about, Dad?"

"It's so bizarre, but in today's world, perhaps it's realistic. All these unhappy husbands and wives looking for excitement in all the wrong places."

"I'll watch a little with you," I said. "The hospital personnel discuss it every Monday morning."

During the next commercial, I said, "How is your left arm feeling?"

"You tell me," he said, lifting his arm twelve inches above the table. "I couldn't do this yesterday."

"That's great, Dad. I see you've been doing a lot of physical therapy with Radcliff and Louisiana."

On Monday, three days after the second chemotherapy session, Dad developed a high fever, a runny nose, and a swollen right eye. I heard about this from Russell, who'd seen him in the morning. I called Mom and recommended doses of Clarinex and Tylenol. That evening at the house, I held his hand, but his eyes were closed as he lay in his recliner.

"How was your day?" he asked.

"Just one simple operation, typical office visits, catching up on administrative decisions. How about your day?" I said.

"Not great," he said, and then he asked me about the timing of the upcoming chemotherapy on Friday.

"The probability is high, as you've had few side effects from your second session."

My cousin Joanie—Miriam's daughter—sat with Mom playing Rummikub. For some thirty-five years, Aunt Miriam, along with Cousin Joanie, ran Miami Beach Auto Tag Agency on Tenth and Washington, in the Galbut Building, which also housed Dad's law practice. Almost everyone in Miami Beach went there to renew their auto tags. My aunt would always ask her customers, "Do you know my nephews Dr. Robert and Dr. David Galbut?"

And countless times, patients asked me, "Are you related to the woman who runs the auto tag agency in the Galbut Building," and I would say, "That's my aunt," to which they would say, "I really love your aunt Miriam. She is a great lady. I've known her for all these years. She makes me feel so wonderful, and I enjoy seeing her, you know, for the annual renewal of my license tag."

Mom accompanied me to the door and we leaned against the Remington statue of the American pioneer on horseback, leaning backward, descending a mountainside—a keen example of the promise of the American West. To Dad, that statue represented the American spirit, including adventure, challenge, and the fulfillment of responsibility and dreams. Mom, who had tears in her eyes, was beautifully dressed in a shirt and a belted skirt. "David, at times I'm very scared."

Friday morning, Al B and I met Dad at the house at 6:30. He'd been up since 4:00 and had already been out with Radcliff to drive by Hebrew Homes on Biscayne Boulevard, a reflection of his need to structure the early morning hours and to manage his relationship with his aide. For the past three years, as Chairman of the Board of Hebrew Homes, he created an era of economic prosperity and state recognition for excellent patient care. In recent weeks, he had taken to having Radcliff drive him and Mom around town at odd hours to pay homage to various locations that represented his years as a vital contributor in South Florida.

For our caravan to Sylvester, I drove Dad in his car, with his wheelchair in the trunk. Al B followed. From approximately

7:00 to 10:30, we sat in the waiting room until his blood work came back. The results were satisfactory, so Dad was able to receive his Zofran and Gemzar in the treatment bay, which took another two hours.

In waiting in the reception area, Al B and I saw Billy Sotchkin, who was back for his own chemotherapy. He was more frail than the last time but seemed happy to see us. He tearfully commented how much he loved our Dad. "Hymie is such a great man," Billy said. "I receive inspiration from your father's attitude about life. I always have. Such enormous strength! Seeing him here saddens me, but his courage motivates me."

"That's very kind of you," Al B said.

Russell stopped by for a few minutes on his way to an urgent business meeting. As I walked him back to his car at the valet entrance, Russell pondered the process of dying. "Is this the best way?"

"As long as there's no pain or mental anguish," I said, "and so long as there's the opportunity for him to reflect on his accomplishments, and to share love and warm moments with all of us, then yes."

"He has the opportunity to say goodbye on his own terms."

"That's an extraordinary blessing. What's better, to go suddenly without consideration, or to have a chance to live with some hope, to enjoy love, and to stage the important elements of the legacy for those who really count, the ones you really love—your spouse, children, and grandchildren?"

Russell kissed me goodbye. "Thanks, David," he said, before ducking into his car and driving off.

Back inside, Al B and I sat with Dad. We sipped coffee and ate muffins as we watched a History Channel program about World War II. Dad discussed Guadalcanal, Germany, and the impact on Volkswagen and Mercedes. He was wrapped in blankets and his port was functioning properly.

Around ten o'clock, Al B left for a meeting, and I waited for Robert, who was completing rounds at Mt. Sinai. When he arrived, we reviewed the blood work numbers and discussed the relative ease of treatment, and thanks to the Zofran, he wasn't nauseated.

"The hematocrit is over 30, and the platelets are greater than 120,000," Robert said, reviewing the printout.

"Fortunately the prior chemotherapy treatments haven't suppressed his red cells or platelet production."

About noon, I drove Dad home.

"What's left on your schedule today, David?" Dad stared straight ahead and glanced side to side, as if he were the one driving.

"Two operations, and seeing hospital patients."

"We've wasted the whole day," my father said.

"The day is long, Dad. It has been a great morning being together." As I drove across the Julia Tuttle Causeway, I reflected on Mom's comments earlier. As Dad had been preparing to leave, she'd asked me to approach Dad with extreme confidence. "Although it may not be true," she'd said, "tell Dad how great he looks, how strong he is, how he is getting better, how the chemotherapy is working, how the fever is improved, and how his overall status is on the mend. Convince him with your smile and give him greater hope. He needs to believe, David. He needs to hope, and he needs to know that you believe in him and his future."

"Mom, I will," I said. And with that, our day had begun. And now, as the morning concluded, I believed my father had received much of Mom's message.

We spent Shabbat evening at home with our children. There was much discussion at the table about the birthright and blessings that a parent gives a child. In the continuity of the family, if parents have more than one child, the responsibility of each one can vary. The birthright, or double portion, is given to the child who exerts the greatest influence in the preservation of the family, and blessings may be given to all children. The Jewish patriarchs include Abraham, Isaac, and Jacob. Abraham had only one son of his first wife, Sarah, which was Isaac. Therefore, Isaac received both the blessing and the birthright. Isaac had two sons, Jacob and Esau, and the former received both the birthright and the blessing, and the latter had to fight for the blessing. Jacob had twelve sons, but the birthright was given to Joseph, who was responsible for the family's survival by being the viceroy in Egypt. During the world's famine, Joseph preserved the families of his siblings and his father with their descent into Egypt. Jacob gave the blessings to his sons at the end of his days. Judah received the greatest blessing, and became the ancestor of the King David Dynasty, from which the Messiah will someday come. Central to his greatness was his ability to recognize his mistakes, to take corrective action, and to place the welfare of his siblings above his own interests.

Gita and I visited Dad Saturday afternoon. He was watching the annual Army-Navy game, which we often watched as a family when I was growing up. The most famous football player to emerge from the Naval Academy was Roger Staubach, who won the Heisman trophy in 1963, served in the Navy for four years, and starred for the Dallas Cowboys, winning the Super Bowl after the 1971 and 1977 seasons, and ultimately, he entered the NFL Hall of Fame.

"This is the most competitive rivalry in college football," Dad said.

"Bigger than Michigan and Ohio State?" I said.

"It is for me," he said, "and through the years, the advertising during the game for Annapolis and West Point has only gotten better and better—Madison Avenue at its best."

The Navy had fostered Dad's code of ethics and discipline, from which he never varied in his personal and professional life. In the early years, our family relied on the Navy as a consistent source of income. In addition, the G.I. Bill had enabled my father to attend law school. Long after he became a successful attorney and no longer needed his Navy stipend, Dad remained in the reserves until his retirement in 1980, when he was 60, at which point he had fulfilled all the officer billets available to a Naval Reservist.

I recalled our visit to the Naval Academy nearly fifty years before. During that time, I'd sensed tension between my parents. The thought of their child going to an academy that did not currently foster Jewish observance disturbed my mother, but my father appreciated how an Annapolis education might prepare me for a supreme rank in the Navy, and he believed I could do so while maintaining my commitment to Jewish observance. Mom asserted that one's commitment to Judaism required immersion in a primarily Jewish environment. Dad believed I could excel as an officer—and as a Jew—in the U.S. Navy, what many considered to be the most anti-Semitic of the military branches. As the navigator aboard his ship, everyone, regardless of rank, depended upon his flawless execution of his duties. During his years of service, Dad maintained a low profile but never denied his Jewish origin. He did not participate in Christian observances, but throughout his naval service, and until his last moment, Dad wore the custom-made gold medallion, displaying the Ten Commandments in Hebrew, which my mother had ordered from a New Orleans jeweler in 1941.

It's the summer of 1956, I'm seven years old, and we're headed to the Pentagon, where Dad will serve this year's active duty. On the way, we stop at the U.S. Naval Academy at Annapolis, Maryland, where officers and cadets—men of honor—come to acquire an excellent education and provide service to their country. In the preceding year, Dad has mentioned how I might study here when I grow up, but I sense disagreement between my parents on this subject, as there is little opportunity to observe traditional Judaism in such a setting. Once Dad said to Mom, "David will be the first to bring a kosher kitchen to Annapolis."

Annapolis is a beautiful campus with rolling hills. The educational buildings are majestic, and the students we encounter exude pride for their country. They dress in white, which Dad explains is consistent with their rank of Midshipmen. On our walking tour, I note Dad's enthusiasm and my mom's indifference.

I am surprised by the beauty of the summer's day and the rolling lawns surrounding each building. After we visit the athletic fields in the center of campus, the classrooms, the student center, and the dining quarters, Dad brings us to the all-purpose chapel. It's a modern building resembling a church, sort of like the ones I've seen in Miami and elsewhere. Inside, Dad explains that religion and belief in God are paramount in the mind of a young soldier charged with the awesome responsibility of defending his country. Dad explains that the Navy is "nonsectarian." He says every chaplain must be able to provide the service and essence of all branches of Christianity and Judaism. He explains that this is an all-purpose chapel where a midshipman or naval student of any persuasion can come engage in prayer. In the large chapel, I notice images of both the six-point Jewish star and the Cross. There are many rows of wooden pews. Upon the altar, beneath a large stained glass window, we see a velvet pillow which my father says is used for kneeling in Christian observances. We're the only ones in the chapel, and I look at Robert in dismay. Al B and Russell hold Mom's hands. Dad says this chapel represents the promise of greatness in our country.

He has explained that while prejudice against blacks still exists, freedom from persecution for religious observance in a courtroom is a Constitutional guarantee, and the military is predicated upon religious tolerance. He points out that this chapel is used mainly by Christians, but during the Jewish High Holidays, the chapel becomes a center for Jews. Impulsively, I walk toward the velvet pillow upon the altar, which Dad says is where Christians receive the Holy Sacrament, and I stomp the velvet. My brothers are watching, and perhaps my motivation is to please my mother, suggesting to her that I'm in tune with her apathetic feelings toward the chapel. Instantly, my three brothers scramble up the steps and pounce on the delicate velvet as well.

My father grabs my arm, strikes my bottom, and he gives a similar punishment to Robert, Al B, and Russell. As we march toward our car and drive away from Annapolis, my parents sit in the front seat with the four of us in the back seat of our mid-fifties Lincoln Continental sedan, equipped with what collectors refer to as "suicide doors."

"I am disappointed in your behavior, all of you," Dad says. "I will never accept religious intolerance from my children. The four of you are punished, and there will be silence for the next two hours. Instead of conversation, you will each sit in silence and think about your actions."

The cold silence served as a constant reminder of Dad's disappointment, a palpable shame I appreciate nearly fifty years later. During the summer of my twentieth year, I traveled with Al B and Russell to Europe and Israel for twelve weeks. Along the way we visited many churches, and I always thought of our visit to the chapel at the US Naval Academy in Annapolis and the lesson we learned about religious intolerance.

In 1980, after completing my five years of general surgical residency and after beginning my two-year thoracic surgery residency, I joined the Navy Reserve as a lieutenant commander. My rank was high because of my education. I enlisted largely because of my father's love of the Navy and his impending retirement, and to provide service to my country. My brother Al B joined the Naval Reserves in the adjuvant or legal division, also entering as a lieutenant. Al B remained in the reserves for four years and defended many enlisted men in Orlando during his periods of active duty, becoming an expert in military court proceedings. My involvement lasted just a year and a half. Although I wanted to continue, additional service was impossible, given with my eighty-hour workweeks as a young cardiac surgeon in Miami and my young family.

The Army-Navy game was over. Navy had won for the fourth year in a row. I sat beside Dad as Radcliff massaged Dad's legs in his ongoing attempt to improve his muscle tone. Dad ate a bowl of spaghetti and some sliced watermelon, although in general, Louisiana was convinced he wasn't eating enough. Sensing that he was particularly alert and relaxed, I thought it was a good moment for us to talk. "Dad, you're an outstanding father," I said.

"I agree." He smiled.

"What has been the key to your success?"

Dad shifted in his chair so that his knees were now pointed toward me. This was the perfect moment for reflection, the eclipse between the excitement of Navy winning the ballgame, the banter of the post-game commentary, and the sweetness of the watermelon.

"It's very simple, David. A father must demonstrate to his children how much he loves their mother. The greater the love and honor and kindness he demonstrates, the more it reflects the unity between husband and wife. There can only be one message and one entity in communication. If a husband and wife are divided, there is disharmony and friction."

"But does the unity create the father's demonstrable love, or does the love create the unity?"

"Your question is too difficult," Dad said. He was wearing a blue warm-up shirt and matching pants. Under different circumstances, he might be taken for an exercise enthusiast who'd just come home from the gym. "The approach must be simple in life. A mother will naturally connect with a child, having carried that child for nine months. The father can only achieve the same emotional bond by making the mother a queen. Naturally, the right mother makes her husband a king."

"But a king and queen do no not naturally reign. There must be some battle in the establishment of the relationship," I said, distracted for a moment by an ad for GEICO auto insurance featuring a talking lizard.

"Sure, but at the end of life, taking—which is the goal of all battles—yields to giving. By giving more, one actually receives a far greater portion. The secret to any relationship is focusing upon what you have in common. Any disagreements I've had with your mother are now meaningless in my reflection as I look at the life we've built together."

"What about divorced fathers?" I said. From the kitchen I overheard a bit of conversation between Gita and Louisiana, something about how they needed to add lettuce, tomatoes, and red peppers to the shopping list for the upcoming Shabbat.

"Those who are most successful keep peace with their ex-wives above all costs," Dad said, "and demonstrate to their children that they are united in the best interests of their children. But you know, there is one other thing, David. A father must help his child find the $1,000 bill, and this varies from child to child. It's not always obvious."

I knew Dad was referring to the O. Henry short story about the indigent who finds the $1,000 bill, and how it changes his life because people see him differently. Through their vision, he begins to see himself differently, and he develops self-esteem for the first time in his life. In typical O. Henry fashion, the concluding paragraph reveals that the bill is counterfeit, but the man's self-esteem remains.

"Do you think I'm succeeding as a father?"

"Of course, but we both know you're too lenient. Some of your children get away with murder."

Now I regretted broaching the subject. "Dad, I disagree. I just don't feel that getting A's is the ultimate accomplishment."

"David, it's not about grades. I care about their being disciplined and achieving to their level of aptitude."

"I concur, but our school has not always done such a great job of identifying and developing my children's specific gifts and skills."

"So you're blaming the Hebrew Academy for not recognizing your children's $1,000 bills?"

"Dad, I'm a heart surgeon. I don't blame people for my mistakes at work. Same goes for my family life. It's my responsibility to provide unconditional love and support, and to always preserve the self-esteem of my children."

"David, I love you, but you're still too lenient."

Dad grew up in a home in which the parents were not united in purpose and in which profound sibling rivalry was left unchecked. Wisdom comes from experience, and the best experience comes from our failures. I understand this from my experiences as a heart surgeon and as a father. In both roles, I've found failure to be a great teacher. It can also be quite painful.

As I completed the Sabbath in his home, Elle and Jaime arrived. Their two children marched around the house as if they owned the place. As Yakira and Eme walked into the room, Dad said to Gita, "Please give them some chips," referring to the endless supply of Pringles they kept in the kitchen. Elana had also arrived. Both Elle and Elana were nearing their due dates, four days apart. Some days I was convinced that Elle was larger, while other days Elana appeared bigger.

"The race is on," Dad said.

Chapter 8: Days to Remember

Sunday afternoon, the Dolphins defeated Buffalo with a four-yard touchdown pass with six seconds left in the game. They had triumphed against the odds, winning the game by one point, a bright spot in a season of mediocrity and disappointment.

Al B and Nancy had come over. My brother sat on the footstool and massaged Dad's feet and legs. "His legs are so thin and atrophied," Al B said. "Would electrical stimulation help?"

"Unfortunately that's mostly for spinal chord injury patients hoping to preserve muscle tone." I told Al B that we were meeting Dr. Rosenblatt on Tuesday to discuss Dad's condition and future chemotherapy plans."

My parents spoke with Nancy about her and Al B's son Jason, a painter living in New York, and his upcoming exhibit at Art Basel. I walked into the living room with Al B. Model railroad magazines were stacked on an end table, and on the glass coffee table stood an assortment of Dad's sailboat models, which had been identified for distribution to friends and loved ones.

"Is the chemo helping?" Al B asked.

"Perhaps the cancer in the liver is being halted, but the loss of protein metabolism and the breakdown of the structural elements is still underway, contributing to his atrophy, which has been ongoing since his bilateral knee replacements."

Radcliff told me that Dad's alertness had been good overall, and that he'd been up and about a little bit more, going from chair to chair, room to room. He'd enjoyed a pizza for lunch. He'd also developed a cough, with some sputum production and hoarseness, probably a consequence of Friday's chemotherapy.

Russell arrived with food from Sam's, a kosher restaurant on 41st Street. He loaded the takeout containers into the refrigerator, which since yesterday had been purged of lots of old food and was now stocked with vegetables, drinks, and fruits, and the dinner Russell had just brought over.

As Russell and Al B spoke with Dad, I joined Mom in the bedroom, where she was playing Rummikub with Rachel. She'd spent the day without an aide, preferring to spend time with Rachel. Their activities often included visits to Publix for groceries and occasionally lunch at Shem Tov's, a kosher pizza place near the house. Mom enjoyed her intellectual exchanges with Rachel, discussing her graduate courses, of course, hours of Rummikub.

After dinner Russell received a phone call from an Israeli faith healer, Dr. Daniel Woda, who visits Miami about twice a year. Ronalee had seen him once for knee pain, which he diagnosed and treated. He received his training in alternative medicine in France and in Sefat, the town in Northern Israel where Kabbalah, or Jewish mysticism, emerged over the centuries. After they spoke awhile, Russell handed me his phone. Dr. Woda told me he was interested in treating my father, and he assured me that his methods were harmless. "If a child should take the potion by accident, it will cause no harm."

"What are the ingredients of this therapy?" I asked.

"It is a stone extract, which takes me several hours to prepare. We could begin tomorrow."

"What about side effects?" I said. Skeptical of any benefit, I focused on any potential risks.

"None," he said, "with the remote possibility of diarrhea."

"If it comes from stone," I said, "then it must contain calcium, carbon, and oxalates."

"That's correct," he said.

I had reservations about the ingestion of the oxalate, which has some degree of toxicity, but the risk seemed minimal, and I recognized the potential psychological benefit. I've always believed that the more a patient participates in his own care, and believes in his recovery, the better will be his outcome. This may reflect a mentally directed, perhaps hormone-mediated, stimulation of the immune system to higher efficiency. In a strictly medical sense, I hadn't seen replicable and objective improvement in patients treated with alternative medicines, but some do better than expected.

In the dining room, Al B, Russell, Robert, and I agreed that this treatment could be initiated the following evening. Robert and I agreed that the toxicity would be negligible.

I kissed Dad goodnight. "How're you feeling?" I said.

"It was a great day of football."

Dr. Woda arrived at 6:30 Monday night. He was a slim, intense man in his mid-fifties, about five-foot-nine. He wore a white open-collar dress shirt and dark slacks. He and Dad exchanged accounts of their respective military careers. We learned that Dr. Woda had served as a helicopter pilot for the Israeli Defense Forces prior to his health training.

He opened a large briefcase, withdrew a corked bottle, and explained that his grayish, chalky "medicine" included "two herbs" derived from local stone. Instead of herbs, it probably contained calcium and oxalate. My brothers and I tasted the bitter liquid, which smelled like licorice. Dr. Woda suggested Dad take two tablespoonfuls three times a day. After Dad took his first dose, Dr. Woda placed his hands on Dad's stomach and chest, and he appeared to pray.

"Captain," Dr. Woda said in his combined French and Israeli accent, his hands still touching Dad's chest and upper abdomen. "The medicine can only help you. It will not harm you."

"I have complete faith in my sons, Dr. Woda."

I questioned the wisdom of resorting to faith healing, as I've never recommended this modality to my own patients. This was a new experience for me, as both a medical advocate and as a loving son. The ultimate pledge in the Hippocratic Oath is "Do no harm," and I felt comfortable that this was being fulfilled.

Although I grew up in American medicine, which relies upon scientific investigation, and although I've authored over a dozen journal articles, I remain open-minded about the prospects of a faith healer adding a modality of treatment. For all I know, there may be some exceptional people in the world with God's gift of the power to heal, and I hoped Dr. Woda was one of them.

Russell tasted the liquid potion. "It's awful," he said. "This may very well be hocus-pocus."

I led Russell out of the room and whispered, "Dad must believe he's taking an active and decisive role in the process of getting better. The risk is minimal, although the chance of benefit is probably the same."

Back in the bedroom, with closed eyes, Dr. Woda remained focused on my father, his hands still palm-down on Dad's abdomen and chest. If he'd heard Russell's comments, he chose to ignore them.

In lieu of compensation, which I suspect Russell had probably covered earlier, Dr. Woda seemed impressed with my surgical scrubs and asked whether I had any extras. So I brought him over to my house, went upstairs, and brought down a sampling of all three colors: green, blue, and gray, and I thanked him for his extraordinary efforts. "I hope we'll see you again soon," I said.

"Thank you, David," he said, "and I'll continue to pray that at least your father should have minimal pain and possibly some healing from his cancer."

"It's in God's hands," I said to Dr. Woda. "Thank you for your efforts. God should give you success in your endeavors."

I turned eight a few months ago. It's summer now, and my father and brothers and I are stepping onto The Reward, a boat designed to accommodate about fifty fishermen. We're going deep-sea fishing off the Atlantic coastline in search of snapper, kingfish, grouper, and maybe a marlin. The boat is anchored, and the fishing lines have been thrown off in all directions. The rods and reels are provided by the staff of The Reward. The fish aren't biting, and the boat is rocking. As this continues, my brothers and I get seasick. My father, an old Navy officer, is not seasick, and mans the fishing rods for all of us as we lie down along the benches of the crowded boat. I'm desperately trying not to vomit. After a half-hour unsuccessful fishing, the motors rev up and the boat begins moving. Finally, I have a moment's relief from the nausea until the next location is found and the anchor is dropped again. The ship begins rocking again, and this time I throw up.

"Sometimes this happens, David, but you can endure, and shortly, the vessel will move again." After four or five more stops, thankfully we're finally heading toward land. With the ship in motion, my nausea improves. My brothers and I haven't caught anything, but my father has caught one small kingfish. As we depart the boat at the dock, there's a large barracuda, which someone caught on another boat.

"May we borrow your barracuda for a moment?" my father asks.

"Excuse me?"

"For my boys," my father says.

One by one, my brothers and I each pose with the barracuda, which is two and a half feet in length, as my father takes a picture with his Yashica 35mm Camera.

While holding the fish, I say, "Dad, we didn't catch this fish."

"No, you didn't, son, but you deserved to, and I want you to remember this day."

After Dr. Woda departed, I wondered, "Are we just fishing for possibilities here? And how different is that from actual fishing? Placing bait on a hook, are we not investing our time on faith and uncertainty? You never know what you're going to catch. And if our father had experienced a remarkable improvement in his quality of life, or if he had enjoyed an unforeseen prolonging of his life, would we have attributed this to the session with Dr. Woda? Would we have dared question it? Either way, it was a memorable day spent fishing.

On Tuesday, December 6th, I met Al B at Mom and Dad's to prepare for another journey to Sylvester, not for chemotherapy, but for an office follow-up with Dr. Rosenblatt. On the causeway, we encountered heavy fog. Our normally limitless visibility was down to maybe a hundred yards.

"Fog," my father said, "results from an inversion effect as a consequence of hot weather being above cold weather, and dissipating with the advance of the sun. The greatest blessing is the dew, because without it, nothing grows."

Al B parked behind us in the valet area, and soon we were upstairs, where Russell met us a few minutes later, carrying his laptop computer. We all sat in semi-circle, surrounding Dad's wheelchair.

We were the first group to be brought into an examination room. The busy clinic had four doctors, each with two examination rooms, a central core of secretaries, and individual nurse practitioners. I spotted Dr. Rosenblatt's appointment list. He was scheduled to see about ten patients that morning.

Inside the compact, efficiently organized examination room, we helped Dad onto the table. The room contained a white porcelain sink, a supply cabinet, and a desk with a computer terminal. Dr. Rosenblatt arrived at 9:00 for the 8:00 appointment, complaining how the fog had slowed the traffic on I-95 South. Robert had arrived just few moments earlier. At this point, there were eight of us in the office: my three brothers, myself, Dad, Dr. Rosenblatt, and two women I hadn't met before—a nurse practitioner and a medical student.

"Everyone's here," Dr. Rosenblatt said to the assembled crowd as he shook Dad's hand. "So how are you feeling this morning, Captain Galbut? Your handshake is very strong."

Dad had always taught us to greet people with direct eye contact and a firm handshake.

"But I'm unsteady, and I'm not mobile," Dad conceded.

"I don't understand why you're having trouble walking," Dr. Rosenblatt said, "unless it's part of the catabolic process, a consequence of the tumor."

"That's true," Robert added, "but it's also compounded by neuropathy, which over time has been worsened by his dual knee replacement surgery and the herniated disks in his lower back."

"You seem pretty strong, Captain," Dr. Rosenblatt said, "but how do you feel in general? Any pain?"

"I have no pain, but I'm very bored. I have no entertainment."

"What do you want, a girl?" Russell quipped.

"I already have one," Dad said, "and it's too costly to have more."

Suppressing a laugh, Dr. Rosenblatt said, "What sort of entertainment would you like, Captain?"

"A movie," Dad said. "I'd like to go to a movie."

"Let's all go one evening this week," Al B suggested.

"No, I want a 12 o'clock matinee."

"Fine," Russell said. "That's what we'll do."

"How is your diet, Captain?" the doctor said. "What are you eating?"

"Not many solids. Mostly ice cream, fruit, and milk. I'd enjoy a nice steak, but my I feel full after the smallest portion of anything."

Al B said, "Dad, I'll barbecue a steak and cut it into small pieces for you."

"I'd like that," Dad said.

The medical student took notes, even on the light-hearted banter. Dr. Rosenblatt asked me and Robert about Dad's medications, with particular emphasis on his digestive aids, as the pancreas was not producing the chemicals needed for the breakdown of food products.

Dr. Rosenblatt examined Dad's exposed abdomen. "Lungs are clear, abdomen is soft, without distention. The liver is not significantly enlarged to palpation." The medical student swiftly jotted down every word.

Having reviewed the blood results, which suggested anemia, Dr. Rosenblatt went to his keyboard and typed up an order for an injection of Epogen. "This should stimulate your father's bone marrow production," he said. "It'll take about twenty minutes for the medicine to arrive from the pharmacy." As Dr. Rosenblatt left, he instructed his nurse practitioner to administer the medicine as soon as it arrived.

Russell, who had assumed responsibility for acquiring and overseeing the eighty family gravesites in Israel, asked Robert, Al B, and me to step outside. He pulled a folded chart from his coat pocket. Russell explained that after much consideration, he wanted to finalize the location of Dad's grave, given the uncertainty of the days ahead. He believed that a diamond pattern surrounding our parents would be most appropriate. Robert will be to Dad's right, Russell will be above Dad, Al B will be below Dad, and I'll be buried between Mom and Gita. This configuration will give my family, the largest, room to expand both in a northern and southern direction. Ultimately, my brothers and I will each rest alongside our wives, with our children, and potentially their children in close proximity. While I am the one brother who will not be alongside Dad, in our eternal resting place, I am more than satisfied with my assigned position, given my interconnectedness with both of my parents. It will be an extraordinary blessing to be next to Gita, and for us to grant our children's families the option of one day resting alongside us.

After the subcutaneous Epogen injection, Dad was ready to leave. By this time my three brothers had returned to their various work commitments. In the car, Dad said, "David, do you think John could help me restore some muscle tone in my legs?" John was Dad's trainer from the 51st Street Gym in Miami Beach. For the five years since his knee replacement surgeries, Dad had worked out there as often as three times a week.

"I'll call him," I said, but in my heart I questioned whether Dad was up for it.

At 11 a.m., I began my workday, which included rounding in three hospitals, one thoracic operation, five consults, and forty-eight office visits. I then attended a meeting with potential investors at Miami Beach Community Hospital, formerly South Shore, a struggling facility in the heart of South Beach on Alton

Road between West Avenue and Ocean Drive. I believed the hospital could be made profitable if the mission was to provide quality service. Russell's company owned the real estate, and to protect their interests, they needed to revamp the business plan. As a limited partner, and as a physician, my goal was to advise the clinical managers and to preserve this important community asset in South Beach.

The following day, after many surgeries and other business, I realized that this was December 7th, the anniversary of Pearl Harbor. Dad was a proud member of "The Greatest Generation." Idealistic, brave, and generous, he and his cohorts gave their youths—and many gave their lives—to protect and build America. So much of his didactic code has been instilled in his children—his work ethic, his dedication to his family, his community commitments, and his service to country. My own work ethic, which I learned from Dad's example, keeps me going during my eighty-hour weeks, and during a trip I took over three decades ago, I caught a glimpse into the root of Dad's lessons.

It's the summer of 1972, and I'm in Hawaii with Mom, Dad, and Russell to tour Pearl Harbor and enjoy some recreation. I'm in medical school and Russell's in college. It's been at least a decade since I'd traveled with my parents. Dad enjoys reminiscing about his time here. During his service in the Pacific, Dad came to Pearl Harbor periodically when his ship required maintenance and supplies. Frankly I don't have time for this trip, given the minimal time off we're given from school, but I couldn't refuse the opportunity to visit Pearl Harbor while I'm about the same age Dad was when he served here.

I'm also enjoying the opportunity to spend time with Russell. He's nineteen now, and a sophomore at Cornell. From what we're hearing, he's made the Dean's List, and is now driven to succeed.

We step across the memorial and look down upon the carcass of the USS Arizona, part of which, depending on the tide, is barely six feet below the surface.

"Over a thousand crewman are entombed down there," Dad says. "It's hard to imagine."

A tourist standing nearby remarks to his wife and kids that oil continues to seep from the engines.

As we leave the memorial, I say, "Dad, how does it feel being here again?"

"I grieve for my comrades. They never had a chance, but this is a fitting memorial to their sacrifice. But today I'm happy that I could return with you boys and your mother. I only wish Robert and Al B were here too. Maybe next time," Dad said, placing his arm around Mom. "The way Pearl Harbor and all of

Honolulu have been rebuilt is a true testament to our winning the war and the greatness of America. It's truly something."

Afterwards we walk to the commissary, which is basically a super-department store but with huge discounts like I've never seen back home. The pride Dad exhibits showing his military I.D. card reminds me of our Navy trips in the '50s. Here in Hawaii, we go on the greatest shopping binge I can remember. They buy me and Russell all the clothing we'll need for the coming year. They also buy me a new Harmon Kardon stereo with Panasonic speakers. I can't overlook the irony—two countries we defeated are now producing products that are superior to anything America makes, and it's all for sale in a U.S. Navy commissary. And the real kicker is that all over town, we're finding Pearl Harbor souvenirs that were made in Japan.

After the shopping splurge, perhaps Dad senses my uncertainty about my future. Beyond the checkout lines, but still within the atrium of the commissary, we spot a young female artist who produces whimsical watercolor portraits. "Your work is beautiful," Dad says. "I have a handsome subject for you."

At this point, Russell is still shopping with Mom.

"Dad, I'm too young for this. Portraits should be of accomplished men. I haven't done anything yet."

"Sit down," he says. "She's a great artist, and very interested in painting your future." I try to get comfortable in the

little wooden chair beside the easel. "My son is an artist too, but he performs his craft with a knife."

"I hope he's not a serial killer," the artist says. Then she looks at me. "Are you a sculptor?"

"He's studying medicine to become a great surgeon," Dad says.

"Your eyes are green," the artist says as she begins sketching a caricature of my long hair, green eyes, and youthful grin. "Are you right-handed?"

"I'm a leftie," I said. "Why do you ask?"

"You'll see," she says, dabbing her brush in a puddle of green paint that will form the surgical scrubs she envisions for me.

About twenty minutes later, I see the results of her work. In the picture, I am performing surgery on the chest of a Frankenstein creation, who is thinking "MMM... The Greatest Surgeon in the World!" while giving me a look of serious doubt. On my left is a happy blonde nurse who resembles the artist. I realize that she is communicating with me in her art, but with my father in attendance, this is not the time or the place.

Over the next three days, Russell and I explore Honolulu as two carefree young men while Mom and Dad seem content to relax at the hotel. Dad has already fulfilled his goals for the trip, having visited the memorial at the Harbor and having shared his thoughts on this sacred place with Mom, myself, and my brother.

The next morning after breakfast, Dad pulls me and Russell aside, gives us some cash, and tells us about a glider excursion he read about in a brochure in the lobby. He hands me the keys to the rent-a-car and explains that the landing strip is on the other side of the idle Honolulu Volcano in the center of Oahu.

An hour later, Russell and I are standing bare-chested in our bathing suits and sandals beside the wooden glider, which is attached to a single-engine plane by a thick rope. The airstrip is on the northern edge of the island, a thousand feet above a beach dotted with surfers. "At least if we crash, we can swim to shore," I say, glancing over the cliff at the Pacific Ocean.

"David, we're nuts for doing this," Russell says, looking at his signed "waiver of responsibility" document.

"C'mon," I say as the pilot arrives. He takes our waivers and ushers us into our seats, single file, in the enclosed panoramic cockpit.

"Hold on," the pilot says as the glider accelerates behind the small tow-plane. We gain about a thousand feet before we're released, and then we bank over the beach in pure silence as intense sunlight permeates the clear glass above.

"Good thing we had a light breakfast," Russell says.

Floating above the ocean, like a bird in flight with open wings, I recognized that I would never again possess such a rare combination of time, daring, and absence of responsibilities. On a glider, as on a sailboat, I've learned that you can't control everything. You jiggle the jib and adjust the sail, but you can only control so much. You must be willing to run with the currents.

My father had lived such a diverse life, always seizing opportunities, including those things that can't be controlled. He found opportunity in everything, and that's the essence of being that our father personified. And he was always teaching us things a family unit. It wasn't enough to have certain experiences, but he wanted us to relive them in our minds—hence, his concern with photographs. A successful event had to have a record that could be looked back upon. A persistent goal of mine has long been to write a book and collate these memories. Until my dad's illness, I never saw the opportunity. Writing a book is perhaps a futile attempt to cheat time.

Floating over Honolulu, my brother and I peered down at a spectacular landscape, where, coincidentally, Russell would later become a prolific condominium and hotel developer. In retrospect, we must have been just a little crazy back then, placing our lives into the hands of that glider pilot, a total stranger, who, for all we knew, had been kicked out of the Air Force or an airline training program. But how different is that from my patients, who place their lives in my hands, having little or no prior knowledge of my training and experience?

After twenty minutes of sailing over the ocean, Russell and I returned to the landing strip, gaining speed on our approach. And as we landed, despite my joy and exhilaration, I knew that I would never repeat this adventure, and I knew I would never forget it. In recent years, several of my daughters have expressed an interest in skydiving, which I adamantly opposed, which is ironic, because had I been given the opportunity to freefall from an airplane that day in 1972, I would have jumped at the chance.

Mom, Dad, Radcliff, and Louisiana spent Pearl Harbor day at the Intracoastal Theater, viewing *Ushpizin,* an Israeli film about two paroled criminals who celebrate the Jewish holidays with a fellow criminal from their past who has become an ultra-orthodox Jew who is married but without children.

At the house that night, Dad said, "The movie was fair, but your mother loved it." I sensed Dad's pride in attending his first movie since his diagnosis.

"Gita and I enjoyed it."

"Well, I'm just glad it was short, because frankly it was boring," Dad said. He held a can of chocolate Boost. In recent weeks, a good portion of his diet constituted three cans a day of that high-calorie supplement.

"I felt like I was in Jerusalem," I said. "Despite the abject poverty, the spiritual richness was tangible."

Dad placed the empty Boost can on the glass table beside his chair. "The two cities in the world I love the most, David, are Miami Beach and Jerusalem."

"They're both timeless," I said.

In bed that night, I thought about time. It's not our friend, but rather it's our enemy. We say, "Spending time," but is that always accurate? We "spend" time, but can't we also "invest" time? On one hand, Dad hadn't been thrilled with the film, but he was proud of his accomplishment of bringing my mother to a movie again, but more than anything, my parents shared some final moments together in the Holy City of Jerusalem. All for the price of movie tickets.

The next evening, following our Shabbat meal with our children, I visited my parents with my son-in-law Jamie. Robert's family had spent the evening there. When we arrived, dinner was over and they were serving a birthday cake for Erica's husband, Ari. Dad was sitting in what had become his bedroom, with Radcliff, watching an episode of *Law and Order*. It's not that Mom had kicked him out, but rather he had taken to watching TV at all hours of the night, and Mom's medication schedule required that she be awakened at odd hours. Between the two of them, nobody would have gotten any sleep.

"A person could be prosecuted for rape in one state, but not another," Dad explained to us. "There is such ambiguity in these matters. Sometimes it's difficult for a jury to determine consensual activity."

"So can we learn from the show, or is it Hollywood fluff?" Jamie asked.

"They do a reasonable job on this program," Dad said, "but they're forced to squeeze a complicated matter into forty-four minutes of screen time between all the commercials for sports cars and perfume."

As Jamie discussed the virtues of the TV show with Dad, I caught up with Mom at the dining room table, amid a scattering of desert plates covered with cake crumbs and half-empty coffee cups.

"These Shabbat meals are exhausting," Mom said, "but I enjoy them."

"Dad seems in excellent form tonight? Did he eat at the table?"

"He stayed in his room, but he sampled some of the brisket."

"The Boost should help," I said. He's only been on it a few weeks."

"He's losing more weight, David," Mom said. "He's barely 190 anymore." In health, my father's weight had remained a steady 215 pounds.

"Has he said anything to you about bringing Dr. Woda back again before he leaves town?"

"Yes, and he's absolutely not interested. Dad said the taste of that drink was awful."

"Bessie, where's my sleeping pill?" Dad called from his bedroom. Radcliff was in there with him, but with the various aides coming and going, it had remained Mom's job to dispense the medications.

"Bessie!" Dad shouted from the bedroom. "Did you hide my pills?"

"I'll be there in a minute, Dad."

My father had the greatest love for my mother and his family, but Mom had become the inevitable outlet for his occasional anger in this new monotonous, dependent existence.

Jamie and I said goodnight as the credits scrolled on *Law and Order*, alongside a split-screen promo for the Channel Six late news. Dad apologized for yelling and expressed his excitement about the upcoming births. Elana and Elle were both due next week. "More great-grandchildren," Dad said with a smile. "I can't wait."

I went home that night, anxious for a good night's sleep and a pleasant morning at the synagogue, but life doesn't always go as planned. At 4:45 a.m., Elana called the house. "Dad, I think I'm in labor."

We had agreed beforehand that if her labor should occur on the Sabbath, I would bring them to the hospital and allow Yochai to observe his commitment of not driving on the Sabbath. Normally he wouldn't even be a passenger on Saturday, but this was an obvious time for an exception.

We arrived at the obstetrics floor at South Miami at about 6:30. This would be the first of my grandchildren to be born there. As Chief of Heart Surgery, and as the face of recent print ads, I've become well-known throughout the hospital family. Elana was having irregular and mild uterine contractions. The supervising nurse determined that the cervix was not dilated and that she was not in active labor. At the shift change, the nurse said to me, "Walk with your daughter awhile, Dr. Galbut, and see if that helps." After an hour of pacing the halls, and a walk across the third floor from the Pavilion to the North Tower and across the bridge over 62nd Avenue, we returned to the Labor floor where the nurse determined that Elana's cervix was now dilated to approximately 3 cm and slightly effaced.

Within sight of Elana, Yochai sat in a chair, saying his Sabbath morning prayers and reading a book of Psalms. He felt most productive in this effort, and was happy that I was being the medical advocate for Elana.

For an hour, I visited patients in the Intensive Care and Telemetry units. When I returned, Elana's contractions had improved, and she was in the early stages of labor. She was moved to the delivery floor, where Elana continued in labor. Her obstetrician, Dr. Rafael Perez, broke the amniotic sac, and after much discussion, he ordered a Pitocin drip, a uterine contraction stimulant, just after 2:00 p.m. An hour later she received an epidural for her pain.

I sat in her room and watched her sleep. I sat in a chair near the window, which revealed a receding sun. We had been up since about 1:30 a.m. I sat and monitored the screen, complete with data on the baby's heartbeat, Elana's heartbeat, Elana's blood pressure, and the magnitude of her uterine contractions. Her pressure had dropped to 70mm systolic pressure as a consequence of the epidural narcotic. Following an ephedrine injection to increase her pressure, the baby had a reflex tachycardia, or rapid heartbeat, interspersed with a mild bradycardia, or slow heartbeat with Elana's contractions, an indication that the cord might be tangled around the baby's neck.

Most of the time, the baby's heart rate remained in the normal 155-160 range, and Elana's pressure stabilized at 90mm systolic. At 6 p.m., she moved into the final phase of labor.

Diana, the head labor and delivery nurse, began coached Elana. "You must be strong—push with every contraction," the nurse said. "The baby's almost here and the mystery will be solved," she said, a reference to the baby's unknown gender.

Dr. Perez opened the sterile kit and laid out the instruments for the episiotomy, often required with a first-time mother. As Elana began the final phase of labor, with her cervix at 9 cm, I stood beside Diana, and between us stood Dr. Perez. Diana held one leg and I held the other.

"Elana, the baby's almost here. Be strong, sweetheart. One more push. Push!"

As the baby crowned and the head came out, we saw that the umbilical cord was coiled several times around the neck, strangling the baby. Dr. Perez swiftly placed two clamps on the cord. Much like the choreography I know from the operating room, Dr. Perez exposed the section of cord between the clamps, allowing me to reach in and make the cut with the metzenbaum scissors, releasing the neck and permitting the delivery.

Within seconds, Dr. Perez placed a beautiful baby girl, with magnificent, delicate features upon Elana's chest, initiating the imprinting of the greatest natural bond known to the human species. Within fifteen seconds, the baby cried and her bluish hue gave way to a pink complexion. As Dr. Perez delivered the placenta and repaired the episiotomy, I took the baby girl from

Elana and placed her on the newborn table, where the neonatal nurse examined and measured her. My own inspection revealed a perfect newborn, which coincided with the nurse's Apgar scorings, which were both nine out of a possible ten points. The Apgar measures a newborn's health with regard to heart rate, respiration, muscle tone, color, and reflexes.

Yochai, who had quietly observed the closing of the Sabbath to what degree he could in the hospital, was now a jubilant young father, snapping pictures with the new digital camera he'd bought for the occasion.

"I'm so happy," Elana said. "our daughter is so beautiful."

"Like her mother," Yochai said.

Upon her arrival, Gita cried at the site of her newest granddaughter. She kissed and hugged Elana, welcoming her fourth daughter to the club of motherhood. My wife then caller her own mother and her siblings, and I called my parents. Mom answered and placed me on speakerphone.

"Mom and Dad...guess what? Elana delivered!"

Before I could continue, Mom asked, "A baby girl?"

"What else?" I said. Now I had six daughters, six granddaughters and one grandson."

"We're coming over, David. We'll see you tonight. We are so excited. We love baby girls." This was my parents' nineteenth great-grandchild.

Within an hour, Elana's siblings, save for my daughter Dani in Toronto, had arrived. We shared coffee and sandwiches and the love of being together. I was excited to introduce Elle to the labor and delivery staff, as we expected her delivery within a few days.

I met Mom and Dad, who'd arrived with Al B, Radcliff, and Louisiana in the Emergency Room. In my green scrubs, I functioned as my father's transporter, pushing his wheelchair, surrounded by his entourage, through the first floor corridors, into an elevator, and up to the Labor floor.

"I want to see my princess and the new addition to our family." I knew Dad was referring to his special relationship with Elana, forged during the two-year period in which he'd been her high school advocate and mentor. Each day, Elana studied at my parents' home. Dad had devoted himself to being her tutor and interacted with her teachers. He affirmed her self-esteem and brought out her thousand-dollar bill, which was her artistic gifts.

"I love you," Dad said to Elana, still lying in the birthing bed. He handed her an envelope containing a beautiful note, written by my mother and signed on behalf of both of them. The envelope included two $500 checks, one for the newborn, and the second for Elana to purchase some new clothes for herself. Following birth, the protocol is to permit the mother to rest a few hours while the baby is further evaluated by the neonatologist and specially trained neonatal nurses.

I escorted my parents along the corridor toward the large glass wall revealing the nursery. A nursing supervisor for the neonatal unit spotted us. We'd met a few months earlier when I performed an aortic valve replacement on her husband. In a gesture of professional reciprocity, she brought the bassinette within inches of the glass wall and lifted the baby toward us. Dad sat upright in his wheelchair, smiling, with tears in his eyes. "She is beautiful," he said. Mom stood behind Dad's wheelchair with her hand caressing his shoulder.

As the baby was moved toward the glass, within three inches of Dad's face, she cried in a crescendo of defiance.

"She's got my stubbornness," Dad observed.

I stepped back and considered the contrast. Four generations, the eldest in the last days of winter, and the youngest, my seventh grandchild, in the first hours of the dawn of spring. I recalled the Welsh poet Dylan Thomas, who gave us the beautiful words: *Do not go gentle into that good night ... Rage, rage against the dying of the light.* Although I know better, I wondered whether the newborn could see her great-grandfather's face behind the glass. Was she raging on his behalf?

Chapter 9: Generation to Generation

On Tuesday, Al B and Nancy were the honorees at the Talmudic University Annual Dinner held at the Deauville Hotel on Collins Avenue. This award recognized their distinguished service and charitable contributions over many years. I attended the ceremony with Gita, Mom, my brothers, and their wives. Dad wanted to attend for Al B, of course, but was reluctant to be seen by some five hundred people, most of whom knew him as vital and vigorous. "They don't need to remember me like this," Dad said one night at the house, gesturing at his wheelchair with his swollen hand.

"Dad, whether you attend or not, they'll remember you as the Captain."

That same night, Nili spoke to him about her day, and the excitement of earning her driver's license.

"You'll be a great driver," Dad said. "Your hand-eye coordination is outstanding, as evidenced by your basketball skills."

"We have chemotherapy in the morning, Dad," I said, noting his skin to be pink, and not pale. His respiratory rate was in the normal range. "Your lungs are clear and your left upper extremity is less swollen than yesterday. Both legs are less swollen than yesterday, and your mind is sharp," I said, knowing he needed to hear this. "Dad, I think you're doing well."

"David, it's time for you and Nili to go home. I can't wait to see Elana and the baby." Outside, I handed Nili my keys. She climbed into the driver's seat, tuned the stereo to her favorite FM rock station, and drove us home.

On December 14th, Russell and Al B brought Dad to Sylvester for his chemotherapy, now beginning the second cycle. There had been an off-week, necessary to permit his bone marrow to recover from any toxic affects.

I arrived about 9:00 a.m. Dad lay in a recliner in the treatment bay, covered by a tan blanket. A month had now passed since the consultation with the oncologist who'd predicted Dad's imminent demise, Dad had increased difficulty ambulating, but his spirit and mind remained strong, and he had only minimal abdominal pain. This morning he was listening to Russell and Al B's son Eric discuss the headlines in the paper, included something about General Motors and their ongoing financial woes. Russell left shortly after my arrival to attend a meeting with underwriters from a local bank.

I was pleased to share these moments with Eric, who'd spent Sabbath afternoons in our home when he was growing up. "It's wonderful that you're here, Eric," I said, "both as an education and as an opportunity to demonstrate your love for Zayde. With this experience, you'll be able to take care of me someday."

"With your wife and daughters and sons-in-law, I think you'll be well-cared for, Uncle David," Eric said.

Robert arrived a little after 10 a.m. We reviewed the chemotherapy dosage. "Has there been any difficulty with the port?"

"It's working beautifully," I told Robert.

We all left the unit at 11:00, with Eric pushing Dad's wheelchair. We waited under the awning while the valet retrieved Robert's car. We all helped Dad into the front seat and placed his wheelchair in the trunk.

"Good afternoon, Captain," the attendant said as Eric pushed the door closed. Dad responded with a wave through the window.

As Robert drove off, Eric and I waited for our cars. I reflected over Dad's special relationship with each of his sons. "You know, Eric, Zayde worked hard throughout his life to be even-handed with us. Today you assumed the role of a son representing *your* father, and therefore, as a brother to me."

As Eric's car approached, he turned to me. "Thank you, Uncle David."

Elle went into labor the morning of her due date. I was preparing to fly to New York to spend the day with Russell and to participate in a Chabad dinner at the New York Hilton in honor of Russell, Ronalee, and Mayor Michael Bloomberg. I looked forward to speaking in tribute of Russell and Ronalee's philanthropy and service before over a thousand guests. I'd planned to speak about the influence of our parents, and although I never delivered my extemporaneous speech, I know exactly what I would have said:

"By paying honor to an individual, one honors that individual's parents. Russell's father, our father, is a renaissance man in his interests, abilities, knowledge, wisdom, and deeds. Our mother is devout in her faith and unswerving in her commitment to Torah. This combination helped Russell become a man of dreams and action.

"In last week's Torah section, Jacob is a young man who leaves his father's house, dreaming of a ladder with angels in ascent and descent. As he awakens, he realizes the holiness of the site and says to God, 'If you will watch over me, give me bread to eat and clothing to wear, and return me in peace to my father's house, then you shall be my Lord and I will build a house of God and I will tithe from all that I will receive.'

"As Russell went into the world and pursued his dreams, he encountered Ronalee, his soul mate, who has established the immutable values in their home. My brother is also diversified in his accomplishments and never swerves from his sense of Jewish values. As in his youth, he understands caring and sharing, and sharing means giving and receiving. He has followed the example of our Patriarch Jacob by giving generously from all of God's rewards. As a brother, I am proud of your accomplishments and cherish the love of family that we share."

But as my thoughts developed that morning, Elle went into labor with her third child. I met her and Jamie at the South Miami Hospital labor and delivery floor. We can't dance at two simultaneous weddings. My love for Russell is great and the importance of family unity and preservation is paramount, but a father's unconditional love and commitment to his child is greater—only secondary to the bond with his wife.

I promised Russell that I would try to catch an afternoon flight. He emailed me several times that morning to check on Elle's status, and each time assuring me that he understood if I couldn't' make it. "Your responsibility is with Elle," he said, adding that he hoped that I could also attend the dinner and share in his honor.

Gita and I arrived at South Miami at 10 a.m. Elle is a courageous woman with a beautiful smile and a spirit in tune with her faith. Soon after we arrived, Dr. Starke broke Elle's amniotic membrane and initiated the Pitocin drip to further strengthen the uterine contractions. As her cervix dilated, one of my anesthesiologist colleagues administered an epidural. As Elle dozed off, Jamie leaned down and kissed her cheek. "You're doing great, and you're so beautiful. I love you."

I stepped outside to call Russell. It was now 4 p.m. and I'd missed my chance to fly to New York. "Russell, forgive me but I'm not on an airplane. Ellie will probably deliver in the next one to two hours. I'll be with you in spirit."

"You are where you need to be. The most important thing is Elle and the baby's good health."

In the birthing room, Gita sat beside Elle, held her hand, and I watched the monitor, documenting the increased frequency and intensity of her uterine contractions. With a perfect mother and fetal heart rate and blood pressure, we waited for the moment of arrival. With the cervix completed dilated and the baby low in the birth canal, delivery occurred after three to five pushes coinciding with Elle's contractions. Gita and I witnessed the birth of our eight pound, ten ounce granddaughter. After the nurse determined perfect Apgar scores of ten, I examined the newborn and said to Jamie, "Another perfect baby girl. You're halfway home," I said, thinking of my own family of six daughters.

"I am home," Jaime said.

Whereas most newborns are exhausted and feed within a few hours, Elle held this baby within five minutes of the birth and began breastfeeding. I pondered the beauty of God's creation, with birth being the greatest of all natural experiences.

I called Mom and Dad. "Elle's had another girl."

"There's nothing better, and you should know," my mother said.

"Is that David?" I heard my father ask in the background.

"Hymie, we have another granddaughter. Pick up the phone."

"Mazel tov," my father said from an extension. "We'll see you tonight, right after your mother's breathing treatment. Meantime, I'll rest another hour. Kiss Elle for us."

That evening, before picking up my parents, I had dinner at the Gourmet Carrot on West Avenue, with Gita and our daughter Dani, who was five months pregnant. She and Josh were visiting from Toronto during her law school winter break. After dinner, I picked up Mom and Dad and Louisiana and brought them to the hospital. Jamie greeted us at the ER entrance and helped me get Dad into his wheelchair. Dad cradled her portable oxygen tank in his lap. The oxygen lines draped over Dad's chest and led to the nasal prongs in Mom's nose. Jamie pushed my father's wheelchair, and Louisiana followed us, carrying my mother's purse. Hospital personnel, from custodians and transporters to nurses and colleagues, congratulated me and my family on the new birth.

Upstairs, Elle held the baby. "Bubby," Elle said, handing Mom her twentieth great-grandchild.

Mom sat in the rocking chair beside the bed and held the baby, rocking gently. "I can't believe she's just four hours old. She's the size of a two-month-old. Hymie, she's looking at you."

Dad leaned forward in his wheelchair. "I'm your great-Zayde, your mother's grandfather. Your mother will tell you all about me one day."

We drove home to Miami Beach after midnight. Dad suggested we take the MacArthur Causeway, which runs alongside The Miami Herald Building and the Port of Miami, full of dazzling cruise ships, preparing for their weekend voyages. I forced myself to stay awake as I listened to Mom whispering to Louisiana. Dad and I listened to an Andrea Bocelli CD. In recent years, Bocelli (when singing in Italian), Yanni, and Beethoven had become regular performers in my operating room.

"God has blessed us with such a large, close family," Dad said. "Not everyone has this." In a lower voice, he continued,

"David, you are a wonderful son. Your mother and I are overjoyed."

"Dad, when you were a teenager, did you ever envision the life you've had?"

"My parents had no money and the times were uncertain," Dad said, a reference to the Great Depression, when his family catered to Miami's winter tourists, and the summer tourists in Monticello, New York, to whom they sold ice cream, newspapers, souvenirs from the race track, and other odds and ends. "Along this causeway, I learned to fly a seaplane when I was fifteen."

I nodded, glanced over at my father beside me, and then I went into the left lane and accelerated a bit.

"I also wrecked my motorcycle in front of Star Island and was thrown twenty feet, onto the shoulder of the road." My brother and I had heard this story a few times when we were growing up, which made it easier for us to adhere to his wishes that we never ride motorcycles ourselves. "I've had many adventures and uncertainties," Dad said. "Perhaps what I've always been most certain of has not been my future but my love of your mother, your brothers, and yourself."

It doesn't get much better than the day your daughter gives birth to a beautiful baby, particularly when the day is witnessed by your own parents, and yet the inevitability of time marching on hovered all around us. I'd become a grandfather twice more that week, and I still felt the vigor of a young man in both my family life and in my work, but my parents' decline recalled my own mortality. Once they traveled with suitcases and my brothers and I in tow, and now they couldn't leave the house without wheelchairs and oxygen tanks and paid assistants.

The next evening, it was my family's turn to celebrate Shabbat at "Zayde and Bubby's house." Gita and I had Elle's two older daughters, Kira and Eme. Our daughter Dani, her husband Josh, and their daughter Yve also joined us that night. They visit from Toronto about four times a year, and Gita and I go up there when we can.

Before dinner, in my parents' room, toddlers Kira, Eme, and Yve played catch with Dad, using Mom's Nerf basketball.

"Dad, we're ready for Kiddush," I said as everyone gathered around the Shabbat table.

"David, I'm exhausted. I'll stay in the room. Let's say Kiddush in here." Dad was dressed in matching blue sweatpants and sweatshirt.

As I said Kiddush, I thought about how it had taken Dad almost eighty years before he felt comfortable enough to say the Kiddush in Hebrew, further testament to Mom's perseverance, similar to how she'd accepted my father at all levels of his pilgrimage—from his lack of Hebrew education as a young man, fresh off active duty in the Navy, to how he'd put himself through law school, and how, in his spiritual life, he ultimately mastered the Hebrew prayers. After Kiddush, we sat around the table, with Mom alone at the far end of the table. Several times during the meal, Rachel got up and brought Dad small servings of the meal. In the distance, I heard Dad's TV, but some twenty minutes into our meal, I no longer heard the channels changing. He'd either fallen asleep or he'd finally settled on a program.

As we ate, Evy and Eme, cousins born two days a part, asked to sit on my lap. As the three of us ate, I was reminded how privileged I was to help raise my grandchildren, and in my parents' case, great-grandchildren.

As we completed the dinner and said our goodbyes, Dad swallowed his sleeping pill with a gulp of water. "David, before you go, please help Radcliff bring me to the other room." Radcliff turned off the TV and pushed the button on Dad's chair, bringing him upright. We lifted Dad to his feet and helped him walk into the small bedroom for the night. Radcliff turned on the TV, a sleeping aid Dad had relied upon for years. As we said our goodbyes, Louisiana sat down with Mom to assist with her evening respiratory and inhalational treatment.

As we walked home, there was a beautiful breeze in the air. It was one of those dry, cool nights we don't get enough of in Miami. Our version of winter was now upon us. "I hope Elle and

Jamie are having a good night with the baby," Gita said in our
room that night after we'd put Elle's kids to bed.

"Elle is your daughter," I said, "Always graceful in the line
of fire, and she has your smile. I'm sure they're fine." But I
couldn't shake the striking contrast between birth and the process
of dying.

On Saturday, I rounded early and arrived at Shaare Ezra,
the Sephardic synagogue on Arthur Godfrey, for the naming of
Elana's baby. Robert and Al B were waiting for me, along with
my nephews Daniel and Eric. In the sanctuary we recited the
Torah blessings. Then Yochai recited the closing blessings during
the Torah portion, at which point, the assistant rabbi prayed for the
mother's health and announced, "Noa, the daughter of Yochai and
Elana," to the community.

My granddaughter's name was the topic of Rabbi
Galimedi's sermon. He emphasized that Noa is one of the five
daughters of Zelophehad, who is mentioned in the Book of
Numbers and in the Book of Deuteronomy. This is a man who had
five daughters and no sons. The daughters approach Moses and
exclaim that their father's inheritance will not be passed on to
them. In the absence of a son, inheritance is typically passed to the
father's brothers. After consulting God, Moses validates their
claim, and they inherit their father's property. This passage recalls

one of the earliest chapters in the history of women's rights. Noa is described in the Talmud as the second most intelligent, and most endearing daughter of Zelophehad.

As Rabbi Galimidi completed his comments. "You have chosen a valiant name," I whispered. Although it is customary for a newborn to be named for a deceased family member, it is not mandatory. Jewish tradition believes in the importance of a name, and in its potential to convey the qualities of those who came before.

I spent Sunday with Nili, who was turning sixteen that week. That morning, she chauffeured me for more than fifty miles as I did rounds in South Miami and Aventura. She shadowed me, eliciting many warm smiles from my patients as I scribbled orders and progress notes. During her year with a learner's permit, Nili's driving had improved admirably.

"You ready to solo?" I said, as Nili navigated my Hummer north on I-95.

"I am, Dad," Nili said.

"For the first six months, no driving on the highway without me or your mom, and you can only chauffer two friends at a time, and speaking on the phone is forbidden."

"I know, Dad."

"And finally, I'll say this for the hundredth time, but as a driver, you're responsible for your own life, and as importantly, the lives of your friends. If something ever happened to you, I'll cry forever. Promise me, you'll never drink and drive and that you'll never do drugs. The same goes for your passengers. Finally, my expectation is that you'll always be the driver among your friends."

"OK, Dad!" she said. "I heard you," but I knew her challenge would be overcoming peer pressure and becoming a leader. As we neared Mom and Dad's house, I wondered whether my parents had felt this anxiety with me and my brothers.

Mom was weaker than she'd been in the past few weeks. Her cough had intensified, decreasing her appetite and impairing her sleep. "David, should I take an antibiotic?"

"You're bronchitis has worsened acutely, but we can minimize this with Levaquin." Mom had taken this newer generation and broad-spectrum antibiotic in the past. "I'm certain you'll be able to continue physical therapy this week."

"Bubby, I'm getting my license this week!"

"At your age, I was already earning a living as a bookkeeper," Mom said. "My first car was a stick-shift Studebaker."

"A what?"

"They stopped making them a long time ago," I said.

I found Dad in his room, in his recliner, watching an Ed Bradley segment on *60 Minutes*, a piece about African-American Hurricane Katrina evacuees who'd been stopped by police as they attempted to escape New Orleans via the Mississippi River Bridge. Gone were Dad's days of multi-tasking. Within the last few weeks, he'd given up reading. Not long ago, when I'd visit, Dad would be listening to the TV while he read *Newsweek* or *Model Railroad* or the *Wall Street Journal*. And prior to that, and for much of his life, he's spent his evenings hands-on, working on his model ships and trains.

"The Dolphins won again," he said, "but I'm tired and bored, and I'm still having trouble moving my left arm." I examined him, and indeed he was weak. Most of the muscles of his left biceps and triceps and deltoid had atrophied, a consequence of his catabolic state, compliments of his relentless tumor.

I lifted his arm and examined it. "Press against me with some resistance and work your muscles the best as you can." I felt minimal resistance, and I knew the arm function would not return. "Dad, your right arm is good, and it can compensate."

"Zayde, I'm getting my license this week," Nili said.

"You're better looking than Radcliff," Dad said. "Maybe you can drive me around from now on."

"Any time, Zayde," Nili said, winking at her grandfather as she left the room.

At the front door of the house, Mom held Nili's hand. "Every day he gets a little weaker," Mom said. "Is this it? Is this how it's going to be until the end?"

"Unfortunately, these are signs of a breakdown of muscle from his disease, but his mind his strong. He's still Dad."

Monday morning at 6:45, I met my sons-in-laws Jamie and Josh, and my three brothers, at Beth El Synagogue in the Hebrew Academy. It's customary to name a newborn girl during the Torah reading, which occurs on each Saturday, Monday, or Thursday. The naming typically follows within a few days of birth. In honor of my father's mother, Elle and Jamie's newborn daughter was named Kaelly, the Hebrew version being Kelilah Tiferet. The name refers to a crown of splendor, which was seen in the Aura of Moses, the great law giver, when he brought the two tablets of the Ten Commandments down to the Chosen People, the Children of Israel.

Russell held his cellphone open, allowing my parents to hear the naming at home. He also emailed the name to many of our relatives from his BlackBerry. After the forty-five minute service, we all dissembled to begin our respective chores and daily works. My day included an open-heart, a pacemaker, and many office patients. On my visit with Mom and Dad that night, Dad was watching Monday Night Football. Mom was sorting her medications into the compartments of her days-of-the-week pillbox. She seemed to be coughing less. That morning, she'd attended a respiratory therapy session at South Miami Hospital, and in the afternoon she and Dad and Radcliff had driven up to North Miami Beach to visit a Hebrew Homes facility under renovation. If not for his illness, Dad would have been actively involved with Al B, the architects, and everyone else in the oversight of the project. But now, the visit mainly provided Dad a chance to get out of the house for a few minutes, a break from his daily routine, and maybe the little field trip recalled the leisure of wonderful summer memories on the road.

In that morning's prayer service, five generations of our family, beginning with my father's mother, and concluding with his great-granddaughter, had been acknowledged before the community. This young four-day-old girl, born December 15, 2005, bears the name of my grandmother, her great-great-grandmother. The Jewish custom is to memorialize departed loved ones on the anniversary of the death, and coincidentally, this was the week we remembered my grandmother. Through baby namings, and through Yartzeit prayers on the anniversary of a loved one's death, our people foster continuity and perpetuate the qualities of the departed.

"Generation to generation," Dad said to me that night. "We're all part of an everlasting chain." As I walked with Mom to the door that evening, I thought about how our days are long, but our mission is short. We must maximize the value of every single day and cherish the time we have together with those we love.

Tuesday morning, five days before Christmas 2005, the valet parking attendant greeted me at South Miami Hospital, asked about my parents, and wished me a happy Hanukah. When Mom was hospitalized earlier in the year, he and Dad had spoken many times. The driver was a Lebanese Christian whose three sisters had all converted to Judaism and married Jewish husbands. "Give my regards to your parents," he said as I entered the hospital, where my day began with an open-heart procedure, followed by the placement of a pacemaker in a 90-year-old woman.

As I scrubbed for surgery, Patrick, my surgical nurse, asked me about Dad's progress. Patrick had participated in the surgery for Dad's Infuse-a-Port, which was placed by one of my South Miami colleagues.

"He's holding his own," I said.

After seeing two dozen of patients in my office, I attended a meeting regarding the South Shore Hospital deal with Russell and several advisors at the Starbuck's on West Avenue. We addressed the question of whether we should take over the failing facility, with its unknown debt and obligations, or permit its current ownership to lapse into bankruptcy. The advantage of the latter scenario would be the opportunity to completely disassociate ourselves from the failing regime and start anew.

Afterward, at my parents' house, I found Mom organizing the household payroll and preparing the paperwork for their year-end taxes. Dad was resting, watching the *O'Reilly Factor* on the TV in the big bedroom.

Gita and Rachel arrived shortly afterwards, with a prescription for my mother and a quart of strawberry ice cream from CVS.

"I hate this monotony, my backside is getting sore, and I'm concerned as to what it portends."

With Radcliff's help, I examined my father and found only superficial redness. "Dad, I'm sure we can prevent any worsening," I said. "Radcliff, you're doing a terrific job with him, but let's make sure he spends time each day resting on his side."

"Can you try Balmex?" Gita suggested, referring to a strong zinc-based diaper rash medication she had used on our kids.

"I'll go right back to the CVS," Rachel volunteered."

Gita reminded my parents about the upcoming engagement party for Rachel and Ethan that Thursday night at our house. Rachel and Ethan had been best friends since kindergarten.

"Red's a fine young man from a great family," my father said. He always referred to Rachel's fiancé Ethan as "Red" because of his copper hair. "He's a great match for you, Rachel, and he'll be a terrific husband. I'm looking forward to the party."

"Thank you, Zayde," Rachel said, pulling her keys from her purse. "I'll be right back."

"Elle and the baby were here today," Mom said, turning her office chair toward us. "They spent a couple of hours, and it was so wonderful. I held Kaelly. They're so easy early on."

"Mom, I'd like a copy of your calendar with all the family birthdays?" I said at the door.

"Come," she said, "I'll make a copy of it for you." Mom dropped her two-page list onto the photocopier in her office.

"Why do you need this now?"

"So I'll know in advance the significant days that are coming up, but mainly I suppose I'm looking for a way to mark time, which may help me understand how to expand it."

"You can't, David, but at least now you'll know when to wish your grandchildren and nieces and nephews a happy birthday."

Speaking of birthdays, as the clock reached midnight, on the eve of December 21st, my youngest daughter, Nili, my 40th birthday present, turned sixteen. She related well to my father and inherited his toughness and determination. She demonstrated discipline in her basketball endeavors, but she had yet to apply his level of focus and discipline to her schoolwork.

All things considered, Mom seemed emotionally and physically strong, despite her chronic obstructive lung disease, but life was marching on, and time, as we all know, has no mercy. I knew we must be thankful for each day. As we age, our two most important emotional needs are to be needed and to have a mission, or in Navy speak, a billet. Perhaps the two are intertwined, but who am I to say? I just knew that we needed Dad and Mom, and I fantasized that surviving for our sake would be sufficient motivation to keep them going.

Two days later, Al B, Eric, Russell, and I accompanied Dad to Sylvester for his fifth treatment. We were the first to arrive at the blood laboratory, and the lab results were optimal for him to proceed. Dad was among the first to arrive in the chemotherapy bay, and fortuitously, he had the most efficient nurse we'd met so far—expedient at retrieving Dad's medication from the pharmacy and a pro in its administration.

Al B and Eric remained with Dad during his treatment, and Russell and I went off to work. As I left, Dad was watching a Fox News report on the Christmas rush at various malls around the country. Prior to Dad's illness, I'd been out of touch with the world of modern daytime television, from the History Channel to CNN, to *Oprah* and *Dr. Phil* and *Jerry Springer*. Whether your tastes run from the didactic to the pedestrian, life could be vicariously lived through television. For much of his life, TV had been Dad's background companion while he pursued other interests, but during these final months, TV had become a reliable friend.

Robert arrived at the completion of the treatment and escorted Dad home. We'd honed this like a symphony, making sure that Dad was never alone, and in our minds, always protected.

Gita had spent the day with Debbie Wasserman, Rachel's future mother-in-law, preparing our backyard and gazebo for the engagement party. The large catered buffet of Middle Eastern food was presented under the gazebo, and the tables and chairs were set up around the pool deck. An Israeli disco band played late into the evening, as everyone danced and ate and drank amid the beautiful backdrop of the city skyline lurking beyond the waters of Biscayne Bay.

All that was missing was Dad. He'd promised Rachel that he'd come, but prior to the party, he developed a fever, probably from the chemo. Mom arrived with Louisiana, although they mostly sat in the dining room, as the temperature that night was hovering around 50 degrees, and the cool, humid air wasn't healthy, given Mom's severe lung disease. She seemed happy to be with us, but I detected sadness in her smile as she greeted the guests as they passed in and out of the sliding doors.

Mom had wanted to stay for the evening's speeches, but the party ran later than we'd expected. "Mom," I said, "we can interrupt the band a few minutes."

"Everyone's having such a good time," Mom said. "No speech could describe the beauty of Rachel and Ethan being in love. Also, I'm tired, it's cold out, and I'm anxious to get home to your father. Let the guests enjoy themselves."

After Shabbat dinner that week, I walked to my parents' house with Miki, my eldest son-in-law. En route, we discussed the challenges of his business in high-end Chinese bathroom sinks, toilets, tubs, and various accessories and the ongoing cash flow imbalance.

"Miki, the difference between success and failure is sometimes a hairline," I said. "Often we can't understand why our predictions don't hold up."

"I believe in this business," Miki said, "but sometimes the pressure is too great."

"The magnitude of the reward is dependent on the difficulty of the pursuit. Don't give up, so long as you can also focus on your family responsibilities."

At the house, I sensed an unusual calmness and tranquility. Dad was resting in his recliner in the big bedroom and Mom was stretched out in bed. She'd had an exhausting week between the engagement party and her physical therapy.

I spoke with Dad about his plan to attend early Sabbath Prayer Service at Beth Israel for the Yartzeit commemorating the death of his mother, Bessie Galbut, in 1958. He also wanted to see a movie. "I love this house, but I'm bored to death. I have to get outside sometimes."

On the morning of December 24th, my daughter Dani's birthday, I returned early to Mom and Dad's house to escort him to the synagogue. As we arrived, Al B was walking up the street from the other direction. Dad's part-time aide Paden had helped him get dressed, and despite Dad's beautiful tailored suit and Zegna tie, there was no denying his illness.

Together, Al B and I took turns pushing our father's wheelchair the half-mile or so to the synagogue. In the library, where the early minyan took place, we brought Dad to his usual location on the left side, in front of the table he'd built and where the Torah was read. The room was approximately thirty feet deep and fifteen feet wide. The side walls were lined with tall shelves housing the synagogue's library. The small rear section, which sat eight, was reserved for women congregants. A large elliptical conference table and chairs occupied in the center of the room. This was surrounded by yet another row of chairs lined up in front of the bookcases along the side walls. The room was lit with white light, the brightest in the entire synagogue. A year earlier, my father had funded and personally supervised the installation of the lighting. The ark my father built about five years earlier housed the Torah my parents had donated on their fiftieth anniversary. The velvet Torah cover included the phrase from Psalms, "Generation to generation."

We suggested Dad sit in a regular seat, but he wanted to remain in his wheelchair. As the moments glided by, everyone joining the service greeted Dad on their way to their seats. He offered each man a warm smile or a handshake or a nod of his head. This was home, the one place my Dad seemed willing to spend time among old acquaintances who would not see him as a man humbled by disease, but rather as a man who'd built a synagogue and fostered the spirit of his community.

My father did not grow up reading and speaking Hebrew, but over the years, he had learned the services and would follow the English translations in the prayer book. My mother had grown up reading Hebrew and was quite familiar with all the prayers. So in the early years, I sensed that many of the members of the synagogue looked down upon my father for his lack of Hebrew education. To compensate, my father became an officer of the Beth Israel Synagogue and became a founder of the new building. He ultimately became the synagogue's greatest benefactor. Furthermore, over the past twenty years of so, he had become a dedicated student of the many scholarly English translations of Judaic texts.

After the service, Robert delivered a word of remembrance for my father's mother, whose Hebrew name was Kayla, and a word of congratulations to my parents on the birth of their great-granddaughter Kaelly, named for her late great-great-grandmother.

During the service, my father, now unable to read due to his failing vision—another consequence of his malignancy—sat patiently in his wheelchair, smiling on occasion and following the services from memory. My mother, famous for her punctuality, arrived about an hour into the service, following her respiratory therapy and Mucinex treatment to clear her secretions.

During the prayer service, my father was surrounded by his four sons, two of his grandsons, and one great-granddaughter, Eme, who attended with her father Jaime. Robert spoke about the life of our grandmother, emphasizing unity and family values, which meant everything to her, and how her reward was in the room, in terms of the ongoing life of the family unit.

The service concluded, followed by a Kiddush, sponsored by my parents, and my children, Elle and Jamie. The informal Kiddush was complete with assorted liquor, wine, herring, beef cholent, salad, crackers, and cake. This Kiddush was given in the memory of my grandmother Kayla—and in honor of the birth of my granddaughter Kaelly. Five generations were celebrated and remembered that morning.

After services, we returned home for a multi-faceted family celebration. And despite the backdrop of our parents' undeniable decline, Robert, Russell, and Al B joined us as well with some of their own children and grandchildren. In honor of her sixteenth birthday, Nili's friends—about six or seven girlfriends and four or five boys forged their own little teenage clique, sitting on and around the chaise lounges along the dock. From a distance, I heard their laughter and playful banter, probably about classmates and teachers and dating and all manner of pop culture. Who can say? All I knew is that they seemed happy. That afternoon we also celebrated Elle and Jamie's fifth wedding anniversary, and the recent births of their daughter Kaelly and the birth of Elana's daughter, Noa.

Our daughter Dani, now a law student in Toronto, had arrived several days earlier, just in time to celebrate her 25th birthday and Chanukah with us. Dani, our third daughter, and most introspective child, is the only one who has spent her early years of married life and motherhood away and from her hometown. She is fortunate to be living in a thriving orthodox community, but in her early years there, maintaining her identity and pursuing her personal and professional goals was challenging.

To her credit, she excelled in law school while fulfilling her responsibilities as a wife and mother.

Her connection with us remained strong as ever, and if my girls ever write a book about my generation, I'm guessing Dani will lead the effort. In recent years, my father had forged a unique relationship with Dani and her husband, Josh, a hobbyist in his own right, who maintains several large aquariums in their home, including an eighteen-hundred-gallon shark tank. Maybe two years earlier, Gita and I flew up there, along with my parents, for a long weekend. Dad spent hours sitting near the shark tank, reading *Toronto Star*, taking frequent breaks to observe the symbiotic interactions of the exotic sea creatures and to ask Josh intricate questions about the process of maintaining the homeostasis of the tank. For sure my father, the noted train enthusiast, was attracted to Josh's passion for his own eccentric hobby, but more importantly, I believe Dad was committed to bonding with his grandson-in-law, despite the thousands of miles and the international border between them. And recognizing the common pitfall among married couples in which the wife outpaces the husband educationally, Dad, as I later learned, had encouraged Josh to pursue a master's in health care administration, advice for which Josh, already an established senior living facility owner-administrator, remains most grateful. Soon after Dad returned home from that visit, he selected some two hundred pounds of his trains, tracks, miniature houses and buildings, and landscaping accessories. He boxed it all up and shipped it FedEx to Josh.

I heard about this one Shabbat evening. "You think he'll set it all up?"

"He's already contacted a local guy to assemble everything in the basement garage, alongside the shark tank," Dad had said, sitting at the head of the table, presiding over the tone and content of our conversation, as it had always been. "It will be quite a sight, and your mother and I will visit soon for a final inspection."

We all returned in June, about four months later. "You see?" Dad said, overlooking the miniature environment the trains had formed. My brothers and I never quite shared Dad's commitment to trains, so this setup represented the first time one of Dad's progeny had featured a completed train display in their own home. "It's really something," my father said, adjusting the transformer to accelerate a passenger train through a narrow tunnel traversing a papier-mâché mountain. My father's smile and expert manipulation of the controller recalled those days on the oak floor in our Coral Gate home in the 1950s, sitting yoga style with Robert, Russell, Al B, and myself. Back then, we had no room for a permanent setup, so a day spent with trains mainly involved assembly and disassembly, with just a few precious moments spent running the trains along the perimeter of our living room. But now, standing before this grand model railroad display, my father seemed unchanged, despite the passing of fifty years and many miles of train track in between.

Chapter 10: A Slow-Moving Cowboy

Miami is never quieter than it is on December 25th. Our normally hectic city assumes a relative aura of calmness, serenity, and relaxation. After three hours of rounds, I came home for lunch, followed by a combination walk and jog with Rachel, my fifth daughter, who was preparing for her wedding over Memorial Day weekend, along with Dani and Josh, who were enjoying the Florida sunshine during their visit. We ran south along the boardwalk, crossed onto the sand behind the Setai hotel and condominium, continued on the beach alongside Ocean Drive, and returned north, a total of about four and a half miles. I was reminded of my youth, and how we'd swum on these beaches and played in the beautiful sand. For my father, these waters had once been his childhood back yard. He'd grown up in the Crown Apartments, on Fourth and Washington, just one block from Al's Corner, which was taken by eminent domain in the 1960s for the purpose of widening Fifth Street.

Returning from our run, we stopped at Mom and Dad's for a quick visit. Dad, of course, was watching football, and Mom was busy in her office, affixing labels to a stack of manila folders. "Robert stopped by before and prepared the oil and wicks for us, and he'll be here with us to light the menorah," Mom said, turning to us in her office chair.

Mom was referring to the large silver menorahs they had brought from Israel for themselves, my brothers and I, and each grandchild. My parents gave these gifts with love—and with the expectation that they would be utilized and not just placed on a shelf like a museum exhibit.

"Rachel," my father said, lowering the volume on his TV, "you see the beautiful menorah in our front window?"

"Yes, Zayde, it's beautiful."

"We light ours every year," Josh said.

"I have saved one for you and Red," my dad said, "and I'm so excited to give it to you tonight to become part of your home. As you use it, you will always remember Bubby and me."

I saw tears in Rachel's eyes. "Dad," I said, "you'll enjoy Robert's company tonight, and we'll light our beautiful menorah as well." As I kissed my father goodbye, I thought, *Miracles...why not?*

Because Christmas fell on Sunday, the next day, which was also the first day of Chanukah, was a legal holiday. This meant I didn't have any elective surgeries. Russell and I planned to enjoy a movie matinee that afternoon with Dad. In the morning, Gita and I exercised on the beach, and we walked and jogged along the shoreline at high tide, soaking our feet in the cold, refreshing saltwater. After picking up Nili from basketball practice, we joined my parents, my brothers, Radcliff, and Louisiana at the Regal Theater at the intersection of Lincoln Road and Alton for a noon showing of Steven Spielberg's *Munich*.

My father sat in his wheelchair in a section reserved for handicapped patrons. Our entourage filled the remainder of that row and several seats behind. Gita, Nili, and I handed out popcorn and soft drinks.

The exciting but disturbing movie explores the futility of terrorism and questions how society should best respond. The film paints a historical doctrine, as established by Golda Meir—that of targeted assassinations of all terrorists, no matter the cost. It also reaffirms Israel's non-compromising position of not negotiating with terrorists. The decision to hunt down and kill those who masterminded and executed the murder of Israeli's 1972 Olympic athletes was driven by Israel's commitment to making the value of Jewish blood so costly as to become a deterrent for future terror. The Holocaust taught Jews that they must defend themselves. The movie attempts to be evenhanded about the horror of the murders in the Munich Olympic village, and also the horror of the Israeli response. The concern for not injuring civilians and the humanity of grappling with these decisions is what sets the movie apart.

One of my great pleasures has been attending movies, a pastime that began with my parents on Saturday afternoons in Coral Gables. After Shabbat services at Temple Zamora, we often walked to Miracle Mile for cheese sandwiches and French fries at the Woolworth's luncheonette, just blocks from our house in Coral Gate. Then we'd see a film at the Miracle Theater. In those early years of my parents' marriage, they were evolving in their understanding of religion and raising children. Income and leisure time were scarce. Dad attended law school full-time and worked full-time, and my mother raised us while working full-time at Three Sisters, a ladies clothing store on Miracle Mile, so the only day available for our family outings was Saturday. But to Mom, the Sabbath was sacred, and to my father, the family unit was paramount. In the early to mid-`50s, my parents reached an understanding that perhaps observed the letter of the Shabbat law, but compromised the spirit of the day. Although my father paid in advance for our Shabbat lunches and our theater tickets, these activities violated the spirit of Shabbat, which dictates that we study Torah and rest.

I am seven years old in 1956. After the synagogue service, we walk to Miracle Mile for lunch at Woolworth's—a cheese sandwich and French fries. Then we attend a movie at the Miracle Theater. Mom, Dad, and my brothers and I go upstairs to the mezzanine, which is otherwise vacant. My parents sit together while my brothers and I play cops and robbers in the aisle. My parents hold hands as they watch Love Me Tender, *the movie in which a popular new actor and singer, Elvis Presley, sings his hit song, also called* Love Me Tender. *It's like a Western, my favorite kind of movie, but even so, this one has little action, except for the ending, when Elvis Presley dies and Richard Eagan gets the girl.*

During the film, I go, "This isn't much of a cowboy movie or Western. There's no gunfights, no stampedes, or anything exciting."

"This is a slow-moving cowboy," Dad said.

I guess Dad knew I wouldn't appreciate the concept of a love story. Even though my brothers and I were disengaged from the screen, I cherish the time I spent with my brothers, creating scenes and playing the roles of imaginary soldiers in the safety of the Miracle Theater in Coral Gables, Florida.

After Dad finished law school and began his practice, my parents changed their perspective regarding Saturdays, choosing to observe both the letter and the spirit of Shabbat. So instead of matinees at the Miracle, we spent many Saturday evenings at the Lejeune Drive-in, a property since converted to car rental lots and other support facilities for Miami International Airport. Money was scarce for us in those years, but for about two dollars, Dad paid for the carload, all six of us, to see a double feature. Mom often packed peanut butter and strawberry jelly sandwiches, which always seemed to taste better at the drive-in than they did at home. Intermission wasn't complete without a trip to the refreshment stand for popcorn, sodas, and Good Humor ice cream. We'd either watch the movie from inside the car, with the metal speaker tilted into the side window, or sometimes the six of us gathered on a blanket on the hood of Dad's car, or we'd sit on the chrome front bumper. We all derived a certain comfort from being together on those evenings, complete with mosquitoes and no-see-ums and a star-filled sky.

As for our screening of the disturbing *Munich*, I found solace in our decision to attend a movie as a family one last time. In the course of aging and infirmity, patients often find comfort in the pleasures of youth. But in retrospect, I wish my dad's last movie had been one that celebrates life rather than destroys it, perhaps a slapstick comedy, or a sports movie, or better yet, "a slow-moving cowboy."

Despite all we'd been through, 2005 ended quietly. That final week, book-ended by Christmas and Chanukah and New

Years Eve, Dad seemed in good spirits, but I knew this was the proverbial "calm before the storm." That week, Dad enjoyed the string of endless bowl games and a freedom from chemotherapy. At the house on Wednesday, Mom was playing Rummikub with Elana and Louisiana.

"Dad, your hair and moustache look great," I said.

"Lisa, that stylist you found, was here this morning. She does a fine job. Look at the color in your Mom's hair."

I was comforted by Dad's continued interest in his appearance. "Dad, I apologize for suggesting that movie the other day. If I'd known it was so graphic…"

"It was difficult to watch because it portrayed the futility of terror, but that's part of life."

"A lot changed on September 11th," I said.

"Americans lost their sense of invulnerability, and the true nature of radical Islam became apparent in this country.

"Did you ever think that we would live to see such a large-scale act of terror against the United States on our soil?"

"If terror remains unchecked, it will always escalate. Also, America had been warned that this might happen. It's documented that the Mossad had given information more than six months before."

"Yes, I read that, Dad, but what do you think this act means to America?"

"David, it's the end of the innocence that we have enjoyed in America, but perhaps it will help Americans appreciate the great gift of freedom and the prosperity and greatness of our country. We must be responsible for each other, and that certainly was the feeling of my comrades in the Navy during World War II. The 1950s was a decade of readjustment, optimism, and prosperity. In the 1960s, civil rights, particularly in the South, helped establish integration. Then in the late `60s and into the `70s, the response to authority became one of disrespect, probably a consequence of Vietnam and the baby-boomer population reaching adolescence and adulthood. In the `80s, there appeared to be little concern for other citizens. Americans seemed to mind their own business, and we suffered as the nation became less sensitive to caring about each other. In the 1990s, because of our country's wealth and the boom in the stock market, we developed a sense of arrogance and we lost our ethical edge with corporate dishonesty and deception. With arrogance often comes impaired understanding and a lack of sensitivity. We were unprepared for Islam becoming such a force in the world. There are many Muslims in America, most of whom are fine Americans, but there is a radical arm that does not value human life and is committed to sowing destruction for all infidels or nonbelievers."

"Dad, you know my partner Naaman and I are close and in many ways. I feel I treat him like a younger brother."

My father responded, "Naaman is of superb character, which reflects his parents and upbringing and the true values of Islam. If there is a criticism for some of America's Muslims, it is their failure to denounce the extremists' commitment to terrorism."

"Dad what do you think will happen, especially as the world becomes a smaller place and the Internet facilitates global communication?"

"I believe in God and I believe in humanity, and I know that one philosophical change could destroy the basic tenants of radical Islam."

"What is that, Dad?"

"Female equality. If Muslim women were granted the equality of American women, they would not permit their children to be suicide bombers, and they would restore the unbridled male ego of many radical Muslims."

"Dad, do you expect more events such as 9/11 in America?"

"I am afraid so, David. The proliferation of weapons, including nuclear arms, will continue as long as governments act in accordance with their individual selfish interests."

"Dad, are you concerned for the safety of your children and grandchildren and great-grandchildren?"

"I'm always concerned for my family, but I have faith that one day there will ultimately be peaceful coexistence."

On the final day of 2005, I greeted Al B in front of Mom and Dad's house. Without prior discussion, Al B and I both arrived on foot at 7:05 a.m. to share the privilege of escorting Dad to the synagogue. We took turns pushing Dad's chair, with Radcliff following a step behind.

"Who's this coming with us?" Dad said.

"Dad, it's just Radcliff," Al B said. "He can help us out, and besides, he enjoys the services."

"The Bible is the Bible, Captain," Radcliff said, as if reminding Dad that he was within earshot, "and I'm here if you need me."

"Thank you," Dad said.

I pondered this first sign of Dad having memory lapses as we proceeded south on Royal Palm Avenue, and then he asked, "How many procedures are you doing?"

"You mean surgeries, Dad?" I said, startled by his renewed interest in my work.

"Yes, and how is your income derived? How many patients are you seeing in your office and in the vascular lab?"

"Forty to fifty patient visits and approximately fifteen surgeries a week, and the numbers are increasing," I said. Then I described the variety of procedures and their economic value relative to the various insurance plans.

"What percentage of your patients are indigent and comprise pro-bono work?"

Further startled by his specific question, I said, "Approximately 20%, as I must accept all hospital consults. Poor people comprise a large percentage of ER admissions."

"Let the other heart surgeons share in the free cases," Dad insisted. "Why should you work for free?"

"Unfortunately, Dad, the other heart surgeons refuse to do these cases, and I have a problem turning them down. To excel as a heart surgeon, one must maintain a high level of integrity, and this means dissociating economic considerations from clinical decisions."

Medicine is the most integrating profession in the world because the enemy, illness and health misfortune, is an equal opportunity assailant, regardless of wealth and economic background. Ill health does not discriminate. I've operated on vagrants, family members, and celebrities, and from the moment the knife touches the skin and the body becomes the operative field, there is no difference. What kind of physician could I be if I permitted the pursuit of dollars to affect my pursuit of clinical excellence? Key to a heart surgeon's ethic is to treat all patients equally. A dedicates surgeon gives 100% to an indigent, a managed-care patient, or a wealthy patient.

As we crossed Arthur Godfrey Road, Dad said, "You're fortunate to have good people working for you," Dad said.

But I knew my great fortune was having my father's vigorous participation this far into my adult life.

Inside the synagogue, Al B and I wrapped Dad's prayer shawl around him. Josh, who'd arrived a bit earlier, came over, kissed Dad on the cheek, and handed him a prayer book. "I can't see the words anymore, but I'll hold the prayer book," Dad said.

The early service began, and along the way, fellow congregants greeted Dad with a handshake and good wishes. The morning's Torah section began with a dialogue between Judah and Joseph, two of Jacob's twelve sons. Judah is the heir to the Jewish dynasty of royalty, the Davidic chain of kingship. Joseph, who was sold into Egypt by his older ten brothers—and who told their father that Joseph had been killed—becomes the Viceroy of Egypt, saving Pharaoh's kingdom from the world's famine. By ultimately saving his father and family, Joseph merits receiving the birthright, or double portion. Jacob sends his ten sons to Egypt to buy grain, as the famine rages in Canaan. Joseph recognizes his brothers, but they do not recognize him, and he sells them grain. As they depart, Joseph warns his brothers not to return to Egypt without the accompaniment of their youngest brother, Benjamin. The famine continues, and the purchased grain is consumed. In order to sustain his family, Jacob, after much protest, permits Benjamin to return to Egypt with his ten brothers only after Judah becomes his guarantor. Joseph, who has yet to reveal himself to his brothers, tests his brothers one final time by imprisoning Benjamin.

The dialogue between Judah and Joseph depicts the love and responsibility of a son to his father for all eternity. It also emphasizes Judah's unconditional commitment to do whatever it takes to fulfill his guarantee. The strength of Judah's plea touches Joseph, leading him to reveal his identity to his brothers.

As the portion concluded, Dad leaned over to me and said, "Sir Walter Scott described this section as the most beautiful prose in all of literature." Dad appreciated knowledge and once he acquired it, he was happy to share these nuggets of wisdom or interesting facts, sometimes in the most surprising settings.

"This section always brings tears to my eyes," I said, recalling my senior year in high school, studying British literature.

Forty years earlier, in response to what I hoped was the final typed draft of my term paper analyzing twelfth century English life as depicted in Sir Walter Scott's *Ivanhoe,* Dad remarked, "Back then it was fashionable in literature to be anti-Semitic, but Scott was pro-Semitic. You neglect this point in your report. After all, he gave us the Jewish heroine, Rebecca. She was the classic Jewish heroine, combining beauty and intelligence, giving unconditionally and without expectation."

I'd been satisfied that I had prepared an adequate paper, one that would meet my teacher's expectations, but Dad reminded me, as he always did, to look beyond the pages and to try understanding unwritten motivations and messages. So despite my urge to step away from my typewriter and enjoy that spring Sunday afternoon, my father's dissatisfaction became my motivation. For the next few hours, I sat in my room and explored how Sir Walter Scott's words had helped encourage the emancipation of the Jews in nineteenth-century Great Britain. It was the least I could do.

Chapter 11: Dinner on the Patio at Sunset

Gita and I enjoyed a Western-style New Year's Eve party given by our close friends Michael and Chava Genet. I've known Michael since elementary school at the Hebrew Academy, and Chava and Gita are dear friends. We've spent many occasions together, including three trips to Israel. Most of the guests departed after the ball dropped in Times Square, but several couples remained. Dressed in our finest Western boots, denim jeans, wide leather belts, and plaid shirts, we gathered in Michael and Chava's Florida room and discussed our concerns for the new year with regard to our children, and our dreams that 2006 would be a fine year for all of us. Each of us had various concerns about the health of loved ones, but we kept those thoughts private. This was a night for celebration.

We were now in the month in which we hoped my father would celebrate his 86th birthday, on the 21st. I spent much of New Year's Day with Nili, rounding at Aventura and South Miami. Late that afternoon, Gita, Nili, and I shopped on Lincoln Road, and I went into Browne's Salon for a haircut. The facility, which has about fifteen chairs, along with a health spa, is located above a trendy boutique offering a full line of imported beauty products. Nowadays, although my hair is black, it is thinning. Whereas the Navy haircuts always revealed my ears, now my haircuts reveal my increasingly visible scalp.

Near sunset, on this, the last evening of Chanukah, Gita and I stopped at Mom and Dad's to wish them a happy new year and to light the candles.

"Daddy spent the day watching football and napping," Mom said. He's more tired than usual." I wondered if his Ambien and Xanax were metabolizing more slowly due to the inevitable replacement of his liver with cancer.

Dad was sleeping in the recliner in the large bedroom with the TV on. I kissed his forehead, and as he opened his eyes, I said, "Happy New Year, Dad."

With barely a whisper, he said, "Happy New Year to you, David."

I massaged Dad's shoulders, back, and arms, assessing the ongoing loss of muscle mass in his arms and chest.

"Thank you for the Balmex," Dad said. "It's working."

I also examined my mother and determined that she was wheezing, which correlated with her increased shortness of breath. This will be an interesting upcoming year, I thought as we drove home that evening.

January 2nd was a national holiday because New Year's Day fell on a Sunday. I performed an emergency open-heart procedure in Aventura. My first major case of the new year always carries an increased anxiety. I've never lost the first patient of a new year, but statistically it could happen, and would represent an ominous beginning. All went well, and I returned home with heightened energy and satisfaction.

That evening, I found Dad reclined in his chair.

"Dad, how's the football game?"

"Lackluster," he said. For college football fans, these were days to indulge, but Dad was elsewhere that night.

"Who are you rooting for?" I longed for his elaboration on offensive and defensive strategies and his detailed breakdown of matchups at the line of scrimmage.

"It doesn't matter," he said.

I held his left hand and examined his arm. Despite the swelling, the muscle mass in his triceps and biceps had further atrophied.

Mom sat in her bedroom chair, reviewing household bills and a stack of late-arriving Season's Greetings cards from various family members and charities they'd given to during the year. "He slept in the chair most of the day," Mom said, pulling a card from an envelope. She glanced at it and put it back. "I spent most of the day sitting beside him and playing Rummikub with Louisiana and

Erica. Mom seemed like a finely built house of cards, and I recognized both her beauty and her fragility. During the holiday season, she'd missed several sessions in the pulmonary rehabilitation program and she had regressed measurably. Her shortness of breath and increased oxygen use concerned me.

"Mom, we should cherish these moments together."

"I want to be there for Dad, but I must also maintain my schedule, including my trips to South Miami."

"Absolutely," I said, reviewing Mom's handwritten notes of her oxygen saturation and pulse, measured thorough the oximeter I'd borrowed from the hospital. Her numbers were down, and in recent days I'd observed an increased cough with darker sputum production in her discarded tissues, which was consistent with bronchitis. However, unlike Dad's diagnosis, COPD was a disease Mom could survive for years, although there would certainly be some rough days.

The football game reminded me of the old days in Miami, before the powers that be cancelled the annual New Year's Eve Orange Bowl Parade along Biscayne Boulevard. Each year, the road would be painted white so it would look beautiful on national TV.

It's January 1, 1963 and we're at the Orange Bowl game. Dad got us seats on the forty yard line in the fifteenth row. He's

Vice-Mayor of Miami Beach and the commanding officer of the Naval Reserve Training Center. Mom's here too, along with my brothers. We park at the Navy Base, about five blocks from the stadium. The Goodyear blimp floats overhead.

With over seventy thousand fans, the Orange Bowl is an overwhelming place. Mom's a good sport about this whole thing. I'm sure her interest in football has more to do with her wanting to please my dad and my brothers and me. For her, I guess football brings her family together, which is a good thing.

Before the game, between Alabama and Oklahoma, they introduce President Kennedy, who comes to midfield to do the coin toss. "He's a fellow Navy veteran and a great President," my father says, "and his book, Profiles in Courage *is a modern classic. I want you boys to read it."*

"He is so handsome," Mom says, "and this action demonstrates that he is a man of the people."

During the first half of the game, Dad gets us peanuts and sodas from the vendors going up and down the aisles.

During halftime, we watch the marching bands and fireworks. I haven't seen fireworks since the Fourth of July, so that's a treat. Also, many of the floats from last night's Orange Bowl Parade enter the stadium, many of which represent local businesses and TV stations and so forth. Atop the U.S. Navy float, which my father helped design, an attractive girl waves to the crowd.

"That's Sarah," Dad says. Her father sits behind us in the synagogue. I'm the committee of one who crowned her Miss Miami Beach. Isn't she beautiful?"

"Dad, I can't see her from here," I say.

"Trust me, I would only select a real beauty to represent Miami Beach."

During the third quarter, I say, "Dad, how come you love football so much?"

"The competition and the teamwork," Dad says. "All we can ask is for every player to give one hundred percent from his heart."

"Dad, did you ever play sports?" Russell asks.

"Of course, I played football for Miami Beach Senior High School. I've told you boys about that. But did I ever mention how I wrestled in Officers Training School?"

"Really?" Al B says.

"In the annual tournament, I participated in the final match. They pitted me against a much stronger contestant. Let's face it, as a Jewish kid in the Navy with a name like Hymie, nobody expected me to win. But at the last moment, when I was already pinned, I heard the second slap on the canvas, and I mustered all

my strength to turn over my opponent and pin him down to win the match."

"Dad," I say, "how come we never heard this story before."

"David, I rarely spend time thinking of these experiences. It was fun at the time, but I'd rather focus on today and the future."

The Alabama quarterback, a sophomore named Joe Namath, leads the underdog Crimson Tide to a 17-0 win.

After the game, we march back to our car at the Navy base, holding hands as a family, careful not to get separated in the post-game chaos. I can't wait to tell the guys at school that we saw President Kennedy, and I look forward to actually meeting him one day.

"Are we getting anywhere?" Dad said, tilting his head from the white pillow on the recliner.

"How do you mean?"

"The chemotherapy...am I putting myself through all of this for nothing?"

"I believe we're status quo. No major improvement, but no worsening. We're in our second cycle of Gemzar. Let's complete the cycle and let Dr. Rosenblatt review our progress."

Back home, I took a moment to breathe. We had just concluded a long year, another long and perilous year awaited us. Frankly, I was tired. My responsibilities to my parents, my wife, my children, and my grandchildren, not to mention my patients who trust me with their lives each day, weighed on me as I faced the prospect of 2006.

"I'm too tired to cook," Gita said.

So in a moment of surrender, we went out for dinner, just the two of us, for the first time in months. After steaks at La Marais, a short-lived kosher steakhouse on Forty-First and Collins, we saw some romantic comedy starring Kevin Costner and Jennifer Aniston, a thinly veiled sequel to *The Graduate*. Driving home from the theater, Gita and I both felt carefree as we enjoyed our evening escape from real life.

"When I first met you, I fell in love in the first five minutes," I said to Gita.

"Yes, but it took me a year to get you to realize it."

On the third of January, it was back to the grind. Surgery, consults, office visits, phone calls to and from referring physicians who'd been away over the holiday, and an income tax consultation with my accountant.

At the house late that afternoon with Nili, we found Dad in the big bedroom. The heat was on, and the house must have been eighty-five degrees.

"Zayde, what's up?" Nili said. "How come the house is so warm?"

"I want the thermostat at a comfortable level, but your grandmother keeps trying to fool me. She keeps turning it down to sixty-five degrees."

"Dad, are you having chills?" I said, placing my palm on his forehead and then on his back. "Do you feel cold?"

"It's a terrible feeling."

Through the window, I spotted Mom on the patio, looking up at the fichus and palm trees beyond the pool. I stepped outside and pulled a metal folding chair from behind the barbecue. The wind was cool and the sky magnificent, reflecting orange and blue as the sun set. Mom had eaten little of her dinner— roasted chicken, a sweet potato, and a salad of tomatoes and greens—from a china plate on a TV table. She'd been my father's constant companion for nearly six decades, and I'm guessing she'd never before stepped outside to eat dinner by herself.

I kissed her cheek and noticed that her eyes were swollen, probably from crying in the aftermath of the thermostat debate with Dad.

"He's being mean, but I know he can't help it. He's not himself, and I'm sure he feels bad for shouting at me, but it's just too warm. I can't breathe in there."

"The tumor is causing a chill," I explained as Nili came outside and joined us. "I'm hoping this issue will be mitigated as the Gemzar takes effect. But in the meantime, you're right, the heat isn't healthy for you, and we must resolve this. From now on, Dad needs to dress more warmly."

"I keep meaning to ask you," Mom said, "but now that we're into the new year, Dad needs help signing those checks we talked about."

"He's tired and irritated now," I said, standing up. "It can wait until tomorrow."

As I went back inside to speak with Dad, I heard Mom ask Nili if she was ready for school and for basketball season. I paused in the threshold to eavesdrop on my daughter's response.

"I guess," Nili said, looking at the sunset peeking through the trees and between the houses. "It's so beautiful out here."

"I feel very close to you," Mom told Nili, "and I've never spared my words. You're a beautiful girl, but you'll need to watch your weight."

I've cautioned Mom against her constant focus on the ideal weight for her grandchildren. Her standard of personal discipline has allowed her to maintain a constant weight throughout her life, but excessive protests are self-defeating. Fact is, my youngest daughter has become drop-dead gorgeous, but she doesn't see it that way. In my eyes, she has a smile that lights up the world, perhaps a Galbut trait, which I think we've inherited from Mom and Dad.

Back inside, Dad said, "I'm sorry, David. There's no one I love more in the world than your mother.

"I know, Dad, and we'll work this out. You can dress more warmly, especially in the afternoons when you feel the extreme chills coming on."

"I can do that," Dad said. He removed the blanket from his shoulders and pushed it aside. "You can lower the thermostat to seventy. Ask Mommy to come back inside now. I'm ready for bed. Is Radcliff is in the kitchen? Maybe you and he can help me walk to my room."

At this point, Dad could take one or two steps, at most, and only when supported on each side. Mom came in, holding Nili's arm. Then Mom leaned down and kissed Dad on the lips. "Hymie, I love you."

After Radcliff and I helped Dad into his bedroom, I adjusted the thermostats in the house to seventy degrees. Upon leaving, I said to Radcliff, "My father needs to be dressed in layers when he has any fever or chills, which will occur mostly in the evenings or late afternoons."

"OK, Dr. Dave, I'll take care of it."

"Mom," I said, "if a problem like this happens again, call me immediately." Knowing it was time for her respiratory treatment, I kissed her goodnight. "I love you, Mom."

Louisiana, who'd been studying in the living room, put down her textbook, *Physical Diagnosis,* and went outside to retrieve Mom's dinner plate and to bring the folding table back inside.

The next day, Dad's exhaustion worsened and he slept a lot. His appetite was poor in that he was eating only eating some watermelon and ice-cream and his strawberry Boost. His chill had improved, although his temperature had reached 101.6 earlier in the day, which Mom had treated with Tylenol.

That night I found Dad in the recliner in the big bedroom. He was wearing a blue sweatshirt, matching sweatpants, and a red fleece windbreaker. The room felt cooler than last night, and in fact the thermostat was set to seventy-two degrees. Mom was sitting in her office, filling out a stack of checks they would distribute to their children and daughters-in-law in the coming days. "Are you having any pain?"

"You know something, David, this boredom is unbearable."

"I'll get you some DVD movies or some new music … or how about a few audiobooks?

"Can we move time ahead?"

I knew where he was heading with that question, but I didn't know how to answer it. "Is there something specific you'd like to discuss?"

"Maybe it's time for me to stop the treatment. I think it's futile."

"Maybe you're right, but let's see what Dr. Rosenblatt says next week."

My mother came over to us and placed a stack of checks and a felt tip black pen on Dad's portable table. "Hymie, David wants to help you sign the gifts."

"Of course, *Batya*," he said, using the Yiddish name for Bessie.

The checks Mom had referred to the previous night involved the gifts my parents had decided upon in order to minimize estate taxes. They would each give the maximum annual amount to my brothers and myself, along with each of our wives, for a total of sixteen checks.

I handed Dad the pen, placing it into his left hand. He awkwardly gripped the pen with his swollen fingers, but he couldn't lift his arm from the table. "I'm sorry," he said.

"It's OK, Dad. You can use your right hand and I'll assist."

I placed the pen in Dad's right hand, and with both of my hands, my fingers enveloped the rigid instrument that was my father's right hand, and together, we swept a across the signature line of the first check, creating a lazy "H" and "G."

"This is so generous of you, Dad," I said, holding back my tears as I remembered the rare dexterity of his hands, which not so long ago could have been the signature of a master surgeon.

After signing the final check, I read a one-page note Al B had prepared, tabulating their assets and the projected income that would maintain their standard of living. As I read the note, Dad's eyelids kept closing. I sensed that his level of interest was dimmed by the stark reality of his terminal illness.

The first Thursday afternoon of the new year, I was seeing patients in my office when a call was put through from the South Miami Heart Center's Cardiac Catheterization Lab. "Dr. Galbut, are you in the house?" the technician, asked.

"Yes, what's up, Freddy?"

"Emergency in the cath lab."

"What is it?" I said. With the phone cradled between my shoulder and ear, I scribbled notes into the chart of a new patient with coronary artery disease who would need surgery in the next week.

"A patient with a closed artery and an ascending aortic dissection," Freddy said.

"I'll be right over, but Freddy, this is a bad situation. Please type and cross the patient for blood and platelets." I assumed the invasive cardiologist was occupied, trying to stabilize the patient.

I made my recommendation to my new patient, explained the life and death emergency, across the street, and we exchanged cell numbers. I promised to call him the following day to answer any questions about his upcoming surgery. I told my office staff that I would be unable to see my remaining twenty patients, and then I raced over to the cath lab. The timing couldn't have been much worse. This would require my operative commitment for most of the evening and probably well past midnight.

Typically, patients are told that they are to have cardiac catheterizations or angiograms, with the possibility of a balloon or stent placement in a diseased artery. Cardiologists often fail to explain to patients that there is a one to two percent risk that they'll require emergency surgery as a consequence of their cath lab procedure, after which there may be a fifty percent or greater risk of death.

In recent years, the industrial complex has provided us with more manageable drug-coated stents that not only open diseased arteries but also reduce recurrent blockage from the inflammatory reaction around the aluminum cylinder. However, when an injury occurs, which generally occludes one of these arteries, an acute heart attack is induced. In this case, not only was the diseased artery abruptly closed, but a dissection—or break in the arterial wall—had occurred the ascending aorta. When this pathology is seen in patients presenting to the Emergency Room with severe chest pain or dramatically reduced blood pressure, it is an operative emergency with a death rate that approaches fifty percent.

The patient complained of severe chest pain and the monitors suggested an evolving heart attack. Two technicians surrounded the patient and another handed off the blood to a transporter for type and crossing. The invasive cardiologist doing the procedure was reviewing the films with a colleague and a third cardiologist, the patient's nephew, was also discussing the severity of the case.

"It's a bad situation," the nephew said, standing before a computer monitor revealing a series of images. The large right coronary artery, which normally feeds approximately 35% of the heart, had a significant blockage and was now completely occluded. More ominous was that dye from the angiographic study, which filled a false channel in the aorta.

"She'll need a complex combined open-heart procedure," I explained. "A bypass and a repair of the break in the wall of the ascending aorta. The remaining images from the cardiac angiogram revealed that the patient needed yet an additional bypass.

In the waiting room, I encountered the husband, two children, and several cousins, nieces, nephews, and friends, about ten people in all. I was faced with explaining that their loved one, whom they'd expected to return home in the morning a little tired for a week, but otherwise in good shape, had only a fifty percent chance of survival. In fact, in my clinical experience of over twenty years, this combination of an aortic dissection and occluded coronary artery caused in a cardiac catheterization lab has been fatal. There is technical complexity, which is further complicated by the high probability of coagulopathy, or unmanageable bleeding.

"I will do my best, but part of our outcome depends on God … or her fate." The husband's eyes revealed his love for his wife and his understanding that this was not a moment of choice but rather a necessity.

"May God be with you," he said to me.

The next six hours, with various CDs from Yanni, Beethoven, and Bocelli playing softly in the background, I worked with my partner, Dr. Naaman Abdullah, using a biologic glue to repair the dissection of the ascending aorta from the valve up to the arteries that feed the head and arms. We integrated a Dacron graft material into the repaired aorta. We sewed two vein grafts to the distal injured right coronary artery and the blocked circumflex artery, and we connected them to the Dacron graft.

After the repair and bypass, the heart began beating with vigor, and I began imagining that this surgically improved heart reflected the patient's desire to survive. With the assistance of an IV adrenalin drip, we weaned the patient from the heart-lung machine. The patient's heart was now supporting circulation and working on its own, so the next technical problem was stopping the massive hemorrhage. The patient had received large quantities of clot buster medications and blood thinners during the attempted stent placement in the cath lab, and now this operation was expending large amounts of blood. Before an elective procedure, we typically suspend all anticoagulants and anti-platelet medications such as Coumadin, Plavix, and aspirin. Furthermore, we had utilized the left femoral artery, which supplies blood flow to the lower extremity, as one of our access routes for the heart-lung machine. This artery was severely blocked, requiring an extensive surgical repair from the pelvis into the thigh with a patch of Dacron. Finally, after receiving platelets and plasma from the blood bank for many hours, the patient was returning to normal coagulation.

"Dr. Galbut, are you going to tell us we're all winners?" asked Angelica, my regular scrub nurse who'd been called in for the emergency. She was referring to my frequent comparison of surgical success to athletic victories. Except in this business, winning correlates with life, and heroic efforts only count when the patient survives.

"You know we are tonight, Angelica, but I wish we could win every day," I said, making reference to the rare but painful inevitable operative death.

"Hallelujah," I said upon closing the sternum with steel wire, and the layers of fatty tissue and skin above with a plastic surgical technique involving absorbable sutures. It was now after midnight.

Standing in a corner of the hospital's largest operating suite, I prepared to dictate my operative notes. The anesthesiologist and his aide adjusted medications, and a surgical assistant was placing a sterile dressing over the chest incision. Angelica was organizing her instruments on the back table and securing the sharps. The circulating nurse and her assistant were checking blood products, which would continue to be administered during the transport to the intensive care unit. My perfusionist was preparing the heart-lung machine for use later that morning. The board of laboratory data on the wall to my right had over fifty entries. Two large monitoring screens of heart data, suspended from the ceiling, to the right and left of the head of the operating table, provided real-time hemodynamic data. The floor between the table and heart-lung machine was smeared with blood. Behind

Angelica's table was a steel tree with branches containing at least a hundred large blood-soaked laparotomy sponges. My eyes were tired, having worn my telescopic lenses, or loops as we call them in the business, for nearly seven hours straight. My back and neck muscles were stiff from standing in my awkward flexed position over the patient's heart, which unlike some areas of the body, cannot be conveniently positioned for easy access. I shed my gown and gloves, bloodied from the battle. Seven hours removed from the early agony and apprehension of this case, my sense of ecstasy was now indescribable—and so was my loneliness.

In the waiting area, I met the family and discussed my satisfaction with the outcome thus far. "She's still profoundly sick, and it may be several days before we can be certain that she didn't suffer any brain damage. During the first twenty-four hours, there could be additional bleeding, which could require subsequent surgery. We'll monitor the heart and its recovery from the acute heart attack." This was clearly a nightmare for the family, given their lack of anticipation of this untoward event.

Driving home at 3 a.m., I thought about how the general public has little understanding of a surgeon's personal stress when facing such cases. On US-1, heading toward northbound I-95, I lowered the windows and blasted WKIS, Kiss Country 99.9 FM, a station my daughter Elle introduced me to several years ago. I sipped a can of Coca-Cola I'd purchased from a vending machine in the hospital lobby, all in my effort to fight the exhaustion and find my way home.

In the ensuing months, I saw the patient and her husband in my office for post-operative visits. She has since returned to a normal lifestyle and I believe she will enjoy a typical lifespan. She and her husband expressed their gratitude by way of holiday cards and gifts, but my true reward was seeing them together as the husband placed his arm around his wife's back and escorted her from my office.

About four hours later, I was back at South Miami Hospital. After three scheduled surgeries, including a patient with aortic valve disease, I drove to South Beach for a lengthy meeting with a group interested in joint venturing on a drug-dependence treatment program at South Shore Hospital.

My surgical commitment is 24/7, but Friday evening my priority has always been receiving the Sabbath and connecting with my family. Occasionally a surgical emergency arises, which takes preference. This Friday evening, I was mellow from exhaustion, and I particularly needed to reconnect with my children. The weather was unseasonably cool for Miami and just a delight. We gathered in the big bedroom, where my father sat upright in his recliner, my mother standing to his left and myself to his right. Together we held hands and sang *Shalom Aleichem,* or *Welcome to all of You*, a reference to the Angels who join the

Shabbat home. According to Kabbalah, the moments of Shabbat—
a day we pursue peace and inner tranquility—are the closest we
come to tasting the world to come. Next we all chanted *Eishet
Chayil,* a prayer of praise for the women of valor responsible for
the sanctity of the Jewish home. After we sang, there was a
muffled silence during which I performed the weekly Blessing of
the Children. I wanted my father to see me perform this ritual, as I
thought of how he had blessed me, not so much through formal
prayer, but rather through his lifetime examples of kindness,
wisdom, courage, and unconditional support.

I blessed each of my children, from oldest to youngest, first
a husband, then his wife, and so on. Occasionally, I will bless the
grandchildren as well, but I have encouraged their fathers to adopt
this ritual themselves. I concluded with a special blessing to
Rachel, who was then engaged to Ethan, and finally with my
blessing to Nili. In Hebrew, I offered each child the two-fold
blessing. For my sons-in-law, whom I've grown to love as my
own, I say, "May you God make you like Ephraim and Menashe
(the children of Joseph)," which represents the combination of
Jewish learning and secular excellence. For my daughters, I said,
"May God make you like Sarah, Rebecca, Rachel, and Leah," the
matriarchs of the Jewish people. For each child I added the
priestly blessing, "May God bless you, and safeguard you, and
illuminate you, and be gracious to you."

Next we sang the Kiddush, which included the blessing over the wine, followed by the ritual washing of our hands, and then the blessing over the bread, which tonight included Rachel's fabulous whole wheat challahs. My father enjoyed a sip of wine, and a few bites of challah. Although tonight he preferred silence, he communicated with a broad smile and alert eyes, basking in this, his greatest accomplishment. Regardless of his military and civil service, my father's family was the priority of his life. The importance of the Sabbath meal in his house, even though he could no longer come to the table and partake in the actual eating, was that he delighted in the presence of his family.

In the dining room, we discussed a variety of subjects, including Jamie updated us on his progress in his home security business, including an all-night installation his company had completed in a Central Park West apartment. Ethan, a first-year student at the University of Miami Law School, told us about the courses he was taking that semester.

The sisters spoke about Rachel's wedding dress and her forthcoming wedding at the Doral Country Club. Having satisfied the modest appetites, my grandchildren scattered throughout the house, but they found my father in the big bedroom, where he sat in front of the TV with a plate of diced roasted chicken, a small salad, and a serving of raspberry sorbet. Throughout the meal, my children alternated visiting my father, making sure he was never alone, ensuring that he knew how much he was loved.

After dinner, the parents, aunts, uncles, grandparents, and great-grandmother took turns holding the newborn girls, Kaelly and Noa, each less than a month old. After sitting on my lap awhile, Riki's toddler daughter, Leor, grew fidgety, and so I brought her into my father's room and placed her on his lap. She kissed my father on the cheek, and then climbed down, preferring the freedom of jumping on the nearby bed and reciting her newfound vocabulary of ten or fifteen words. The older grandchildren had also migrated into the bedroom and lay on the bed in the comfort of their great-grandparents' pillows.

At the table, amid the paradox of formality and informality on this Shabbat night, I recalled the now completed week, and I silently acknowledged an extraordinary accomplishment that I could not share. Nobody in the room would have understood the complexity of the clinical problem I'd overcome Thursday night, and I wondered how many such extraordinary moments remained in my surgical inventory. Basking in the delight of my family, and seeing my father hunched over in his recliner, with bits of food staining his shirt, reminded me that my greatest purpose is to foster a unity among my children that will thrive beyond the days when I will sit in an adjacent room, nibbling morsels of a family feast, while my children and grandchildren and great-grandchildren carry on our joyous Shabbat traditions.

I sat between Gita and my mother, and considered whether I was taking each of them for granted. As she did most Fridays, Gita had risen that morning and arrived at the supermarket before 7:00 to acquire the food for our evening's feast. She'd spent most of her day marinating and cooking the chicken and beef, brewing her signature chicken and vegetable soup, and preparing the vegetable side dishes, which that night included asparagus, sweet potatoes, and spiced apples. Somehow, each week Gita orchestrates her Shabbat masterpiece in an elegant and pragmatic sequence that accounts for limitations of time and space. And the challenge of tonight was compounded by transporting the meal to my parents' house.

"Gita, everything is delicious," my mother said. "You added something to your recipe for the apple crisp."

"A bit more brown sugar," Gita said. "I'm so glad you liked it."

"As always, you create the standard," I whispered to Gita. Her face alit with pride. Then I added, "And we both know that food is your specialty."

At the table, my children began singing Shabbat songs, and my grandchildren accompanied them. Amid the singing and controlled ruckus, my mother said, "I wish to remain in my house until the end of my days."

I looked at my mother, forced a smile, reached for her hand, and after a moment of thought, I responded, "Mom, it's a noble wish…" I hesitated a moment, trying to understand why she was broaching this subject now. Perhaps she was more capable of accepting reality than I. "Mom, I'm not sure. You might be better offer in an independent area in a son's home. Being alone in this house, with so many memories of Dad, may be unbearable." I didn't have the answer, but the longer we spoke, I was convinced of her resolve.

"This is the house where the two of us have lived, and the memories will give me courage and pleasure. Twenty-four hour aides, with my children visiting on a daily basis, will ease the isolation."

As she pondered the unthinkable, I knew certain questions needed answers. I also realized that my obligation was to honor my mother's wishes and not try to satisfy my own vision for how this should play out.

"David, my lifestyle requires a large income, but my overwhelming expense is the money I choose to give away to my family. I need assurance that this will not change."

"Mom, you'll never have to worry about that," I said. For years, Russell had overseen a family trust fund, owned by my brothers and I, funded by equal contributions, the proceeds of which were available for our parents continued financial well-being.

The grandchildren had fallen asleep on my parents' bed, and the late evening news was ending. An hour earlier, Dad had taken an Ambien, and he was now sleeping in the small bedroom. Gita and my children probably wanted to wrap up the evening, but they had waited patiently for me to announce that it was time to go home. I wanted to be sure that Mom knew her wishes would be honored. "It's been an unforgettable Shabbat evening," I said to Mom.

Until that night, I hadn't realized how important independence was to my mother's existence. I kissed her goodnight and said, "Mom, I have never intentionally lied to you, and I promise you that my brothers and I will honor your wishes. You never need to worry about income, and now matter what, it will always be your choice to live in this house."

That morning I attended a 6:30 a.m. class given by Rabbi Yochanan Zweig, Dean of Talmudic University of Florida. He shared his understanding of a parent's mortality, which helped him recover from his own sorrow after his parents' deaths. Jewish belief holds that throughout life, one must strive to maintain the healthiest body possible. Upon death, as we return to the *kever*—the grave or womb—the flesh then returns to the earth and the soul returns to God. Upon resurrection, the soul returns to an ephemeral form resembling the former physical body. This is based on the fundamental Jewish belief that God will resurrect the dead within the seventh millennium, or the ultimate Sabbath, which concludes with the Jewish calendar year of 7000. We are currently just over 300 years from the beginning of that window of time, which begins in the year 6000.

That night, as Gita and I walked home from my parents' house, we followed Elana and her newborn daughter Noa. "I remember when Elana was Noa's age as if it were yesterday," Gita said.

I knew Gita was inviting me to reminisce about old times, and perhaps to point out how the new times were even greater, but I could not, as I was engaged in my own interior monologue, seeking to understand the matter of eternal life. Does it truly exist? The key must lie in the soul, which along with our abilities to acquire knowledge and to seek wisdom and to speak, distinguishes man from beast. But at the end of the day, what is the ultimate purpose of any of this?

Is eternal life housed in the minds of those who live on and remember the love, kindness, service, and loyalty of the departed? I wanted to believe it was much more than this, and that I could look forward to being with my father again, in days of health and vitality.

I accepted the limitation of my understanding, as the soul cannot be comprehended. Perhaps the soul, which is the energy and essence that makes us human, is best understood as a gift from God. The soul returns to the sender upon our demise, and the bones and flesh dissipate, and that's what's left, or perhaps not? How can we know? It would be nice to believe that in the future, a divine caricature of our unique features, reflected in our new ephemeral bodies, will house our souls and be united with God.

As a heart surgeon, trained to be objective and pragmatic, I see death as a final clinical state. I've never seen a hint of a soul departing a corpse or hovering overhead, although perhaps I've never looked. And yet I desire to understand how my father's soul will be with us in the resurrection. What I do know for certain is that my father's DNA will manifest in his offspring, and the grandeur of his life will live in all those who knew him. Perhaps there is more to it, but as a man, walking home with his family on a Shabbat night in Miami Beach, maybe that is the closest I'll come to understanding eternity.

"I'm sorry, honey," I said, taking Gita's hand as I recalled her observation about Elana. "My mind was elsewhere, and I do remember."

Chapter 12: A Downhill Spiral

We awoke in the morning to temperatures in the high 40s, chilly for Miami Beach. My parents didn't attend synagogue, but I visited them with my grandson Zeev after the Sabbath services. In the big bedroom, Dad was watching an NFL Wild Card game. Not wanting to leave my father's side, my mother drew upon her ability to tune out extraneous noise and silently read her Shabbat prayers. Radcliff and Louisiana were in the kitchen preparing lunch. I kissed Mom hello, nodding that I understood her silence, as she continued her devotion. After Zeev, and I kissed Dad hello, we sat in the rolling chairs, four generations watching the football game together.

"Zayde, will you teach me how to play football?" four-year-old Zeev asked. For a moment I thought he was speaking to my father, and then I realized he was speaking to me.

Early Sunday morning, Gita and I walked on Lincoln Road and Ocean Drive. I spent the middle of the day with Nili, who chauffeured me between rounds at South Miami and Aventura. She is my sixth daughter, but the only one I taught how to drive. My father had taught the others, with Elana offering the greatest challenge. Ironically, Elana, who has developed a keen sense of direction, typically drives when she goes places with her sisters.

At Mom and Dad's that afternoon, they told me how Robert had taken them for a drive throughout South Beach Miami and across the 79th Street Causeway, where they enjoyed the beautiful scenery of Biscayne Bay and observed the recent surge in condominium development.

"How much longer?" Dad asked me. The TV was going with yet another NFL playoff game.

"How do you mean?"

"Until I start feeling better."

I was pleased to hear that he was optimistic about the chemotherapy.

"And when do we repeat the scans?" Mom asked.

"The scans may not be helpful. We know where the tumor is located. What's important, Dad, is that you're comfortable and that you experience pleasure in daily living, such as your ride today with Robert. Each day you give and receive love is a great day."

After we sat awhile watching football, Dad asked me, "How are the collections?"

"This time of year, Medicare pays very slowly, and my cost of living is at a crescendo, between the IRS, college tuitions for my kids, and day school for my grandchildren."

"Your problem, David, is with discipline. If you would make more money, I'm certain you'd end up spending it."

I was unsure where the conversation was going, but it pleased me to see my father passionate again, albeit somewhat critical.

"I have a lot of children," I said, "and therefore, a lot of expenses."

"David, your children have no concept of money. They spend excessively on desires rather than needs. It's time they learn financial responsibility before it's too late."

"Dad, I believe you're right, and the fault lies with Gita and me."

"You must tighten the belt and view money as a commodity to be appreciated and preserved," my father advised.

"Dad, I can't argue with you. You're right, and I have to continue trying to educate my family."

"David, you're very lucky because your brothers love you and they'll never let you down."

On one hand, I felt pride in helping my children to such a degree, and yet I felt like an irresponsible child. I don't appreciate the value of a dollar, having made large amounts of money and saving very little. Perhaps I've been more effective as a donor than as an educator. I knew my father was right. Like in the past, he again proved to be perceptive to my concerns, and adept at cutting to the heart of a matter.

Walking with Mom to the front door, as we often did when she felt strong enough to see me out, I said how pleased I was with her progress. Her breathing was much improved, but her anxiety about my father hung like a shingle in her eyes. "It's not a great situation," I added, regarding Dad's progress, but Mom's faith was carrying her to the next level, bringing everything into balance. "God is in charge," I said. All we can do is make the most of the time we have left."

Dani, Josh, and their daughter Yve have a wonderful life in Toronto, but Dani often feels lonely when she returns after longer visits with us here in Florida. Given everything that was happening, and the particular sadness she felt over her grandfather's illness, Gita went to Toronto with Dani and Yve on Monday to spend a few extra days together. Josh had flown back Sunday to prepare for a Monday business meeting.

That afternoon, as I performed my rounds at South Miami Hospital, I received a thoughtful email from Josh on my BlackBerry. His words reflected his maturity, growth, and understanding of the importance of family and responsibility. Josh told me how much he and Dani and Yve had enjoyed their time with us, and how he'd learned so much, especially from his time with my father. "The love and respect you're showing Zayde is a lesson I'll cherish. I hope to follow your standard when my time of responsibility comes."

A person can only do so much himself, I thought as I walked down a corridor toward a patient's room in the ICU, but our actions inspire memories and convey a life force of their own. As my life moves along, I hope I have inspired my children in some way by sharing my values, motivation, and enthusiasm. Most days, through their words and deeds, my children remind me that Gita and I have succeeded as parents. Some days, when I question my own worth, and the value of my accomplishments, I reflect on my children and who they've become as independent adults. These thoughts restore my emotional equilibrium, assuring me that my life has had meaning.

The next day, I arrived at the house before sunrise to bring Dad to Sylvester. Russell and Robert were meeting us there during the treatment. Al B was up in St. Augustine on business. Despite the early hour, Mom was dressed immaculately, as always, ready to give my father an encouraging sendoff. Dad was bathed and dressed, but he still appeared exhausted. Prior to my arrival, he'd eaten a small breakfast and received his insulin injection. His fatigue, an obvious consequence of his cancer, was intensified by the regimen of his sleeping meds and the Xanax, without which, he wouldn't sleep much at all.

The morning was bright and clear, but not terribly cool. Winter mornings in South Florida are akin to late spring mornings in most other places. I gave Dad a boost into the front seat his Chrysler and placed his wheelchair into the trunk. He could no longer get into my SUV. Radcliff rode with us so that Dad wouldn't be alone if I were called away for an emergency.

After Dad's blood was drawn, we sat in the waiting room for our 8:00 a.m. appointment with Dr. Rosenblatt. Just as Russell arrived, a nurse called us into the examination room. The nurse took Dad's vitals. His weight was unchanged at two hundred pounds. He had experienced significant muscle loss, but his weight had remained steady due to excessive fluid retention in his legs and left arm.

"Good morning, General," Dr. Rosenblatt said. He entered the room just as Russell and I finished helping Dad onto the table.

"It's Captain," Dad said, shifting around on the white paper, "but in the Navy, this rank is equivalent to Brigadier General in the Army."

"Having grown up in Israel, I admire your rank and military accomplishments," Dr. Rosenblatt responded.

"Let's examine you," Dr. Rosenblatt said. Together we removed Dad's shirt and pulled down his sweatpants. We observed an approximately 4-millimeter sacral decubitus—or ulcer—on his buttocks and concurred that we should continue the Balmex treatment.

Dad's lungs were clear, except for the reduced breath sounds on the left, a consequence of his chronically elevated left diaphragm. His heartbeat was regular, his abdomen was distended but soft, his liver was not profoundly enlarged, he had excellent bowel sounds, and there was severe peripheral edema.

"The hematocrit is stable, in the mid-35 range," Dr. Rosenblatt said, glancing at the chart. "The white count is elevated as a consequence of his Procrit treatment. He's not clinically infected. The liver function tests were abnormal, with alkaline phosphatase in the mid-400 range, increased from the prior study, and the CA19-9, a cancer marker, is profoundly elevated in the mid-40,000 range. Although he was speaking to me, I'm sure Russell and Dad had an inkling of the unfavorable results.

"The Gemzar is slowing the process and making your existence more comfortable," Dr. Rosenblatt explained to Dad, looking at him with a lingering gaze, as if to gauge my father's response. "Perhaps we should add Tarceva, an oral agent, which works through a different route to reduce the tumor."

My father shifted around on the table, wrinkling the paper sheet beneath him. "Russell, please hand me that," Dad said, looking at his fleece jacket folded over the back of a chair.

"Captain Galbut, what are your thoughts on this?" Dr. Rosenblatt said.

"Frankly, I'm tired, and I don't see much progress."

"Sir, you have a wonderful, supportive, dedicated family. I wish I could say that for all of my patients. Fortunately, you don't seem to be in severe pain and your remains mind sharp. These are all favorable components for making this current decision. The choice of how to continue is ultimately up to you. Considering the underlying diagnosis of pancreatic cancer, withdrawing from ongoing treatment would be understandable."

Russell zipped dad's jacket up about three quarters of the way and then stepped back and leaned against the wall. He and I made eye contact, and with a nod, we communicated to each other our need to remain silent and let Dad respond.

"The option of hospice exists, and this may make your home care easier," Dr. Rosenblatt said.

"No," Dad said. "Let's continue with my treatments. We'll see what happens over the next month."

"I think that's the right decision, Dad," I said, with Russell nodding in agreement.

In recent days there had been a yin and yang in my thought process as I prepared for this moment. "To be or not to be" in the ongoing chemotherapeutic effort, which we all knew offered little long-term hope. I was convinced that Dad's mind remained sharp, with the exception of some confused moments associated with his nightly Xanax and Ambien. The ultimate decision had to be Dad's, but I was not excused from making the right recommendations. Dad acknowledged his poor prognosis, but he couldn't accept the finality of a no-action decision. Fortunately, he was still lucid and could participate in these tough choices. This was yet another blessing among countless others. Even so, time marched toward the inevitable.

Early Friday morning, we brought Dad to the dedication of the Hyman P. Galbut Jewish Learning Center on 41st Street. The Center is under the auspices of Chabad Lubavitch, an international organization that promotes Judaism through education and practice. Since Dad's diagnosis, Russell had been planning to memorialize our father's life through philanthropy, and to the extent we could, Robert, Al B and I would contribute to these efforts. Dad knew that other dedications would follow, but he specifically wanted to witness this ceremony because he had lived his life in the pursuit of learning. Recognizing knowledge as a universal medium, my father hoped that Jews, regardless of their synagogue affiliations, would benefit from the Center. Dad's multifaceted life of achievement was only possible through tolerance. As much as he encouraged unity among his sons, Dad knew the basis would have be love, which can only flourish in an environment of tolerance, which is the goal of the Chabad Lubavitch movement.

The Learning Center, which was being built in a former office building, had been under construction for about a year. The decision to dedicate the facility to Dad had been made within the past month. The first floor features a high ceiling that accommodates a mezzanine, which was being renovated into a library, with stacks for books and other materials. The first floor, then a concrete shell, has since been completed and now functions as a sanctuary for prayer and as a facility for lectures and social events. The third floor was already functioning as a temporary sanctuary and classroom space.

As we entered the construction site, we received ceremonial yellow hard hats and we were greeted by the Learning Center's spiritual leader, Rabbi Yossy Gordon, and the president, Yossi Duchman. Other dignitaries included Miami Beach Mayor David Dermer, several commission members, and a number of other local rabbis.

Dad sat in his wheelchair, and Mom sat alongside him on a plastic patio chair. My family and I, along with many of our friends, posed for photos, and I'm certain that many of us wondered how many more opportunities we would have to pose for pictures with Dad.

The foyer and the main hall were separated by temporary wooden columns, across which was tied a long red ribbon. Surrounded by nearly one hundred guests, along with Mom, myself, my brothers, and our wives, Yossi Duchman handed Dad a large pair of scissors. Unable to use his dominant left hand, Dad struggled with the scissors in his right hand, now lacking the coordination to make the cut. Without a word, my brothers and I stepped closer to Dad, grasped the large shears within his hands, and cut the ribbon together.

Within the unpainted walls of the future sanctuary, we approached rows of folding chairs set before a temporary podium. My brothers and I pushed Dad's wheelchair to the front row. Dressed in a suit for the first time in weeks, Dad appeared like an apparition. His pale skin was accented by the temporary lighting and his facial features appeared fixed with an intermittent blank stare that gave way to a weak smile each time he was greeted. Starting with Thanksgiving, he had avoided most public and family gatherings, probably because he didn't want to be remembered this way, debilitated and slouched in a wheelchair. I admired his demonstration of courage in attending this event. Certainly he was aware that many guests were likely curious to see his decline in person. I believe that most of us feel sad for a sick person, but secretly we harbor an unspoken relief and ecstasy in our own health. At the same time, perhaps ill people discomfort us because they remind us of our own frailty.

Rabbi Gordon stood at the podium and welcomed our family and invited guests, and paid tribute to my parents. Then he introduced Robert, who spoke about the sons of Jacob and their commitment to each other. Robert's message emphasized that only through unity of brotherhood can a father genuinely know he has succeeded, and this unity is best demonstrated by a lack of jealousy and envy.

Robert invited me to make the presentation to our father. Rather than stand at the podium, I stood before Dad and addressed him directly. Holding Dad's hand, I spoke to the crowd, making certain my words were loud and direct. I wanted my message to sink in.

"As a little boy, I believed my father was the smartest man in the world. As I grew into a young man, this belief never changed. Dad, with your permission, I would like to share a brief story with our guests. When I was about eight or nine years old, we were swimming at the beach at Crandon Park, and being a curious little kid, I asked you about the oblique scar in your right, lower abdomen. You responded that you had been deathly ill with drainage of infected material through your skin from a localized ruptured appendicitis just four years after silent screen megastar Rudolph Valentino died in 1926 following surgery for acute appendicitis. His death, fortuitously for my father and countless others, familiarized the public with this often fatal illness. In your case, diagnosis was also late, but God was kind in that you self-drained the infection through a large abscess in your abdominal wall. You missed a year of school, including almost six months in the Bronx Community Hospital, and your mother was always at your side, and this explains the special bond between the two of you."

I wasn't certain that I had my father's complete attention, as his head had fallen several times during my talk, but each time he lifted his chin and forced his eyes back open.

"Dad, I remember you telling me that during your recovery, how your mother, my Bubby, bought you an encyclopedia set, *The Book of Knowledge,* and that you read it cover to cover in about six months. Growing up, we had a current edition in our thousand-square-foot home in Coral Gate, and we all regularly referred to it for homework assignments. Dad," I continued, "your love of learning and acquisition of knowledge explains why today's dedication is so important to you. I know that the many beneficiaries of this learning center will be inspired by your life."

I was concerned that Dad was no longer following my words, but I needed to share with the audience some thoughts about my mother, the love of my father's life. "Whereas my father has always understood the importance of knowledge for its own sake, my mother grew up in a family where the acquisition of knowledge centered upon Jewish values and observance. Mom brought a great passion to their marriage about religion, and my father understood how this could be used to build a stronger family. Together, they created a home in which Jewish knowledge was paramount." As I finished my remarks, Dad gave me a rich smile of pride and approval. And at the breakfast reception that followed, Dad greeted everyone who approached him with warmth and good wishes and unspoken goodbyes.

With my partner Naaman out of town, skiing in Utah, I'd spent much of the day rounding in many hospitals between Homestead to Aventura before I could return home to be with my family and enjoy Shabbat. "Dad spent a wonderful day remembering yesterday's dedication and he's looking forward to having another good day tomorrow," Mom said at the house that night.

"David," Mom added, the optimism gone from her voice, "I never expected I would outlive your father, especially not since what happened last summer."

I couldn't fully appreciate Mom's agony, nor would I want to. Only the life-partner understands this process. My mother must have felt guilty for being the likely survivor. She continued, "It won't be easy for me without your father."

Her words assured me that Mom would have the strength to continue. She hadn't said she wouldn't survive, but rather that it would be a struggle, and ironically, those words comforted me.

Life has a way of marching to its own beat. We are perhaps the drummers, and if we can modulate the music to be in synchrony, we can enjoy its greater meaning. Sometimes going against the current is important because it is not the destination—which is the same for all mortals—but rather how the journey is made. And as we age, it's the balance between mind and physical being and God's plan that shapes our perceptions and determines our reality.

Sunday morning it got down to about 45 degrees. Gita and I celebrated the relaxing air with a walk in South Beach. Because of the full waves, some forty or fifty surfers had ventured into the high surf off of Third Street. Together we watched those opportunistic athletes, dressed in wetsuits, oblivious to the cold and the inherent risks of gliding along unpredictable roads through the surf. These are the same men and women who ride the waves that precede the hurricane winds when our panicked community is otherwise shuttering windows and stocking their homes with water, canned goods, and generator fuel. And maybe that's how life is best lived, facing the adversary head on, ready to ride the waves.

At a brunch at Russell's house, we celebrated his daughter Marisa's nineteenth birthday and her brief return from her year-long college exchange program in Israel. Despite Dad's increasing frailty, he and Mom seemed to enjoy the event, and even though it was Marisa's birthday celebration, my parents were the center of attention. Overall, the mood in the house was jovial, but Dad's waning strength and alertness were undeniable, as was his silence. He smiled on occasion, but more often, his eyes remained closed. Here and there he added a phrase or two to the conversation, and he joined us in singing "Happy Birthday" to Marisa. Despite his waning energy, I know Dad shared in nineteen-year-old Marisa's joy and anticipation as she prepared to grab life.

My mother's brother, Rabbi Label Dulitz, sitting across from my father, spoke with tears in his eyes. What began as a younger brother-in-law resenting the loss of his doting sister to her new husband who'd taken her from New Orleans to Miami had evolved into a relationship of true brothers. Uncle Label referenced how life is a cycle of nineteen years, as demonstrated by the Jewish calendar, which is lunar based and includes 354 days in a year, thus necessitating an additional month every few years. But the entire cycle lasts nineteen years, and Marisa had now completed one such cycle. He prayed that we would all be together in another nineteen years. I appreciated the sincerity of his love, but I could not overlook the obvious. Robert noted that all of us will have surpassed our seventieth year.

"God should be so generous," I prayed silently. I could see the picture of four brothers, shoulder to shoulder, with graying and receding hair, and perhaps not standing quite as straight, but being supported by each other as always, and praying, albeit a bit less optimistically, for yet another nineteen years.

At the house that evening, I sat and held Dad's hand. It was just Mom, Dad, Radcliff, and myself. I dozed off every five or ten minutes, but Dad seemed alert as we watched the fourth quarter of the NFL playoff game between Chicago and Carolina. I overheard Mom, speaking on the phone in her office, probably speaking with some of her grandchildren or great-grandchildren.

"How are you feeling tonight, Dad?"

"The players are so tired," Dad observed.

I reminded him that the next chemotherapy was planned for Tuesday. And then I said, "I'd love to have a birthday party at our house toward the end of the month to celebrate your birthday, Daniel's birthday, my birthday, and Zeev's."

"That will be a wonderful thing," Dad said.

In Louisiana's absence that night, Mom said she planned to sleep with Dad in his room.

"I'm very happy, Bessie," Dad said.

A hectic surgical schedule awaited me Monday, and on Tuesday there was an important meeting regarding South Shore Hospital, and on Thursday Gita and I were planning to fly to Los Angeles for an Israeli real estate show. I hated to leave my parents, and I needed to see how the week evolved before making a final decision.

Monday morning, I called Mom on my way to South Miami. She said she'd held Dad's hand throughout the night in the bed, despite her discomfort in the smaller bedroom.

Mom and Dad spent Monday night watching a Clint Eastwood movie on TNT. Dad was reclined in his chair, while Mom sat upright beside him, wrapped in her vibrating vest.

"Discouraged," Dad said during a truck commercial when I asked how he was feeling. "It's a downhill spiral."

"With the combination of chemotherapy and the oral doses of Tarceva, we might add a plateau to the downhill spiral."

Dad nodded.

"Did you enjoy yesterday?"

"It was great," Dad said, recalling the party at Russell's.

"You still have time, Dad, God willing. Time for more birthday parties. You're still the patriarch of this family."

Tuesday morning, at 6:25 a.m., I arrived at the house. Al B was already there and the household was alive with activity. Paul,

Dad's new home health care nurse, checked Dad's blood sugar and responded with an appropriate insulin injection. That week we'd hired Paul, a polite and respectful man of about forty-five, to come in twice a day to monitor Dad's insulin and blood sugar. That morning, Louisiana was preparing Mom's breakfast.

"Good morning, Dr. Dave," Louisiana said, standing at the kitchen counter, placing slices of rye into the toaster. "Your Mom finished her treatment and she's inside with Mr. Al B helping your father get dressed."

In the bedroom, I kissed Dad good morning. He was seated in his wheelchair, dressed in blue sweatpants and a matching shirt.

With his eyes closed, but with a faint smile that assured me that he was awake, Dad said, "I'm ready, bright and early." I thought about Dad's favorite Hebrew song, which he still insisted we sing every Shabbat. The refrain translates to, "The entire world is a narrow bridge, and the essence is not to fear at all." Perhaps for him, the bridge had become narrow as a tightrope, and yet his iron will propelled him forward.

How does one go through life, recognizing danger on all sides, in a place where the walkway is narrow and strength begins with oneself? Is it the courage to subjugate fear that makes our life carry opportunity and fulfillment of accomplishment?

"Don't be afraid to try," Dad often said when we were growing up. "The impossible takes a little longer."

In front of the house, I examined the live oak, which Dad had planted a few years earlier. In October, Hurricane Wilma had blown the tree across the driveway, where it lay for several weeks, losing lost most of its leaves and smaller branches. Reluctantly, the landscaper replanted it and to our surprise, it did quite well, but now, two months later, it was back in the driveway, courtesy of a thunderstorm on Friday afternoon. The roots appeared small for the diameter of the branches and leaves, and I questioned whether it could ultimately be saved.

"We'll need to get this tree replanted," Al B said.

"Absolutely," I said, thinking how the rise and fall of that tree, which Dad had planted, signified our father's illness. A person can survive heavy gusts, but sometimes even the strongest roots give way to life's storms. But I knew my father's influence would live on through his children, and if the tree could survive, it would be a constant reminder.

After many weeks of trying, Dad, Radcliff, Al B, and I were finally the first to arrive at Sylvester. "Good morning," said the secretary in the chemotherapy unit. "All the prescriptions and paperwork are ready." We met Al B outside the blood laboratory at 6:55 and waited for it to open. Five minutes later, we were escorted inside where the phlebotomist, Carmen, drew Dad's blood. "Poppy, you have wonderful children," she said.

At the clinical treatment unit, Dad was first in line for a chemotherapy bay. I kissed him goodbye, as I was running late for a 7:30 operation, but I was slow to leave. "Dad is this channel OK?" I said, reaching for the remote control. "We can find something else."

"I love you," my father said in response to my hesitation. "Go to work, David."

Chapter 13: Cardiac Surgery and Kickboxing

The next evening, three days before Dad's 86th birthday, I found him resting in his recliner. Mom sat beside him, reciting psalms from a new large-print prayer book.

"Mom, I want to review your meds and daily schedule. Perhaps we can consolidate a few things."

Louisiana went into the kitchen and came back with a printed sheet which Mom had prepared and regularly updated. "Here's the list of everything she's taking and her daily schedule."

"David," Mom said, "promise that you'll help Louisiana find a suitable job when she graduates from nursing school. She's been so extraordinarily kind to your father and me."

"It will be my privilege," I said. "When the time comes, and Louisiana is ready, I will be her advocate."

Dad had dozed off, his right hand touching his chin. His weight loss had been obscured by the dramatic decrease in muscle mass and the substantial increase in fluid retention in his abdomen and fatty tissues. His belly was somewhat distended, even more than in recent days. As I held his hands and gave him a kiss, Dad opened his eyes. I spent a few moments massaging Dad's neck, shoulders, back, and swollen left arm, my warm hands against his cold skin. His once muscular torso, now atrophied, revealed the skeletal form of his spine and shoulder blades. "Dad, when is the Super Bowl?"

"In a few weeks," he said. "I don't know exactly."

"It's the first Sunday in February," Radcliff said as he massaged my father's feet with a moisturizing cream.

"How about a big party in two weeks to celebrate your 86th birthday, my birthday, Daniel's, and Zeev's?"

"I look forward to it," Dad whispered, leaving me unconvinced.

"Overall, Dad, how are you feeling?"

"I see no progress. I'm bored and uncomfortable. My voice is going, I can't lift my left arm, and I'm unsteady on my feet."

As the days and weeks progressed, I'd been seeking the right moment to ask Dad some big questions. I wanted to understand his courage and how to face life's greatest adversary. I didn't want to miss any opportunities for meaningful conversations. In short, I didn't want anything left unsaid. Then again, maybe this was more my need than his. In Dad's eighty-six years, he'd done it all and had said what he needed to say. And if I was unfulfilled, I could only blame myself for not paying closer attention when I had the chance.

At the front door, Mom kissed me goodnight. "The tree is down again," she said.

"It's already demonstrated its desire to survive, having made it through last year's storms. We'll save the tree, Mom."

I kissed my mother goodbye, got into my car, and headed home.

On Thursday, Gita and I flew to California for the Israeli real estate show, held at the largest synagogue in Los Angeles. Gita is the international sales manager for a five-hundred-unit apartment development in Jerusalem. The weekend represented a great opportunity for her to introduce her product to the West Coast. Of course I wanted to support Gita's career, which has enhanced her personal and professional self-esteem, but I didn't go with a full heart. My mind returned to my father, who would celebrate his eighty-sixth and final birthday without me. I prayed that he would have a comfortable day.

We spent Friday morning at the Santa Monica Pier, overlooking the Pacific Ocean, watching the fishermen bait their hooks and cast their lines, as young couples milled up and down the pier, enjoying the sunshine and brisk morning air. Gita and I reminisced about our visit to Los Angeles with Riki, Elle, Dani,

Elana, and Rachel about twenty years ago, about three years before Nili was born. The girls had enjoyed Disneyland and the tour of Universal Studios, not to mention our walk along this very pier and our ride along the beach on rented bicycles. In my eyes, Los Angeles hadn't changed much in the past twenty years, but I couldn't say the same for us. Our sixth daughter was now in high school and we were now grandparents.

The real estate show didn't begin until Saturday evening, so after a quiet lunch at The Coffee Bean & Tea Leaf in Santa Monica, we drove to Beverly Hills, where Gita spent the afternoon looking for a dress for Rachel's wedding. After several hours of studying the designs and fabrics, she decided that her dressmaker back home could produce something comparable and for thousands less.

Friday was as carefree as I'd been in the past year, free of time constraints, surgical commitments, rounds, consults, and family obligations. Well, maybe not that last one. Throughout the day, my thoughts returned to my father. That afternoon, about 2:00 p.m., about half an hour before Shabbat in Miami, I called Robert from a bench on Rodeo Drive, outside a posh hair salon where Gita was getting her hair styled, in preparation for her presentation tomorrow night.

"Dad's had a terrible day," my brother said. "His abdomen is extremely distended and painful, and he was up most of last night.

"He may have a fecal impaction, or ascites," I said, referring to a collection of fluid in the abdomen as a consequence of his liver failure. I spotted a young blonde actress coming out of the salon, someone I recognized from a movie I'd seen awhile back on TV. "Dad may need to be hospitalized for a course of enemas and possible lower endoscopy."

Mom, who'd been listening in on an extension, said, "I think Dad will feel better if we can get him to eat something tonight."

Robert said, "I'm concerned that the underlying disease, which may reflect liver and intestinal metastasis may be causing these symptoms. In addition, Dad is weak and his level of alertness is diminished."

"Robert, Dad may require hospitalization. I'll call Dr. Rosenblatt to prepare a bed at Sylvester for treatment with hydration and intestinal decompression."

Within minutes, I'd spoken with Dr. Rosenblatt, who was kind enough to accommodate my wishes. Next I called American Airlines, and then I called Robert to inform him that a bed was available, and that unless he saw significant improvement, Dad should be admitted. "Robert, I'll be back in Miami early Sunday morning. "I just reserved a seat leaving LAX at midnight."

"Thanks for expediting the admission," Robert said. "Tonight, let's pray. Enjoy Shabbat with Gita. Here, Daddy wants to speak to you."

After a moment of muffled sounds, probably Dad struggling to steady Robert's cellphone between his ear and his pillow, my father whispered, "How's the weather out there?"

"It's beautiful, Dad, but I'd rather be with you tonight, celebrating your birthday and Shabbat." I continued, "You may need to go to Sylvester for a few days to get your bowels working again. I plan to see you Sunday morning, directly from the airport, just after 8:00 a.m. I'm sure you'll feel better. I love you, Dad."

"Thank you, David."

All around me, opulence abounded on Rodeo Drive, while Gita enjoyed the royal treatment—not yet aware that was leaving early—and probably enjoying this rare opportunity to keep me waiting, much as I've done to her throughout our marriage. Gita emerged from the Salon with radiant, flowing blonde hair.

"Can I have your autograph?" I said.

Gita smiled and I knew she was enjoying the moment. Despite my decision to return to Miami early, I was determined to enjoy a peaceful Shabbat with my beautiful bride, and to make her feel like a queen.

"Gita, we're going to have a great Shabbat," I said as we walked back to the hotel, "but I need to leave on a midnight flight tomorrow after we get your booth set up."

"How bad is he?"

"Dehydrated, and his abdomen has changed, with severe distention. He should be admitted this weekend."

After Gita lit the candles in our room at the Beverly Hills Hotel, we enjoyed a romantic Shabbat meal consisting of roast chicken, mixed salad, hummus, and chocolate cake that we had purchased that afternoon at Kotlar's Kosher Market on Pico Boulevard. Following dinner, we spent several hours on the balcony, overlooking a quiet residential street, sharing a bag of pistachio nuts and a carton of strawberries. And like that, we shared our fears and dreams. I told Gita how much I loved her, and I thanked her for raising our children to be centered, kind, and so appreciative of life. I slept better that night than I had in weeks, and better than I would in the weeks to come.

The fact that I didn't awake to my cellphone ringing assured me that Dad's condition hadn't changed much overnight. It was now his eighty-six birthday, and I wanted to be with him, despite the agony I would have felt, seeing the reflection of the candlelight of his last birthday cake in his eyes, his once-youthful optimism wrecked by the undeniable truth that he had no future.

As I was anxious to return, I was also committed to enjoying Shabbat with Gita. We attended morning services at the large Persian synagogue in Beverly Hills, where the real estate show was scheduled to begin after sunset. After a delicious lunch of schnitzel, cold chicken, coleslaw, and cucumber salad, we meandered through the residential streets of neatly tailored apartment houses and estate homes. After the Sabbath ended, I assisted Gita in setting up her booth, and after the show began, I kissed her goodbye, returned to the hotel room for my suitcase, went downstairs, and caught a cab to the airport. On the way, I called Robert, who informed me that Dad's dehydration and abdominal distention had worsened. That evening he'd been brought to Sylvester Cancer Institute for admission.

On the phone with Russell, I explained what he already knew, that this was a bad situation and that we needed to do our best. "There are two possibilities. The first is an impaction of hard stool, which could be disimpacted with dramatic improvement. Second, it could be the spread of cancer, which would make bowel function impossible without surgery."

"Thank you, David," Russell responded. "When are you getting in?"

"In the morning, about 7:30. Rachel's picking me up and taking me to Sylvester. I'll see you there."

"David, here's Mom," Russell said.

"Dad had a great birthday with his children and grandchildren after Shabbat," Mom said. He deliberately waited until after the party before going to Sylvester. We celebrated with pizza and a birthday cake."

"Mom, it's a great accomplishment for a man to reach his eighty-sixth birthday. Although Dad couldn't enjoy the food, I'm sure he loved the company and the recognition of this milestone. I'll see you tomorrow morning."

"David, promise me you'll get him home as soon as possible. This is very important to me."

"I understand," I said as my cab pulled into the departures ramp at LAX at about 9:30 p.m. California time. "I love you, Mom. Good night."

I realized that it was 12:30 back in Miami Beach, well past Mom's bedtime, but for sure the excitement of Dad's birthday party, followed by his hospital admission, had disrupted her routine.

During the flight, I considered the unanswerable. Have I been a good son? What have I left unsaid? What have I failed to demonstrate? What defines a good end? Is there such a thing as a good death? Can you have a good death without having had a good life?

In Western culture, we avoid thoughts of death, and consequently, we avoid thoughts of what constitutes a good life. Do we see it in others? Do we seek it in ourselves?

After midnight, as the jet engines roared and the cabin lights dimmed and the airplane ascended, I felt myself in a state of hyper-alertness. Despite being buckled into a cramped airline seat, I was comfortable, as the night has always been my friend. Remaining awake with my father, driving through the night on our Navy trips, had given me a sense of security despite the darkness. Throughout college and medical school, I grew accustomed to studying into the early morning to meet academic deadlines and expectations. During my seven years as a surgical resident and fellow, I used the nights, devoid of elective surgeries, to concentrate on the post-operative care of my sickest patients. Although this practice wasn't unique, I often took it upon myself to sleep in a recliner beside a patient, ready to be awakened by a dedicated nurse every one or two hours so that I could make appropriate adjustments in care. Some patients would not survive, but for those who did, I believe my management—often quite subtle—made a positive impact. Most nights, I found an hour to review a didactic technical section in one of my well-used books or in my personal surgical notebook. In those years I could function on two to three hours of sleep per night during the week, and on the weekends, I would try to catch up. At home, I always studied with a newborn or toddler on my lap, but during those training years, I spent every other night in the hospital and worked six days a week.

During my years in private practice, my daily routine has been centered around elective and emergency surgery, but I've continued to use the late afternoon and evening hours for reviewing patient care. Before going to sleep, I prepare mentally for my procedures the following day. A prioritization takes place. The patient requiring the most challenging judgmental and technical decisions occupies my thoughts. Not everything in medicine is black and white, and I must be certain that I perform the correct operation, based on my objective and subjective analysis of the data. For example, does the patient in heart failure need one or two valves repaired or changed? Is there sufficient clinical benefit to justify a particularly high-risk operation? Some complex cardiac operations involve a combination of two or more procedures, such as a valve replacement, coronary bypass, and/or a carotid endarterectomy. In these cases, the sequence of steps must be orchestrated for time efficiency and technical perfection. During the night, I perform the surgery in my mind several times, until I reach a level mental preparedness for the day ahead. And only then, do I allow myself to sleep.

Years of experience and technical excellence have established a standard that I am committed to upholding. These procedures don't get any easier, and confidence must not give way to arrogance. Every day is a new battle, and as an advocate for my patients, I must be in top form. The practice of medicine changes with technology and our better understanding of the disease process, but the ultimate outcome in a patient can never be guaranteed. Medicine is humbling, and the best physicians remain modest students.

I believed I had been a good son, but I knew for certain that Dad was an extraordinary father, and that I would always feel his imprint in my behavior and accomplishments. Settled in for the long flight back to Florida, I wrapped myself in a blanket, but rather than using the darkness and impending slumber to review an upcoming surgery, I needed to chart a sequence of a different sort—my preparation for my father's death. No two surgeries are exactly alike, but the steps are logical and we can learn from our experiences, but now I faced a challenge for which there was no preparation, no training, no rehearsal, and no second chances.

In my work, I've learned to accept death. It is always painful, and I used to believe that part of me dies with a patient whose death is an immediate consequence of my surgery. If I didn't acknowledge my finite abilities—and accept that ultimately God controls a person's destiny—my sense of guilt would overwhelm me and render me ineffectual as a surgeon. Prior to surgery, I offer full-disclosure to patients and their relatives regarding statistical expectations. This sets the stage for all possibilities, including those moments in which I'm faced with informing the family of a death.

So my thoughts returned again to the question? What is the difference between a good death and a bad death? A mortality in the operating room is a bad death. Most patients enter surgery expecting to survive, and anything less is a tremendous shock to a family. Even in the most critical situations, the acuity of the clinical presentation is difficult for a family to accept.

In feudal Japan, the Samurai warrior lived life according to bushido, a code of honor. His purpose was to protect the underclass and to preserve their nation's ideals. He prayed for a good death, which ideally was to die heroically in a great battle. Occasionally, if defeated, he would perform hari-kari or seppuku, the ritual of suicide, to avoid bringing dishonor to his family. Death would occur by the code in which he lived. He would live as a warrior and die as a warrior.

Even half asleep at 36,000 feet, I recognized that my father was not a Samurai, but perhaps the lesson of the warrior death is to die in the act of fulfilling one's greatest purpose. My father's greatest accomplishment, in my view, was the family he and my mother created and nurtured. In that light, perhaps he could achieve a good death by experiencing the unity and love of his sons and his wife, and the assurance that this would endure beyond his final moments and for future generations. Death cannot be defeated, but by attending to the dying with love and compassion, we may be encouraged to live more meaningful lives.

I awoke as the plane descended toward South Florida. Within an hour, I expected to be with Dad. I was ready to participate in the medical decisions, but I feared that my father had lost all hope and would be definitive in his desires. I decided that this would be entirely about him, and I would remain his faithful son. With birth begins the process of dying, but we live our lives ignorant of the time and circumstances of our future death. Once we know that death is imminent, our mindset changes and we risk becoming consumed with this end. Until now, I knew Dad had still been enjoying life, but this was changing. I began to cry as the plane touched down at MIA, thinking about my father—always a man of action—and how he was probably ready to die.

At the gate, from my seat on the plane, I called my mother and Elana. My mother was having a respiratory treatment and expressed her desire to see Dad at the hospital. "I want him home, David. Is that possible? Even if he just spends his days in a chair or in bed. I want to be with him."

"Mom, yes, that is our goal."

I hung up and called Elana, who welcomed me home. "I'll be there in a second, Dad. I'm just taking a final circle through arrivals."

Walking through the terminal after deplaning, I called Robert to let him know I'd landed and to see if there had been any changes with Dad overnight.

"He's worse," Robert said with a sad, defeated voice. "Yesterday's CAT scan revealed an ileus. He's demoralized like never before. I'm glad you're here."

"Do you think his ileus reflects a spreading of the tumor in his abdomen, or is it a consequence of a fecal impaction?"

An ileus is a distention of the large and small bowel, caused by an obstruction or a paralysis. Given Dad's condition, the worst scenario would be an obstruction due to a new cancerous growth. The best scenario would be an obstruction due to rock-hard stool in the lower intestine or rectum, which could be addressed with enemas and mechanical disimpaction.

"Robert, I appreciate the update. We'll talk later, and God knows we'll do our best to give Dad the love he deserves."

After retrieving my suitcase from the carousel, I met Elana at the curb, kissed her hello, and thanked her for picking me up so early in the morning. As she merged into the traffic flow, I called Al B.

"I assume Robert's already given you the update," Al B said. "Can surgery help?"

"Maybe, but I doubt Dad's willing to go that route," I responded, thinking that if Dad's bowel distention were due to an obstruction from tumor, then a colostomy would be the only realistic option to achieve additional days.

Next, I called Russell to discuss the gravity of the situation. Speaking with his voice mail, I told him I'd be at the hospital and that I looked forward to seeing him soon."

I arrived at Sylvester around 8:00 a.m. I'd only been away from Dad for two days, but during that time I could see that any remaining satisfaction with his existence had deteriorated to misery. He lay in a bed near a second floor window, framing a large ficus tree. His head rested upon one pillow and his abdomen now rose several inches above his chest. A plastic naso-gastric tube, draining stomach contents, exited through his nose and was connected to a two-liter reservoir hooked into wall suction.

My father's trademark warm smile was absent, and I knew his spirit had been broken. I kissed my father and held his hand, noting the intravenous line, providing saline and minerals. "I'm sorry, Dad."

"For what?"

"For not being with you on your birthday."

"How is Gita doing with the show?" Dad asked. He lay perfectly still, as if bound in position by his IV and his nasogastric tube and oxygen prongs.

"She's still enthusiastic. I'm sure she'll fill us on her sales when she gets back tomorrow."

"How long will I be here?" Dad said, "and is there any purpose to this treatment?"

"I hope just a few days, but let me review the CAT scan and the medical record."

As I walked over to the X-ray department, I passed through the lobby, filled with empty chairs, artificial plants in large plastic pots, wall paintings of European landscapes, and an undeniable sense of abandonment.

I reviewed the films of the CAT scan. The ileus Robert described was clearly present throughout the small and large bowel. The liver was extensively infiltrated with tumor. The mass in the tail of the pancreas was large in the left mid-quadrant. The descending colon had no air fluid level, suggesting either an obstruction at this level or the presence of a fecal impaction.

In the ward, I spotted Russell at the nurses' station. He was wearing an embroidered Crescent Heights polo shirt and khaki slacks. "As a family, we are very appreciative of the excellent care here," Russell said to our father's nurse, who was reviewing his medication record.

"Is this the end?" Russell said as we walked back toward Dad's room. He held a cup of coffee.

"His prognosis is certainly dismal," I said, "and I believe this will be his last admission. But I am committed to getting him home, both for Mommy and for his dignity. It shouldn't end here. The only hope is a fecal impaction, which can be mechanically broken up, but I'm not sure Dad has any interest in prolonging this."

Back in the room, Dad's position on the bed had not changed. Radcliff had now arrived to spend the rest of this Sunday with Dad.

"Dad, I believe your abdominal distention may be temporary. I think the stool in your rectum is like concrete because of your recent diet and impaired digestion. Very often, this condition can be resolved, either with enemas, and possibly endoscopy. In the interim, the naso-gastric tube will make you more comfortable, removing air, and the IV will provide hydration."

"Here you go, Captain," Radcliff said, holding a spoonful of ice chips to my father's lips.

"David, my father said, with melting ice chips still on his tongue, "I'll give it a day."

I called Gita that afternoon. She was on the floor at the real estate show. "Many lookers, but no buyers. Is it me they want to say hello to, or is it the free candy and ballpoint pens?"

"I'm sure it's your charm and beauty," I said, adding, "I really enjoyed the trip, and I wish I didn't have to leave early."

"How's Dad?"

"Not good," I said, explaining the clinical circumstances to Gita. "Unfortunately you, like me, know too much."

"I'm so sorry, David."

I had dinner with my family at home that night. Mom was there, along with five of my daughters, two sons-in-law, and several of my grandchildren. My mother had requested Chinese food, which we had ordered from Kikar Tel-Aviv here in Miami Beach. Mom displayed a strong appetite, if she were seeking nutrition not just for herself, but for my father as well. Although sadness had permeated my visit at Sylvester, here at home, at my dining room table, I could palpate the love and concern that was directed toward my mother, who would soon become a widow.

After dinner, I returned to Sylvester with Rachel. As we entered Dad's room, I saw tears in her eyes.

"The Captain has received his enemas," Radcliff said, "and this evening he passed some stool and gas. I believe his belly is less tense."

Dad's belly was, in fact, less distended. The head of the bed was more elevated than it had been that morning, and Dad was moving a bit, having made peace with the tethering Naso-gastric tube and IV line. Dad displayed a weak smile, and as a parent myself,
I knew it came from a place that supersedes distress.

"How's Red, Gorgeous?" Dad said.

"He's good, studying very hard, at your alma mater, the University of Miami Law School. Zayde," Rachel added softly, "Ethan and I really want you at our wedding."

"I'll be there, Rachel," Dad said, although I knew he meant in spirit.

From the corner of the room, I watched the two of them chat awhile about the University of Miami and about Rachel's menu plans for the reception, even though it was a meal Dad knew he wouldn't share. But his courage didn't waiver as he lifted Rachel's spirits with these moments.

The dictionary defines "courage" as moral or mental strength emanating from the heart in the face of adversity, danger, or hardship. It is a reflection of a person's character. I believe my father had accepted his fate. On this, the day after his eight-sixth birthday, my father, embodied courage despite being bound to a hospital bed by tubes, wires, and disease.

So at the age of eighty-six years and one day, my father continued to face his terminal fight with grace and dignity. Six years earlier, at the age of eighty, he taught me the most important lesson of my professional life.

In June of 2000, Mount Sinai Medical Center, founded in 1946, decided to purchase Miami Heart Institute, established in 1944. The merger between the two hospitals, about a mile apart in Miami Beach, would be effective midnight of July 1st. This happened after many months of confidential discussion between the administrative leadership of the two hospitals. The transaction was approved by the City of Miami Beach, with temporary financing for the approximately $70 million purchase price coming from the City of Miami Beach. The transaction still required the approval of the Heath Advisory Board and the Miami Beach Commission for the permanent financing. Under the plan, within the first year, Miami Beach would induce the issuance of $250 million in hospital bonds, which would pay off prior debt, along with the $70 million, at a reduced rate of interest, thus saving Mt. Sinai some $6 million annually.

On Friday June 30th, as I scrubbed for an aortic valve replacement, my secretary brought me a certified letter, which she insisted required my immediate attention. I dried my hands and took the letter over to the surgical scheduling desk. The gist of the document was this: I had one month to complete my clinical obligations to my patients at Miami Heart Institute. On August 1st, I would no longer have privileges in cardiac surgery at the new Mt. Sinai/Miami Heart facility.

By this time, I had been practicing for nineteen years. In fact, in 1999 I had been the busiest cardiovascular and thoracic surgeon, both in terms of number of cases and hospital admissions, at Miami Heart. Perhaps equally important, I was the main author of a series of papers establishing the mammary artery conduit as the preferred method in coronary bypass surgery. I presented these findings, on behalf of my former group at Miami Heart, at national meetings from 1985 through 1995. This was pioneering both in technique and long-term results, and represented Miami Heart's most important scientific contribution to the academic community, and it helped solidify our international reputation.

I finished my surgery that afternoon and began a troubled July 4th weekend. As I investigated this cataclysmic event in my professional career, I received no explanation from the powers that be, and no apologies for the subsequent upheaval in my personal and professional life. I received little support from my former colleagues at Miami Heart. To my knowledge, I would be the only cardiac surgeon excluded from practicing in the new combined facility. The other cardiac surgeons, who had been independent at the old Miami Heart Institute, would now become employees of

Mt. Sinai's chief of cardiac surgery, who had participated on Mt. Sinai's strategic committee to acquire Miami Heart.

That Sunday, I attended a kickboxing class with Gita. Always athletic, I had only recently ceased playing pickup basketball at Polo Park. Over time, the opponents had gotten younger and more aggressive. After a few ankle injuries and finger sprains, I acknowledged the possibility that a severe hand injury could end my career. As the Miami Heart merger played out, I was fifty-one. Around this time, kickboxing was emerging as a popular vehicle for aerobic exercise. In my effort to address my anger physically, I was probably overzealous in the high-kicking exercise, and in the process, I injured my lower back but completed the class. Over the next twenty-four hours, the pain developed into a constant radiation from my buttocks into my right thigh. Over the next two days, July 3rd and 4th, I took anti-inflammatories and muscle relaxants and adhered to strict bedrest. An MRI later that week documented a lumbar-5, sacral-1 right-sided disc herniation, which explained my sciatic pain, but I was determined to complete my busy July schedule of elective surgeries. As of the first day of August, I faced an uncertain future, but for the month of July, I committed myself to serving my patients and completing my tenure at Miami Heart.

Indeed, despite unrelenting pain and a limp developing from atrophy of my right calf muscle, I fulfilled my surgical obligations. Now my major concern was economic. I needed to find a new facility where I could rebuild my practice, but my herniated disc had not improved, and the weakness in my right leg suggested the need for surgical decompression.

Since the June 30th letter, I had received only vague responses to my multiple inquiries regarding my termination. Then and now, I have maintained that a monopoly that eliminates a patient's choice of physician is inherently wrong. The termination of a physician's privileges should be subject only to peer review. The record shows that in my nineteen years at Miami Heart, my clinical performance had been exemplary. My ouster had been a business decision, but I couldn't understand the economic basis. My office records indicated that in the previous year I had been responsible for nearly $5 million in gross revenues from hospital admissions and outpatient services.

I had been elected secretary and treasurer of the Miami Heart Institute Executive Committee in the preceding term, but no fellow members volunteered to fight this injustice with me. I had been a popular surgical consultant, and my referring physicians expressed concern, but the majority were reserved in action, probably out of fear of repercussion.

I felt so alone, and my professional confidence was shaken. For an instant, I believed that I was not good enough to practice heart surgery at the new entity. Demoralized, I accepted the verdict as I prepared to reestablish my surgical practice elsewhere. I tapped into my savings to meet my economic responsibilities, which included my family, Dr. Naaman Abdullah, who was then my associate, and other members of my office. Gita's love and belief in me, my commitment to nurturing my children, and my need to reestablish my career and my self-esteem were all motivating factors.

On August 1st, after completing my last month at Miami Heart, I called Dr. Barth Green, chief of neurosurgery at Jackson Memorial, who had treated me since my back injury. I indicated that I was admitting myself for surgery. A subsequent MRI reconfirmed the pathology, and with my muscle atrophy and neurological deficit, Dr. Green added me to his elective schedule for the following day. The afternoon of my surgery, Gita, my daughters, my parents, and my brothers assembled in my private room. I recall telling the nurse who pre-medicated me that my wife Gita, who has no medical training, is in charge of all injections. I was kidding, of course, but I enjoyed all the attention. By then I had received an injection of Toradol, a moderate pain reliever, but my words both eased the tension in the room and reaffirmed the intimacy I share with Gita.

As they wheeled my gurney toward the operating room, I saw my father in tears, and I overheard Robert ask him, "Dad, why are you crying."

"You should never have to know why," my father said.

I held Gita's hand, watching the ceiling tiles go by, and said, "I love you all. I'll see you in a few hours."

Chapter 14: A Time to Act

At fifty, when you're a surgeon encountering back surgery, there's always the fear that your career is over and that you're facing an extended retirement and a reliance on disability insurance. For me, this would be the kiss of death. Being productive is the only life I've known, and I couldn't accept anything less than a stellar outcome.

Thanks to the Toradol, my mind was befuddled, but I was seeing some things more clearly. Gita was my soul mate, of course, and I believe she experienced my fears along with me.

That day I underwent a microdiscectomy of my lumbar-5 and sacral-1 herniated disk. I was discharged the following day, and six days later, I began performing surgery as a cardiac surgery attending at Cedars Medical Center.

Many of my first patients had followed me across the Bay from Miami Beach, but by October, Cedars physicians were calling me and Naaman for consults. Within eighteen months the number of surgeries had increased by about thirty percent, whereas most Miami-Dade programs had realized a decrease in the number of cases. Furthermore, the Cedars mortality rate for cardiac surgery decreased by about one-half during this period.

During my years at Miami Heart Institute, I had achieved among the lowest mortality rates of my cardiovascular colleagues in Florida, and I have continued this success over the past seven years in the hospitals where I now practice. Starting in 2000, I helped Hospital Corporation of America (HCA) build its open-heart program at Cedars, and in 2003, I was the signatory on the "certificate of need" for heart surgery at HCA's Aventura facility, where I've continued to practice. Also in 2003, I was recruited by Baptist Health to become Chief of Cardiac Surgery at South Miami Hospital. In the past two years, my partner Dr. Naaman Abdullah and I have achieved the lowest mortality in South Florida— according to the Florida Board of Cost Containment—an accomplishment the Baptist Health System has featured in its promotional campaign.

In the months that followed my ouster from Miami Heart, I detected a changing mood in my father. Initially he was concerned about my back injury, surgery, and recovery. In September, I committed myself to twice-weekly physical therapy, and worked harder than I had in years.

Dad is proud of my determination and focus, and he believes in my future success, but all along I've sensed his smoldering outrage. "You'll build a bigger practice, David," he says to me at my house in early November 2000 at a Sunday afternoon barbecue. We're standing on the dock, watching a pair of cigarette boats speed by. Dad's wearing shorts, leather loafers, a monogrammed Crescent Heights polo shirt, and a baseball cap with an emblem of the Israeli Navy. "But this is an injustice, and I take it personally."

"Dad, it's been a whirlwind summer of unexpected sad endings and preventable injuries, and, thank God, promising beginnings. Why distract myself from this new opportunity at Cedars? Is it worth the inevitable disharmony just to make a point?"

"David, I came to Miami Beach in 1930. We've built our family and lived our lives here. All of my sons went to college in the Northeast and you all returned. You must fight for your right to perform heart surgery here in Miami Beach."

"Dad, I have to meet my financial obligations to my family. Secondly, I have no support. Mount Sinai is an unyielding Goliath."

"David, your family will always be there for you, and if necessary, your brothers and I will chip in. What's more important is that you do the right thing."

"Dad, I can't turn back the clock. I can't practice here anymore."

Everyone else is under the veranda, enjoying the buffet. The aroma of barbecued steak and chicken waft over us, I want to be with them and enjoy a hearty meal. I place my arm on Dad's shoulder. "I'll think about it," I say.

"I want more than thoughts, David. You've ignored this long enough. It's time to act."

"Dad, is it wise to grandstand for something that cannot be? We don't need the turmoil of a losing battle. What's the value in that?"

"The outcome is not relevant to the issue of justice. The issue now is not whether you will again practice in Miami Beach at the combined Mount Sinai and Miami Heart Institute—that is not necessary. What does matter is your courage to fight the injustice."

"Dad, I believe I'm a courageous person."

"You're not, David."

"Courage is mustering your commitment to do difficult things," I explain, trying to refute his criticism.

"That's partially true," Dad says, "but courage also requires doing the right thing. Outcomes won't always be favorable, but you must fight do things for justice. Even if losing is inevitable, you win by standing up for what you believe in and for what is right. I don't care whether you practice again in Miami

Beach, but you must defend your right to practice here, which reflects your family's commitment to this community."

Over the next three months, I addressed the Miami Beach Health Advisory Board and the City Commission. Although I had a personal grievance, my presentations emphasized Mount Sinai's failure to fulfill its commitment to the best interests of the city, most notably their decision to establish a monopoly in the area of cardiac surgery.

Russell was instrumental in providing strategic and technical support in building the case that it was in the best interests of the citizens of Miami Beach that Mount Sinai be held accountable to the promises it made when presenting the merger to the Miami Beach City Commission. This included preserving the emergency departments at both Mount Sinai and Miami Heart, permitting all physicians from Miami Heart Institute to practice at the combined facility, and maintaining Miami Heart's reduced rates for the care of Miami Beach pensioners and their surviving spouses. Prior to our presentations before the City, Mount Sinai had reneged on all of these promises.

Some two hundred community members filled the Commission chambers. Many of the attendees understood my situation and the injustice to the population at large. Others, including board members from Mt. Sinai, believed that the hospital's survival was in jeopardy.

I fondly remember the late afternoon and evening meetings in the Miami Beach Commission Chamber. Along the way, many friendships were strengthened, some were tested, and others were born. Throughout these public sessions, my father, dressed in a formal black suit, sat in the front row beside my mother. Although he did not speak from the podium, his presence exerted a tangible intensity. And throughout these proceedings, I took pride in the eloquence of my speeches, which I knew were testimony to my father's persistence as my mentor. I realized that my father's smile reflected a moral victory, and pride in our family's demonstration of unity in cause and principle. His presence in the chamber was that of a man of strength, accomplishment, honor, and purpose. The experience, beginning with that June 30th letter, continuing with my father's admonishment of my cowardice on the dock, and culminating with the proceedings before the Commission, reinforced Dad's doctrine that victory can be achieved through loss, and that dignity can be preserved through adherence to principle.

Ultimately, the Commission supported Mount Sinai's decisions, enabled the hospital bonds, and suggested that I pursue my grievance in a different venue. Although I was never invited back to practice cardiac surgery at the merged facility, now known as Mount Sinai Medical Center & Miami Heart Institute, I wish it well, as the people of Miami Beach deserve a center of excellence.

First thing Monday morning, I visited Dad at Sylvester before heading down to South Miami for a 7:30 coronary bypass procedure. At that early hour, he was still under the influence of his sleeping meds. His substantial abdominal distention remained, with incomplete decompression following the enemas. When I came back in the afternoon, Dr. Rosenblatt informed me that Dad had signed a DNR, or "Do Not Resuscitate" document earlier in the day.

"It was his idea. He's refusing further treatment."

I sat alone with Dad, holding his hand. "I'm ready to go," he said.

It disturbed me that he hadn't discussed the DNR with me, as I had been involved in all other medical decisions thus far. Was he simply a father trying to protect his family from the agony of his decision? I had to keep reminding myself that this experience was not about me.

"Dad, if we could improve your abdominal distention, perhaps with a colonoscopy, would you consider it?"

"I have no future." Although Dr. Rosenblatt had consulted a general surgeon for a lower endoscopy, Dad had refused to see him. "When are we going home?"

I visited Dad at Sylvester three times on Tuesday. In the afternoon, despite a limited response to the enemas, he was unconvinced that it mattered anymore. That night, his distended abdomen was back to where it had been that morning.

"Where have you been, David? It's time to end it. Let's go home."

"We'll follow your wishes, but let's wait a couple of days to see if there is any improvement."

"I'm not interested."

"Dad, I'm with you, but the house isn't ready. We need a day to organize and to get some things in order."

"OK, but tomorrow is the deadline."

On Wednesday I completed an open-heart operation and a pacemaker procedure at South Miami, and then I went to Aventura for a consult. I stopped by and saw Dad about 3 p.m. Russell was there, and he was pleased to inform me that Dad had passed a large bowel movement subsequent to several enemas. Then came a large spontaneous stool, which had given Dad significant relief. Still, he was emphatic about going home.

"Let's end it," he said. "I want to go home and end it."

I looked at Russell, not sure if he'd heard this before, and the look on his face assured me that he had not. Russell turned away and stared out the window.

Out in the hall, I said, "Russell, I'll bring him home tomorrow, but first I need to speak with Rosenblatt about ordering hospice care. This will permit us to use narcotics, if necessary for pain management."

"I don't know how you do it, David, dealing with illness every day and night. I know I couldn't."

"It's a matter of habit," I said. "I really don't know any better."

Driving north on I-95 to Aventura to see patients, I contemplated Dad's words. With his inability to move, and with his compromised digestive capability, he was doomed to days and nights of persistent abdominal distention. This was the clinical manifestation of his loss of independence and dignity. Dad had decided that in this fashion, life was not worth living. I had to be his son. The time had come for me to understand his wishes.

That night I met Gita at a restaurant in North Miami Beach for a reception celebrating the wedding of her best friend's daughter, which had taken place in New York the previous weekend. I then returned to Sylvester. Radcliff was spending a second shift with Dad. Radcliff was half asleep, and I couldn't blame him, but he perked up and updated me on Dad's vital signs: a pulse rate of 70, blood pressure of 130/70, and respirations of twenty per minute. Dad seemed to be resting comfortably and his abdomen appeared smaller. He opened his eyes and I held his hand.

"Dad, how are you doing?"

"Not too much pain."

"You'll sleep well tonight, and I will see you in the morning. You're going home tomorrow. Do you prefer to ride in my car or in an ambulance?"

"An ambulance would be better, David, but with you."

"I'll arrange it for tomorrow evening. By then, the house will be ready."

Driving home, exhausted from the day, I kept thinking about Dad's decision to come home via ambulance. He had no confidence that he could sit up for the thirty minute ride home. The time had come to minimize my elective surgical schedule.

I had now entered uncharted waters that conflicted with my code of conduct as a physician. While I would not facilitate my father's death, I had agreed to avoid any attempts to prolong his life. I felt as if I, the child, had become the father, as the executor of his wishes. Despite this terminal illness, my father remained a grown man, a dying man, yes, but always the Captain, and always in charge.

Wednesday morning I visited Dad at 7 a.m. before shooting over to South Miami Hospital for a double valve replacement. Dad's vital signs were stable, his abdomen was less distended, and upon palpation, I felt a mass near his umbilicus or belly button. This undoubtedly was a malignant lymph node, a further reflection of widespread metastasis.

At the house, Russell and Al B were organizing Dad's room with a hospital bed and other durable medical equipment. In addition, Robert was supervising Mom's home care, making sure she kept up with her breathing treatments.

"Dad, the house will be ready this afternoon. We'll go home around 7:00, after my surgery.

"Not a minute later," he said.

During the open-heart procedure, I struggled to control the patient's bleeding as a consequence of coagulopathy, requiring plasma and platelet transfusions. Finally the patient improved, and she was brought to the intensive care unit in stable condition. I returned to Sylvester at 6 p.m., where I spoke with Dr. Rosenblatt at the nurse's station.

"Thanks for waiting," I said.

"Russell and Al B were here much of the afternoon, keeping an eye on your father and working on their laptops. I also spoke with Robert over the phone. Your father is adamant about going home. Sometimes a few more days of gastrointestinal decompression can make a big difference, but your father is probably right in that his future is dismal."

"I guess it's time for home hospice," I said.

"I'll make the arrangements," Dr. Rosenblatt said.

I met my Mom and Gita in Dad's room. I kissed each of them and observed their teary smiles. "Gita, if you don't mind, please take Mom and Radcliff home and I'll ride in the ambulance with Dad. I'll get my car later tonight."

About 6:30, we left Sylvester as a cold spell enveloped Miami. The two medics had transported Dad on a gurney from his room, down the elevator, and outside to the waiting ambulance. There was sweetness in holding Dad's hand, which conveyed love. He had always been the protector, and just as I was coming to terms with becoming *his* protector—as his medical advocate—this role was coming to an end. After the paramedics positioned the gurney on the right-hand side of the ambulance, the two of them sat up front. I sat on the bench beside Dad in the passenger compartment. He wore nasal prongs connected to a portable oxygen tank, and a Foley catheter was draining his bladder.

We were about an hour past sunset and the chill in the air had found its way into the ambulance. I pulled a white blanket from the shelf and placed it around Dad.

"Thank you, David."

"I thank you, Dad, for so many things."

As the ambulance crossed the Julia Tuttle Expressway, heading toward Miami Beach, Dad and I stared through the back window, revealing a narrow patch of Miami skyline, particularly the lights emanating from the new condominiums along Biscayne Boulevard. I glanced up and down at the clear compartments containing all manner of lifesaving equipment from intubation and respiratory equipment, defibrillation paddles, intravenous tubing and plastic bags containing various solutions, to basic sterile trays, gauze packs, and plastic splints. I was an expert in the deployment of each lifesaving item on those shelves, but it was all useless to me that night.

"I've always loved traveling with you," Dad said, "especially those long summer Navy trips. We always had the best time at night."

"There was always so much to do and see," I said.

"It was the greatest time, because at once I had the opportunity to demonstrate love of country, love of your mother, and love for my sons," Dad said, shifting his back slightly on the narrow gurney, probably a futile attempt to turn onto his side. "I'd like something to drink."

"We have apple juice at the house," I said, frustrated that I couldn't oblige such a simple and innocent request. The ambulance cruised along the causeway, keeping pace with the traffic, the weight of the heavy vehicle wafting up and down despite the smooth surface of the road. Dad continued to peer out the back window toward the skyline, but this time, I locked on Dad's beautiful but glassy green eyes, which conveyed both relief and resolve, and I knew he was happy to be going home.

At the house, the two paramedics pulled the stretcher onto the driveway. On cue, the legs popped into place as Dad emerged from the patient compartment. Mom and Radcliff, who had been waiting in the front alcove, came forward to welcome Dad. Mom kissed Dad on the lips. "Hymie, you look good."

"Welcome home, Captain," Radcliff said.

Inside, we got Dad positioned on his recliner in Mom's room, where I brought him a glass of apple juice from the kitchen. He drank that down, and so I brought him another, after which Dad said he needed to urinate.

"Dad, you have a Foley catheter, which is draining all the urine from your bladder. It's giving you the sensation of needing to urinate."

"No, I want to stand and urinate."

Radcliff and I helped him to his feet.

Within a few unsteady seconds, Dad commanded, "I want to sit down."

But once again, Dad insisted that he wanted to stand. We went back and forth like this at least a dozen times over the next five minutes or so. Each time Dad stood, he looked forward, blankly, as if not sure what to do next. "I want to sit!"

I was puzzled by this illogical behavior, but at least he was exercising his atrophied legs for the first time in the past four days.

"Would you like to spend the night in the chair?" I asked.

"I want to sleep in my bed and I want my sleeping pill now."

Gita arrived at the house to welcome my father back home and to drive me back to Sylvester for my car. Having watched Dad consume two cans of apple juice, and realizing that I hadn't eaten anything since lunch, I took a can of Dad's chocolate flavored Boost from the refrigerator.

"Not as tasty as the strawberry," I said, trying to inject a bit of levity to the grim scene.

"I want to die." My father said this looking at me, but I sensed that he was mainly saying this to Mom.

"Hymie, don't talk like that," Mom said.

I'd heard Dad utter these biting words several times before, but I could tell that this was Mom's first time.

After picking up my car at Sylvester, I still needed to drive up to Aventura to finish my rounds, but first Radcliff and I helped Dad into his new hospital bed, which we hoped would help us position him for maximum comfort. In addition, we had acquired a portable suction device to help clear Dad's secretions. As Radcliff tucked Dad in, we discussed the new equipment. Other than the removal of his old bed, the room looked pretty much as we'd left it, although the air conveyed a hint of scented disinfectant spray. The TV was off, and to my surprise, he never did ask me to turn it on.

"Thank you," I said to Radcliff, who faced a long night in the recliner beside Dad's bed.

At the dining room table, I sat with my mother and Gita.

"Is he going to be all right?" Mom said.

"Mom, do you understand what's happening?" I said, feeling my patience tested. I hated myself for it, but I sensed a hint of anger in my voice.

"Of course I do," Mom said.

"The length of time he'll be home could be very short, possibly days, even hours." I paused for a moment. I needed to clarify her understanding. "This is why we agreed to initiate hospice. They'll come tomorrow, Mom. They can help us legally ease Dad's pain and suffering."

"I understand, and I'm prepared," Mom said, which were lies, of course, lies we tell ourselves and those we love. There's no preparing for this, and of course, no understanding.

After midnight, I was driving home from Aventura when Radcliff called me. "Captain's oxygen level is less than 70%. He has been restless, and over the past hour, he's had me help him sit up and lie down, back and forth, at least fifty times."

"Increase the oxygen to five liters per minute and administer one Ambien to control his restlessness."

I arrived at the house around 1 a.m. By then, probably thirty minutes since the Ambien, Dad was sleeping. Yochai was seated in the chair between the hospital bed and the bathroom, reading the Book of Psalms. Radcliff sat in the recliner, between the hospital bed and the entrance to the room.

Mom was in bed, her room lit by the glow of the computer monitor where Russell was reading and responding to his email. Louisiana was asleep in the chair at Mom's bedside.

Russell turned the chair toward me, as I leaned down and hugged him.

"It's good that you're here," I said. "Dad needs us now."

"How much longer?" my brother said.

"Probably a couple of days—at best, maybe a week."

"I'll spend tonight here," Russell said. "I'll call you if anything happens."

I got home at 2 a.m. When I got into bed, Gita opened her eyes. "How is he?"

"He's not oxygenating well," I said. I leaned over and kissed my wife goodnight.

"You're a wonderful son," Gita said.

Two hours later, the house phone rang.

Chapter 15: Sleeping Fast

In the operating room I'm known for saying we need to "make up time," which generally refers to speeding up the steps of the less critical stages of an operation, such as closure. At home, I've often referred to "sleeping fast," which reflects my attempt to convince my mind and body to feel rested after inadequate sleep. Both are illogical concepts of doing more within a limited, fixed time period.

"Hello … Russell?" I said, emerging from my two hours of "fast sleep."

"Dr. Galbut, your valve replacement patient from yesterday isn't doing well. Her blood pressure, oxygen levels, and hematocrit are dangerously low. Also, her chest tube drainage has increased to 600cc's of blood the past hour."

"She has tamponade," I said to the nurse, referring to a condition of excessive blood compressing the heart. "Please call the operating room and prepare the patient to go back to surgery for the removal of clot or bleeding."

Ten minutes later I was in my car and driving to South Miami, considering my ironic sense of relief. When the phone rang, I expected to hear Russell's voice conveying Dad's rapid deterioration—or worse. Despite the urgency of my patient's condition, the likelihood was high that the surgery would have a favorable outcome. It was a matter over which I at least had *some* control.

In the operating room, I found no active bleeding, and after evacuating the clot, the patient's heart function rapidly improved. I closed the patient's chest with steel wires on the sternum and absorbable sutures on the soft tissue above. She returned to the intensive care unit in stable condition. I arrived back home at 7 a.m. for another hour of "fast sleep" on that already eventful Friday morning.

At 9 a.m. I went to my parents' house to meet with two nurses from Douglas Gardens Hospice.

"They've been here an hour," Mom said, "observing Dad. He is not interested in talking with them. They have checked his vital signs and reviewed all his medications. They're ready to talk with you, David, and they have papers for us to sign."

About an hour later, Russell returned to the house and joined the meeting, the gist of which was that dying is a process, and that it's ethical to use medication to minimize suffering in the terminal patient. It is less accepted, and arguably unethical, to use these medications to hasten death.

To live is to die, and I understood the hospice philosophy, but resented their intrusion into the intensity of our moment. I knew that legally the responsibility for prescribing narcotics resided with the hospice team, and that was, in my mind, to be their only mission. The responsibility belonged to Robert and me, as Dad's medically trained sons, to administer his terminal care. I wanted to be hands-on, accompanying Dad as he completed his final journey.

After the meeting, I returned to South Miami Hospital and found my patient to be doing well. In my office I prepared for my upcoming hiatus. I cancelled my elective schedule and arranged for Naaman to oversee the practice in my absence.

Heading home around 3 p.m. that Friday afternoon, I was exhausted as I drove up I-95 toward the causeway. In the past thirty-six hours I had logged less than three hours of sleep, and but I hoped to catch up later that evening. I needed to visit Dad before Shabbat, as Gita was preparing dinner at our house for our children and their families.

In my parents' house, I spoke with Mom in the dining room. "How's Dad today?"   "He's eating very little, and he's so hoarse he can barely speak."

"Has he complained of any pain?"

"No," Mom said. She poured each of us half a glass of Dr Pepper. "David, the lollipop medication that the hospice nurse ordered…is that morphine?"

"Yes, it's Roxinal, a strong narcotic that is easily administered and absorbed like a lollipop."

"I don't want it given unless Dad is really suffering. I do not want to hasten his end."

"Mom, I agree. God is in charge."

"He is the true judge of the world," Mom said.

"The Captain is up!" Radcliff said, coming out of Dad's room. "He's thirsty and he wants apple juice."

"Hymie, I'm coming!" Mom shouted, her loud voice reminding me of the good work she'd been doing with her respiratory therapy and her excitement over being able to provide a personal service to my father.

Dad drank the glass of apple juice Mom held to his lips. Despite the cancer that had riddled his retroperitoneum and liver and atrophied all of his major muscle groups, he still appeared handsome and powerful, as if with a bit of grooming and a starched, classic white Navy uniform adorned with eepaulettes of his captain's rank, he could be on the bridge of a Naval destroyer, navigating the treacherous waters of the Atlantic Coast.

"Can I get you anything else, Hymie?" Mom said, placing the juice glass on the bedside table near the telephone.

"I'm going to rest now, Bessie. Thank you."

Mom returned to her room to take her medication and to put on her vibration vest. Like my father, Mom exhibited a soldier's discipline, which she displayed through her meticulous attention to her medical routine. Her purpose now was to remain strong for her husband.

"Turn up the TV, David," my father said.

I sat in his bedside chair, took the remote control from the sheet beside him, and upped the volume. It was now about 4:15. On CNN, Wolf Blitzer reported on the day's events from the war in Iraq. Dad wasn't focusing on that, but I could see his gaze aimed at the plethora of assorted family photos on the wall. "How much longer, David? I want it to be over."

I understood Dad's desire to be relieved of this miserable condition in which he was so dependent for the simplest of tasks. "It's happening," I assured him, thinking how time has a way of speeding by when you're running out of it, "very soon, and you will be surrounded by your family."

Dad's swollen hand gripped mine, and he closed his eyes. I spent nearly an hour in and out of sleep, catching glimpses of the news and enjoying the aroma of the hot food Gita had brought from our house. Around 5:20 she came into the bedroom, kissed me, and said it was time for us to get going.

On my way out, I spoke with the hospice nurse. I recommended IV fluid administration of approximately one liter in the evening while Dad rested. Despite the occasional glass of apple juice, he wasn't adequately hydrated. Whenever the moment came, I didn't want my father to die thirsty.

Driving the few blocks home, I felt a little guilty for my joy over the prospect of spending Shabbat with my wife, children, and grandchildren. Life is not lived in an orderly pattern, but rather it delivers a potpourri of happy and sad moments, and perhaps that's how we get by.

Sabbath began, thus ending the longest of days. During dinner, I felt a melancholy that comes from physical exhaustion and sadness, but this was tempered by the playful exuberance of my grandchildren, the eldest of whom would certainly remember Dad, and I took comfort in knowing that he had held and loved all of them.

After dinner, Gita and I walked back to my parents' house, where we greeted Robert and Rita. Mom, who was dressed in a long black skirt and a white blouse for Shabbat, thanked Gita for preparing the delicious dinner. "The chicken soup and roast beef were delicious, Gita."

"Daddy's not eating," Robert said to me.

"I know," I said. "Other than a taste of ice cream or a small glass of apple juice now and then, Dad hasn't been eating since this last admission to Sylvester."

"We'll use the Roxinal if Dad develops any pain or if his respiratory rate increases to the point where he's suffering," Robert said.

"That makes sense," I said.

Mom, who was listening to this exchange, added, "But like I told David earlier, I don't want this medicine to shorten Dad's life."

Before leaving, I kissed Dad goodnight. I had considered spending the night, but after reviewing Dad's vital signs with Radcliff, I was confident that tonight wouldn't be the night. Dad's blood pressure was 120 over 70, his pulse was 90, his respiratory rate was 28, his oxygen level was 93%, and he was still communicating. Anything less and I would have walked Gita home and returned to spend the night at Dad's side.

"Call me at home at any hour if there is any variation, even minor, in his vitals," I told Radcliff.

"I'm on it, Dr. Dave," Radcliff said.

I thanked him, aware that his performance had gone way beyond the call of duty.

We walked home that cool Miami Beach night, the four of us, in a slight drizzle, wearing raincoats.

"This is the great chain of a family's life," Robert said as we spoke about our children and their livelihoods. "I believe we're both working too hard."

"But what can we do? We love our children."

"That's true," Robert said. "Dad set a great example."

About halfway back to my house, Gita and I said goodbye to Robert and Rita in their driveway. Continuing home, Gita and I held hands, and I thought about how lucky I was, how God had given me so much, and how it all started with my parents.

In the morning, I visited Dad at 7:00. He was sleeping and did not appear to be in any distress. At 7:30 services with Jamie, I struggled to concentrate on the service, as my prayers centered on my father. Many friends inquired about his status. My words were few, but I believe the despair on my face and my despondent posture revealed a vivid response to their questions. I would never again see his smile as he greeted me in the sanctuary as if I were the most important person in the world when I arrived late after my early morning rounds. I would never again see the warmth he conveyed upon greeting members of the synagogue community. I would never again feel the sense of pride of sitting in a row with my father, myself, my children, and their children. And I would never again hold his hand as I prayed.

Shabbat lunch at home with Gita, Riki, Jamie, Elle, Elana, Rachel, and Nili was solemn, but Shabbat joy was present, courtesy of our grandchildren. Elle's daughters, Yakira and Eme, ran around the Shabbat table, celebrating their young innocence. Riki's children Motti, Zeev, and Leor played with a tennis ball and intermittently returned to the table for a taste of *chulent,* a medley of beef, beans, and potatoes continuously slow-cooked in a crock pot since Friday. The two newborns, Noa and Kaelly rested in their bassinettes.

"I want to thank all of you for being so kind to my father," I said to my assembled family. "The past few months have been trying, and I'm very proud of all of you."

"How much longer, Dad?" Rachel asked me.

"The next couple of days," I said, noticing tears in Elana's eyes. Of my six daughters, she had probably built the closest relationship with my father. During her last two years of high school, my father had become my surrogate in supervising her education, particularly during the Mt. Sinai saga.

"I learned so much from him," Elana said, "but sometimes it was difficult because he's such a perfectionist. He taught me how to learn with the basic principle of tell, tell, and retell."

"He enjoyed helping you with school the way he helped me in all my endeavors," I said. "You added pleasure, purpose, and maybe a bit of a challenge, but he loved every minute of it."

"Zaide was the greatest teacher I ever had," Elana said.

"Not only did he make sure Elle got her nursing license," Jamie said, "but he also helped me. Sometimes his manner was a little harsh, but he always believed in my ability, and I knew how much he loved me and our children. My biggest challenge was explaining to him about a new phone system for the Hebrew Homes. After an hour of dialogue, he called me an idiot, but in a way that assured me that he still loved me."

"He was only kidding," Elle said.

"Anyway," Jaime said, "I'm not sure he ever understood the full capability of what he bought, but he used what I told him to acquire the system at half the price."

"Zaide was a master carpenter," Miki contributed. "He helped me build my first sukkah, and we worked together repairing the ark in the synagogue. And I was amazed at Zaide's ability to design and build your office here in the house with all those perfectly fitting wall panels and shelves. He could've had his own carpentry TV show."

"*Hymie, the Builder*," Gita said, to which all of us laughed, knowing she was right.

Nili started crying. "My future husband will never meet Zaide," she said.

"He'll learn about him from you—and all of us," Riki said. "We won't stop talking about him anytime soon."

"I owe Zaide a lot," Yochai said. "Thanks to him, tomorrow I'm catering the annual barbecue picnic for the employees of the Hebrew Homes. I'm expecting almost six hundred people."

"Zaide is very proud of you, Yochai," I said.

Last August, my father had personally selected the beautiful Emilia Earhart Park in Opa Locka, adjacent to Mt. Sinai Cemetery. He had worked with Yochai, organizing a cost-efficient menu that would please the guests—and generate a small profit. Originally, the event was scheduled for late October, but Hurricane Wilma cancelled those plans. I considered the irony of a celebration for the Hebrew Homes, for which my father had been chairman of the board the past several years, taking place at the moment of his accelerated decline.

After more reminiscing about my father, we sang Sabbath songs and then recited the grace after meals.

After lunch, I walked over to Mom and Dad's house with Gita. My children and grandchildren would meet us there in the late afternoon and we would conclude Shabbat together. Gita sat with Mom during her respiratory treatment with the inhaler and vibrating vest. She held Mom's arthritic hands as my mother's body shook during the ten-minute treatment. Throughout the treatment, her second of the day, Mom coughed and expectorated mucus into tissues, which she tossed into the nearby wastebasket.

I walked into Dad's room, where he lay in his rented hospital bed. His eyes were closed and he did not react to my presence. I held his hand and softly greeted him. The vigil had begun.

Radcliff rose from the bedside chair. "The Captain has been like this most of the day and he has not eaten anything."

"Has he asked to drink anything?" I said.

"I've brought him apple juice several times and he refused it."

"Has he spoken at all?"

"A few words now and then, asking me to turn him."

"Dad, I'm with you," I said, louder now.

Dad nodded, his eyes remained closed, but I knew he recognized my presence as I stood to the right of his bed, holding his hand and caressing his shoulder.

I am no stranger when it comes to death. Statistically, a certain percentage of my patients will have a bad outcome, be it death, a stroke, a bad infection, or some other poor result. It's the nature of heart surgery. And when the outcome for a patient I've operated on is a fatality, I experience their death as a personal defeat. And while I understand the dying process physiologically,

I had never looked to see how the essence, or the soul, of a human being departs.

I'm not often privy to the real lives of my patients. I learn the basic facts of their circumstances, but I don't see them experiencing life. I don't see them at home, at work, at restaurants, on vacation, or with their families, celebrating their own birthdays, anniversaries, holidays, and religious observances. My focus is upon their illness and the possibility that I can improve their medical condition. While my father's death would not be my professional defeat, I was facing profound loss and untold sadness.

I'm seven years old, and I've recently gotten a beautiful Schwinn bicycle for my birthday. In Coral Gate, many kids hang together and ride bicycles fearlessly through our neighborhood. Five blocks from our house is the Woodlawn Cemetery. Most of it is still open space, a lot like the cemetery my father runs in Opa Locka. To us kids, Woodlawn is a great place to ride our bikes and play. I am probably the youngest member of our group. The other boys are up to about fourteen years old, so I'm usually following them. This particular day, we're crossing Southwest 16th Street, a pretty busy road that separates Woodlawn from our neighborhood. The kids ahead of me are going faster, and I'm pedaling with all my strength—about ten feet behind the last kid.

As they cross the large street, I follow along, without looking to my left.

The car that crashes into the front of my bicycle never stops. The guy, whoever it is, just keeps on going. I've been thrown about ten feet into the grass beside the road. My arms are scraped, my nose is bleeding all over my shirt, and my right shoulder and right hip are sore. I'm crying as I walk over to my bicycle at the edge of the road. My front wheel is twisted, the frame is bent, and bits of red paint from my bike have tattooed the asphalt. And like the driver of the car, none of the other kids look back.

I return home, holding up the front end of my bicycle, rolling it on its back wheel. By the time I reach my house, my nose stops bleeding, but my white T-shirt is covered in blood. I am fearful of my father's response. I know that money is tight. Our housekeeper with the funny accent calls my father at his office. He gets home in less than thirty minutes. "Besides your bloody nose and these other abrasions, does anything hurt?"

"No," I say as my father lifts my shirt and looks me over. He then lifts me in his arms, convincing me that I am safe.

"Daddy, I'm so sorry that I ruined your expensive gift."

Then I see my father's beautiful smile "That has no meaning to me. What matters is you." He puts me down and assesses the damage to the bike, which I left outside the front door

near the stoop. "We'll get this fixed. All it takes is money, but you
are our priceless treasure."

As I recalled those words, sitting alongside my dying
father, questioning whether I had sufficiently expressed my
gratitude and love.

"It's been like this all day," Radcliff said, responding to a
loud knock on the front door. "Many of the Captain's neighbors
and old friends have been stopping by."

I nodded. "Radcliff, you must be beat," I said, getting up.
"I'll tend to him tonight."

At the door, I greeted my parents' neighbors from down the
block. My mother had come to the door as well. She had clearly
lost more weight in recent weeks, the way her blouse and skirt
hung loosely from her tall frame.

"How is he?" the wife said. "Can we pay the Captain a
visit?"

"He's bad," Mom said, "but I'll tell him you came by."

During the last hour of the Sabbath, my brothers and I, and
our sons-in-law, completed prayers in the synagogue and then we
returned to my parents' house where we met our wives and
children and grandchildren for the conclusion of Shabbat. With

stars emerging in the Saturday night sky, we all stood at Dad's bedside and chanted Havdallah.

Then my brothers and I called our out-of-town children, informing them that it was time to come home. Then we all stood in Dad's room. Mom was there too, holding Dad's hand. She kissed his forehead, whispered how much she loved him. "Hymie, we'll only be apart temporarily. I'll follow you soon. I look forward to seeing you in heaven, and I know you'll wait for me. But now I want you to say the *Shema*." As my father listened, I knew where my mother was going. The *Shema,* the most important sentence in Judaism, confirms one's faith and belief in God's unity and the eternity of the Jewish people. It is traditionally the first sentence a Jewish child is taught and the last sentence a Jew speaks as death approaches.

In Hebrew, my mother said, with my father following, "Hear, O Israel, the Lord is our God, the Lord is One."

Rachel and Ethan stepped into the room. At the door, Mom said to all the grandchildren, "This is your opportunity to say goodbye to your Zaide before he can no longer hear us." Mom left the room and I stepped out with her. "David, I want Dad to give Ethan the medallion we put aside for him. It's important for Rachel."

From her closet, Mom retrieved the replica of Dad's Ten Commandments medallion, which had been made from a mold of the original, which still adorned Dad's neck after sixty-five years. My parents had commissioned these replicas for each son, grandson, and current and future husbands of the granddaughters.

My mother placed the replica medallion into Dad's hand, and together, she and I lifted his hand toward my future son-in-law.

"Ethan," Mom said, "Zaide is giving you this medallion today because he loves you and because he welcomes you as the newest member of the family."

In fact, this would be one of my father's final conscious acts, giving of love and giving of himself. Ethan held the medallion and said, "I've loved Rachel most of my life, I am proud to be a member of your family," and with a broken voice, he concluded, "And it's an honor to have this special gift."

When I was growing up, Dad asserted that his medallion had offered him protection. This beautiful handcrafted jewel contains the Ten Commandments, adorned by two royal lions within a circle. The upper part of the circle, which appears in Hebrew, contains a sentence from Psalms: "God will safeguard your going and coming from now until eternity." In the lower part of the circle appears a loose but meaningful translation: "Be guarded and protected."

Mom had given my father this medallion the year he left New Orleans to go to Navy Officer training school and then the

Pacific arena of World War II. She had purchased it from a New Orleans jeweler for about $35, which could have represented two weeks' pay at her bookkeeping job.

Mom caressed Dad's face, kissed him on the lips, and said, "I love you, Hymie."

Dad opened his eyes, just long enough to say, "I love you, *Batya*." And as my mother's Yiddish name lingered on his lips, he added, "Let's go."

After a vigorous life of eighty-six years, and surrounded by those whom he had most touched with his kindness, action, and love, the angel of death now hovered above my dad. Mercifully, he was now slipping into a coma.

Chapter 16: My Father's Final Journey

Since Dad's return home, the house had been lit day and night, much like an ICU or summer in Alaska. The exception was Mom's dimly lit bedroom, where she managed to get some much-needed sleep. Even as Mom slept, her bedroom office continued to serve as our center for email communication. Well into the night, the kitchen and dining room remained busy, and the large sofas in the living room offered us a spot for a brief nap or a place to converse softly.

After midnight came and went, Dad's labored respirations gave way to an irregular pattern of deeper and shallower breaths, medically referred to as Kussmaul breathing. At about 1 a.m., Dad's respirations became fewer but deeper, and his eyes opened widely, revealing a steady gaze at the ceiling. I stood there with my three brothers.

"What is Dad looking at?" Al B asked.

"It's a reflex, perhaps a consequence of his deep breathing," Robert said.

I agreed, but I also wondered whether Dad was watching his soul departing heavenward. Perhaps his mind had directed his physical being to prepare without fear, as had been the method of his life. I had never seen this dynamic before. Then again, maybe I had never looked.

"Should we give Dad some Roxinal for comfort?" Robert asked.

"Is he suffering?" Russell asked.

I didn't believe so, but I wanted to see if I could get a response from Dad. I leaned over, and in a loud but tender voice directly into his ear, I asked, "Dad, are you having any pain?"

He shook his head slightly, and the four of us heard him whisper, "No."

For the next hour, his eyes remained focused on the far half of the ceiling, beyond the fan and above the wall of family photos. In one, I spotted my father's finely dressed parents standing with *my* parents after their wedding in New Orleans. In our own way, perhaps each of us was trying to understand what our father may have been seeing.

Uncle Label, my mother's brother, whom we had alerted a bit earlier, arrived to say goodbye. He stood at my father's side, but only for a moment, and then he left the room in tears. "He's more dead than alive," Uncle Label said in the living room a few minutes later, after which he reviewed some aspects of Jewish law regarding matters of death, preparation for the world to come, and the funeral.

Until now, I had purposefully avoided speaking or reading about this subject, but I accepted the importance of learning my role as my father's son, and the Jewish continuity my brothers and I would now be responsible for maintaining.

"We'll have to watch your mother," Uncle Label said to me in the driveway. I understood his great love for my mother, his senior by eleven years, and a beacon of guidance in his life. "Our goal must be to preserve her health and maximize her longevity. It would be a mistake for her to travel beyond Miami." In other words, Mom should not attend the burial in Israel.

"I'll call you when the time comes," I said, pleased that my uncle agreed with my assessment that any airplane travel would jeopardize my mother's health.

It was now 2 a.m., and at my urging, my children left the house. I hugged and kissed each of them, thanking them for their kindness and love. With tears in their eyes, and broken hearts, they each went home. For the next hour, Gita remained with me as we sat in Dad's room, listening to a CD of King David's Psalms.

Gita had spent so many hours with my father waiting with him and attending to him—in hospital rooms, at doctors' offices, in the chemotherapy sessions, and here at the house. With tears in her eyes, she held my hand. "I've really grown to love your father."

"And he has loved you as a daughter," I said.

I brought Gita home, walked her inside, kissed her, thanked her for everything, and then I drove back to my parents' house. It was almost 3:30 a.m. Rita had returned and was now sitting with Robert on the living room sofa. Eric had arrived from New York City. Mom was sleeping in her room.

Russell was in the study, doing something on the computer. I sat with him and reviewed my printout of the obituary, which I had drafted six weeks earlier. When Rita came in to check on Mom, she joined us in front of the computer and helped us streamline our words.

Louisiana was dozing in the chair beside my mother. Al B had brought Nancy home. Eric was sitting beside Dad's bed, listening to the CD of Psalms, which I had placed on a continuous loop. Russell was now resting in my mother's room, and Rita was napping with Robert in the living room. I joined Eric in Dad's room, and as the night proceeded, we both prayed.

"Let's learn a little bit about this week's section from the Torah," Eric said. And so we reviewed the story of the exodus from Egypt, and in particular, the difference between Moses, who delivers God's message, and Pharaoh, who stubbornly refuses to let the Jewish people go, despite the plagues that destroy his kingdom. Finally, Eric and I closed our eyes. I sat in the chair and Eric lay on the floor. I thought to myself about the greatness of my father's love, which had taught us to blur the lines of distinction between sons and nephews, nieces and daughters.

At 6 a.m., Eric returned home to prepare for morning services at the synagogue. During the night, two major changes had occurred, including the closure of my father's eyes and a cessation of his upward gaze. His respirations were still deep, but far less frequent, occurring ten to twelve times a minute versus thirty times a minute just six hours earlier. He was now cold and unresponsive. The moment of victory for the angel of death was approaching.

Robert and Al B left for the synagogue before 7 a.m. I stayed with Dad. Russell was still asleep in Mom's room. In her housecoat, Mom came into Dad's room, kissed his forehead. His eyes, which had been wide open for a few hours, were now shut.

"Mom," I said. "His blood pressure is low and his pulse is weak."

Steadying herself with the rail of Dad's hospital bed, Mom coughed uncontrollably, loosening the secretions that had built up overnight.

"Mom, you need a vibrating vest treatment. Go ahead. I'm here with Dad."

Without another word, my mother left the room. Alone now, I said, "Dad, please forgive me if I failed to demonstrate proper honor and respect through the years." Although I needed an answer, I knew it wasn't forthcoming.

Nancy, who had just arrived at the house, sat with my father while I prayed in the dining room. Fifteen minutes later, I returned and observed further deterioration. Dad's respiratory rate was five to six times per minute, I could not palpate his pulse, and his nail beds were cyanotic.

By now, Russell had awakened and prayed, Robert and Al B had returned from the synagogue, and now the four of us stood in Dad's room, awaiting the moment of truth. Russell left the room briefly and returned with Mom, who had just completed her respiratory treatment.

At 8:38 a.m., on Sunday, January 29th, 2006, my father stopped breathing. I listened to his heart with a stethoscope and could hear no heartbeat, which corroborated with the absence of any pulse. Within thirty seconds there was one additional partial gasp, and then there was nothing.

My brothers and I each called our wives, and one of my brothers called Uncle Label, as well as Rabbi Turk, our community rabbi.

We covered our father's body with a white sheet and gently placed it on the floor with the feet toward the door. We also opened the window, and then we lit a tall memorial candle designed to burn for one week.

Within the hour, representatives from the Jewish Burial Society arrived to take the body to the funeral home, where several of my father's grandsons and sons-in-law would complete the ritual washing and preparation of the body for the funeral in the morning. They placed the covered body on a gurney. As they left the house, my mother, my brothers, and I followed them through the living room, out the front door, and into the morning sun.

After the black hearse pulled away, I spotted the oak tree in front of the house between the curb and the sidewalk that Hurricane Wilma had blown over. About twenty feet tall, it was now erect, and its symmetric branches were once again sprouting fresh leaves.

Back inside the house, Louisiana, who had been crying herself, kept an eye on Mom. Radcliff sat in the living room, appearing despondent, and perhaps disoriented. My brothers and I met at the dining room table. As Dad's medical advocate, I had played a leadership role, but I was now ready to relinquish the details of the days ahead to Russell, with two exceptions: I wanted to be the last speaker at the funeral, and I wanted to accompany the body to Israel. There was no disagreement. Robert, Al B, and I would go to Israel with our wives. Russell volunteered to make all the arrangements for the days ahead—both in Miami Beach and in Israel. Furthermore, he and Ronalee elected to remain with Mom in Miami Beach for the thirty hours the rest of us would be away.

We then turned our focus toward our exhausted and broken-hearted mother. Throughout the day, we received many friends and neighbors who stopped by to offer their condolences and support. Mom agreed to see a few close family friends, but mostly she remained in her room, where she could fastidiously maintain her medical regimen and get some much needed rest. Ronalee and Gita covered all the mirrors in the house with white sheets. This custom permits the mourners to spend the shivah period (which lasts up to a week) together, without concern for their appearance. The men give up shaving, and the women forgo makeup.

That evening, I was ready to return home to organize my thoughts for the eulogy, but before I left, I went into Mom's room to say goodnight. Her eyes were swollen, but her tears had dried. Her finger oximeter demonstrated a normal pulse and oxygen level.

"Mom, your breathing is good, but are you ready for tomorrow?"

"Your father deserves and a lasting tribute."

"It will be a funeral to be remembered," I said, and then I kissed her goodnight.

As I approached her bedroom door to leave, she added, "And, David, one more thing. I want you to do the same for me when my time comes."

That night, after working in my study for several hours preparing my thoughts for the eulogy, Gita came in to check on me. "David, I've never seen you prepare so long for a speech." She set down a tray containing a cup of tea and plate of sliced strawberries. "You must be exhausted. Eat something."

"This is a speech that I have feared writing most of my adult life," I said reaching for a piece of fruit. The responsibility, and the one opportunity I have, to publicly pay tribute to my father is a high order. There are no second chances."

At 9:20 in the morning, my brothers and I and our wives gathered at what was now "Mom's house." Fifty-six years earlier, in 1950, my grandfather, Al Galbut, was given one of the largest funerals in the history of Miami Beach. An early pioneer, my grandfather had earned the honorable title, "The Mayor of South Beach," in recognition of his twenty years service to the community as a retailer, restaurateur, and political activist. He was also a founder of Beth Jacob. That synagogue—the first in Miami Beach—is now the site of the Jewish Museum of Florida and is on the National Register of Historic Places. My grandfather also provided free meals to prisoners in the Miami Beach jail, which was located near the southern end of the city.

Today, in 2006, my father's funeral would also be an extraordinary Miami Beach event. We had chosen the Hebrew Academy, a school founded in 1947 on Sixth Street and Michigan Avenue, which had moved in 1963 to a sprawling new campus at 2400 Pine Tree Drive. In the early years, my father had joined the Board of Directors, and his leadership and influence continued until his death. My father's funeral was one of just a few ever held on the campus. My brothers and I have each fulfilled leadership roles. I served as president for four years, Al B and Robert have each led the Board of Education, and Russell had been at the helm of our family's enduring commitment to the school's financial well-being.

Nearly nine hundred people filled the auditorium, while another two hundred or so gathered outside. Russell had met with city officials regarding parking and a police escort from the Hebrew Academy to the Opa Locka Airport. After some discussion, the police chief told Russell, "Miami Beach takes care of its own." Pine Tree Drive, a heavily trafficked, four-lane, north-south road, became a single lane in both directions, allowing the middle two lanes for almost ten blocks to become the site for parking. During the police escort of the funeral procession, entrance points along I-95 between the Julia Tuttle Causeway and Northwest 135th Street were temporarily closed.

The funeral consisted of eulogies from fifteen speakers, including one great-granddaughter; several grandchildren; two rabbis, including my father's brother-in-law, Uncle Label; Colonel Jacob Goldstein, the highest ranking chaplain in the US Army Reserve; my three brothers, and then myself. I sat with Mom and held her hand during the service. Before going up to the podium on the stage, I whispered to my mother, "Is there anything specific that you would like me to add?"

"Tell them how your father made you into a great extemporaneous speaker," Mom said.

Standing at the podium, for the first time I realized just how many people had come to pay their last respects. "This is a day I have dreaded most of my adult life." I went on to speak about my father as my teacher. "Even during his final journey, I learned how to express appreciation to people. My father thanked everyone early and profusely for even the smallest deeds or service. He believed in the inherent goodness of people. He was a master teacher who demanded that each son reach his potential. He never lost sight of building and preserving the self-esteem of his children."

I then spoke about my father's love of my mother. Their relationship was united, and their major goal was the building of their family. "Although my father may have appeared dominant in the relationship, theirs was an equal partnership. My mother was more verbal, but my father epitomized the saying, 'Say little, do much.' To quote Shakespeare, 'Eloquence is action,' and my father was the most eloquent man I've ever met. He excelled in multiple interests, what we now call a 'Renaissance man.'

"No matter the endeavor, my father was committed to excellence." And to fulfill my mother's request, I shared the story of how my father had developed my abilities as an extemporaneous speaker during my participation in the Optimist International Oratorical Competition.

"My father taught his children to overcome fear through self-esteem and hard work. He also taught us not to fear failure and that the lessons learned could yield future success. As a student athlete, and now as a surgeon, I have often questioned my abilities. To achieve greater confidence, I often remind myself that I am Hymie Galbut's son, reflecting on his unconditional belief in me. My father believed that the impossible could be achieved through a greater effort if the cause was right and just.

"My father lived by principal. His fear of God was rooted in his understanding that actions have consequences. Sir Isaac Newton's third law of motion is that every action has a reaction, and perhaps this helped me understand the importance of doing the right thing, because then the consequence of the action would not be something to fear.

"In today's world, many say, 'What have you done for me lately?' My father disagreed. He recognized that a good deed or service deserved an everlasting debt of gratitude."

In conclusion, I added, "With my mother by his side, my father succeeded in raising a family who will continue his legacy. My father taught us that the reward for kindness toward everyone is self-fulfilling.

"Dad," I said, addressing the coffin, "I hope I told you enough that I love you."

Upon completing my eulogy, I looked at the audience and appreciated the extreme silence. I sensed that many of the attendees were only now learning about the character of a man who they really never knew. They appreciated his longevity and his demanding and sometimes abrasive persona, but did they understand his unyielding and unconditional dedication, love, and commitment to his wife and children?

A Navy honor brigade of three enlisted men, one officer, and a bugler approached the casket, draped with a flag from President George W. Bush. As the audience rose, the bugler played "Taps." With precision and perfection of movement, two enlisted men lifted the flag from the coffin, folded it into a triangle, and delivered it to the officer, a lieutenant commander, who gave the flag to my mother, along with a note of condolence from the President. Holding my mother's hand, I sensed her strength and her belief that she had loved and honored a man with one hundred percent of her being. As she cried, she walked behind the coffin, which my brothers and I, and several of our children, carried to the hearse.

The funeral procession, spanning over ten blocks, made four stops, including my father's home, his synagogue, the Jewish Learning Center, and the Mount Sinai Greater Miami Jewish Cemetery. The caravan continued to the Opa Locka Airport, where my father's coffin was placed aboard a corporate jet owned by a subsidiary of Crescent Heights, of which Russell is a principal owner. With approximately twenty people including Robert, Al B, myself, our wives, and some of our older grandchildren and several close friends, the plane flew directly to Tel Aviv.

Ten hours later, we arrived in Israel, late in the morning on Tuesday, January 31, 2006. In an unmarked gray van, my father's body was transported from the airport to the Land of the Living, on the outskirts of Jerusalem. Our entourage followed in a chartered bus. The oxymoronic name of the cemetery is indicative of how the ideals, beliefs, and commitments of the departed are carried on by subsequent generations. Many Israelis, including Yona Metzger, the Chief Rabbi of Israel, along with about a hundred American exchange students from the Miami Beach Jewish community attended the burial. Robert, Al B, and I accompanied our father's body to the grave, but the actual interment was managed by the Burial Society of Jerusalem, whose custom is to shield family members from viewing the placement of the body into the ground and the filling of the grave with the displaced earth. In Israel, the custom is to bury without a coffin, so as to expedite the Biblical dictum of every man's fate of "dust to dust." Our father's body, covered in a white linen shroud, was laid to rest. For now, Dad would rest there alone, surrounded by the empty land we had set aside for future graves.

It was late afternoon, about 3 p.m., and already the sun was low in the western sky. The cemetery, surrounded by a forest, was desolate, despite the many friends who'd come to pay their last respects. Robert, Al B, and I approached the grave, which only moments ago had been empty. We stared at the mound of earth covering our dad's body and together we recited Kaddish, the prayer of sanctification, which emphasizes our acceptance of God's judgment. We would then recite this prayer daily for the eleven months of mourning.

From the cemetery, we returned to the airport and boarded our refueled airplane, restocked with food and beverages, for our flight home. We departed Israel at 8 p.m. During the return flight, about two hours longer, given the strong headwinds, I recalled seeing my father with me during the many stages of his adult life, and I pondered his statement of having no regrets, and his affirmation that his life had been complete. He had fought to preserve his independence as long as possible, as his mind remained strong in contrast to his failing body. The importance of striving for independence as a means of preserving dignity is a lesson I'll never forget.

After partaking of the in-flight buffet of sandwiches and fruit, most of us slept during the return flight, but not me. Accompanied by my time capsules of memory, the night was my friend, and I enjoyed the calming hum of the engines and the darkness. I contemplated my father's influence upon the tangible love our family had shared during the preceding months. To my father, love meant a total giving of himself, and he and Mom exemplified this ideal. He could be a harsh taskmaster, demanding performance from his children and grandchildren commensurate with each one's aptitude. He never accepted credit for our accomplishments, but always assumed responsibility for helping us overcome our failures. My father wasn't a physician, but I credit him with much of my success as a heart surgeon. During my early years of practice in Miami Beach at Miami Heart Institute, patients often asked whether Hyman Galbut was my father.

"Yes," I would say. "How do you know him?"

Almost always, they would recall a service my father had provided. As the plane thundered through the night sky, I questioned my professional life. Am I in the service business?

It is the summer of 1964 and I'm fifteen years old, working in my father's law practice. My job is to sort through ten years' of documents and destroy the inactive files. The work is boring, but I enjoy spending time around Dad. As I sift through papers, most of which I discard, I have the opportunity to watch my father in action. One morning at approximately 11 a.m., I walk toward his office to discuss a few files. He is having a serious discussion with a client regarding a family partnership in a real estate venture. The client, a man in his 60s, seems upset. He asks my father, "Do I have legal grounds, and if so, is it worth pursuing?"

My father responds, "It depends on you." The man seems puzzled, so my father continues, "Do you want me to answer you as a friend or as a lawyer?"

"As a friend," says the old man.

My father looks into the man's eyes. "You're legally right, and you would probably win in court, but you would lose in life. The legal judgment would utterly destroy your relationship with your children."

The man sits back in the leather armchair before my father's large mahogany desk. The surrounding walls are covered with Dad's university degrees and all sorts of plaques denoting civic leadership, along with photographs of our family participating in various community events. The client smiles. "Thank you, Hymie. I understand your point."

After the client leaves, I say to my father, "Dad, it sounds like that could have been a profitable case. How do you decide what to turn down?"

"Lawyers are counselors, David. He sought my advice on the best course of action. And even if he hadn't, I still would have shared my opinion on what I believe is the right course of action. Even the answers to simple questions carry important consequences."

Later that afternoon, while Dad and I discuss a number of old files, some of which we decide to retain, a disheveled man walks into the office and without even saying "Good afternoon," he launches into a nonsensical, five-minute tirade about city politics. My father stands there and listens to the man, but never says a word. When the man finishes, he turns and leaves the office.

"What was that all about?" I say when the man shuts the waiting room door behind him.

"He comes here two or three times a week," my father says. "He spends a moment, speaks without purpose, feels better, and then he leaves."

"Dad, he is really disruptive."

"Yes, for a moment he may be, but son, like I've told you, I am in the business of providing service."

"I don't understand. What service do you provide for this bum?"

"I provide him an audience for his tirades, but more importantly, the derelict provides the service for me."

"I still don't get it," I say.

"That man gives me the opportunity to refine my character. Always remember, David, the mark of a man is his attitude toward one who can no longer be of service to him."

"I understand," I said.

But of course I didn't, not at the time. The image of my father, in his office, acting in truth and kindness, has remained with me, even though it took me many years to grasp the magnitude of my father's belief.

After a brief refueling stop in the Azores, we resumed the journey home. During those remaining hours, I reflected on the intensity of Dad's final journey and my recurrent question: Is there such a thing as a good death?

Can this be experienced only by someone who has lived a good life? Does the loss of dignity or independence—or the presence of fear—prevent the experience of a good death? I concluded that there is no answer. Death is a departure. There is no return, and no sharing of the experience with the living. During Dad's illness, perhaps I had gained some additional insight from him. He suffered a major loss of dignity during the final week of his life, but this was counterbalanced by his family's love. When I asked my father if he had any fear toward the end of his final journey, he always responded that he had none, nor did he express any regrets about how he'd lived his life.

He never shared with me his belief in the world to come or the afterlife, but I learned later that he had promised my mother that he would be waiting for her in heaven. My father knew his life would continue as an inspiration to his sons, his grandchildren, and to future generations. On the last day of his life, my father received death on his own terms, sharing love from his wife and family, assured that his death would breathe an even higher level of unity in his sons.

As the plane descended toward Miami, a new day awaited us, and yet I felt a great sense of loss. My brothers and I had become the older generation. I would mourn in the months ahead, commencing with the week of sitting shivah. Friends and extended family would visit and comfort my mother, my brothers, and me. After a week, we would return to work, but for the balance of the first thirty days, we would remain unshaven as a public symbol of our loss. For the remaining year, we would continue our mourning by avoiding movies, concerts, parties, and other enjoyable pastimes. In addition, we would make every effort to fulfill the commandment of attending the synagogue daily and saying Kaddish. I was committed to keeping my father's memory alive. It was also time to become a better husband, father, son, and person.

Epilogue: The Kaddish

Over the next eleven months, Mom spent most of her time at home, assisted by Louisiana. Her children, grandchildren, and a handful of close friends enjoyed a routine of daily visits and activities with her. In her effort to achieve a sleek, dust-free, clutter-free, toddler-friendly environment, Mom gave away many valuable possessions to her children and grandchildren. She replaced the hurricane-damaged roof, she removed the carpeting, and she installed marble and wood. She also redid much of the interior lighting and she purchased several new flat-screen televisions. The house had become *hers*.

As scheduled, Rachel and Ethan were married on May 28th. It was the only celebration I attended with my mother and brothers during the mourning period. During the year, Mom gained five new great-grandchildren, two of whom were named in Dad's memory.

Mom continued her strict adherence to her medical regimen, and each day, she impressed us with her positive attitude, her mental strength, and her ongoing family leadership.

On Sunday, December 17th, nearly eleven months after Dad's death, our family and friends gathered in the social hall of the Mirador Condominium in South Beach to celebrate the first birthdays of Noa and Kaelly, the children of Elana, Elle and Jaime. We were also gathered to observe Hanukkah, the Festival of Lights. Elana had assumed responsibility for providing food and entertainment for the approximately ninety guests.

The large room was decorated with party balloons, colored tablecloths, and a toddler bounce house. In preparation for this first Hanukkah without her husband, Mom had organized an array of gifts for her children, grandchildren, and great-grandchildren. The party began with a dance-fest. Many of the twenty-five great-grandchildren, some with parental assistance, followed Elmo, who danced to familiar *Sesame Street* tunes. I sat with my mother on the fringe of the dance floor. She held Ariana, Dani and Joshua's eight-month-old daughter.

"Dad always loved music and seeing his family celebrating together," Mom said as she fed a bottle of formula to Ariana.

"You and Dad were always a team," I said. "It's inspiring how you have carried on, Mom."

"Dad was a great guy," she said. I pondered their courtship nearly seventy years earlier in New Orleans.

"You have continued to live life with enthusiasm and purpose," I said, watching cousins playing together, mesmerized by Elmo who was concluding his performance.

After Elmo departed, we remained in the social hall to enjoy a Middle Eastern buffet. The offerings included hummus, grilled eggplant, Baba Ghanoush, garden salad, steak, hamburger, chicken, shish kebab, potato latkes (or pancakes), jelly donuts, and tea.

It was now time to celebrate Hanukkah, which represents a time of great miracles in which the Maccabees, a smaller Jewish force, defeated the larger Greek Army. A limited quantity of sacred oil, expected to burn in the candelabra of the Holy Temple for one night, lasted eight nights. But to most of us, Hanukkah is a time for exchanging gifts and love. As everyone enjoyed their meal, I stood up to introduce Mom, so she could begin her presentation of gifts—a moment she had been planning for months.

Mom stood beside me and I held her arm as she began. "This party is very difficult for me without your dad, and your Zayde," Mom said. "During the final week of his illness, Dad said to me, 'I am going ahead to heaven, but you, Bessie, must wait. You will have the job of caring for the boys.'" My mother laughed, adding, "He was referring our sons, who are all grown men. He also said to me, 'Bessie, you have two choices in life—to be happy or to be sad. If you are smart, you will take the first choice...and I know you are a smart lady.'"

During the preceding months, Mom and Louisiana had catalogued the portion of Dad's new trains and accessories that still remained in factory-sealed boxes. These items filled most of a spare bedroom at the house. This was in addition to the elaborate collection that filled the shelving that lined the two-car garage. Mom and Louisiana further organized the items into boxes of train sets for her grandsons (including her granddaughters' husbands) and her great-grandsons. One by one, she called each recipient forward to receive these unique gifts. Mom's unmarried granddaughters, including Marisa, Nili, and Jenna, also received boxes of trains.

The younger great-granddaughters received a Cabbage Patch doll, and the older girls received an ornamental, international doll, with a porcelain face, and a formal dress, representative of one of various foreign countries. The dolls reminded me of the international figures in Disneyworld's *It's a Small World*.

At 4:45, as the children delighted in opening their gifts, the adult men gathered in an adjacent room, separated by a glass wall, to say the afternoon prayer. The devout Jew prays with a minyan three times a day, and only in this forum can a mourner fulfill his eleven-month obligation to recite Kaddish. Although the words don't refer to the lost family member, Kaddish is a constant reminder of the person who once was.

Thirty-five years ago, as a college student, I went to the New York Public Library to study the writings of Abraham Reisin, my father's uncle, particularly his short story entitled, "The Kaddish." The protagonist is an old Jew from the shtetl in the town of Koydanovo in Belarus. He and his wife are childless, and as the man grows older, he prays for a child, and finally his elderly wife gives birth to a son. He raises the boy until the bar mitzvah age of thirteen, the time of communal and personal responsibility. The father soon passes away, comforted with the knowledge that his son, representing continuity, would say Kaddish for him.

We had now reached the end of the first eleven months after our father's death, according to the Jewish lunar calendar. After concluding the afternoon prayer, my three brothers and I lined up shoulder-to-shoulder and recited our last Kaddish for our father, in unison, as if this prayer emanated from a single voice. I believe my father never doubted the completeness of his life and its meaning in fulfilling his obligation to establish continuity. Perhaps this prayer served as a confirmation to the community, and I hope Dad was listening and smiling in heaven.

As the father of six daughters, five of whom are now married, I understood the reality of my being without a son to say

Kaddish for Gita and me. Perhaps our sons-in-law, whom we've grown to love as our own children, will one day accompany us on our own final journeys and recite Kaddish in remembrance.

As we concluded the afternoon prayer, the adult men returned to the social hall, but I lingered for a few moments, peering through the plate glass window. The children played together, and I could almost hear their laughter, and I wanted to hear it. I doubt anyone noticed me, as they were immersed in the celebrations of the two birthdays and Hanukkah. Was I ready to move on, now that the mourning period had ended?

Mothers and friends were conversing, some holding and feeding new babies, and supervising young children. In the middle of the room, the large chocolate birthday cake was adorned with two lit candles.

The Hebrew word "Hanukkah" means a rededication. Having presented her gifts, Mom, received hugs and kisses from three generations of her family. She was in her glory, having rededicated her life to fulfilling the family mission.

I reached into my shirt pocket for my new Sony digital camera. Looking at the large LCD video display, I recalled that bright summer afternoon on the back porch of my parents' Coral Gate home and the commotion of my three brothers and myself, complying with Dad's instructions to hold still long enough for him to snap our picture for posterity. Now I was the dad, and the grandfather, and the uncle. With my camera in hand, I returned to the social hall. At the entry, I pulled the glass door open, and I too could hear the music and the laughter.

Four Brothers: Al B., Russell, David and Robert Galbut. January 9, 2005.

David and Gita Galbut attending South Miami Hospital Charitable Ball. March, 2007.

Hyman and Bessie Galbut, January 9, 2005.

Leutenant Commander Hyman P. Galbut, United States Navy Reserve. July, 1963.

Four generations including from left to right top row: Miki and Lior Rotenstein, Yochai, Noa and Elana, Joshua, Ariana, Dani and Yve Kuhl, David and Nili Galbut, Rachel and Ethan Wasserman, Jaimie Beinenfeld. Left to right bottom row: Riki, Ziev and Matti Rotenstein, Bessie Galbut, Yakira Beinenfeld, Gita Galbut, Miriam Emunah (M.E.), Elle and Kelila Beinenfeld. April, 2007.

Dr. David Galbut

A Personal Note

It has been five years since my father's death. My mother continues to live independently in her home with the assistance of her children and caregivers. She lives each day with "many people to love, something to do, and something to look forward to". The unity among brothers during my father's final journey has decreased. Perhaps, it is related to each of us becoming patriarchs in our individual families, or different influences in the whirlwind of life.

Gita continues to be the center of my world. Our children are immersed in the challenges of life, but remain our pride, inspiration, and future. I continue to cherish the opportunity to care for patients, be a surgeon and operate on hearts.

I reflect on the legacy of my father almost every day. He understood that life is fleeting and that time goes by even faster in the later years. He never lost his enthusiasm or focus, and was a

Renaissance man. He understood how to love as a husband and as a father. He demonstrated the greatest courage in life and in the final journey. He believed his life was fulfilled, with his greatest achievement being his family. My story of balancing the demands of heart surgery with my most important goal of succeeding as a husband, father and son continues.

David L. Galbut M.D.
DAVID@DGALBUTMD.COM

CPSIA information can be obtained
at www.ICGtesting.com
Printed in the USA
FSHW010513220719
60264FS

9 781456 479510